AN ONI PRESS PUBLICATION

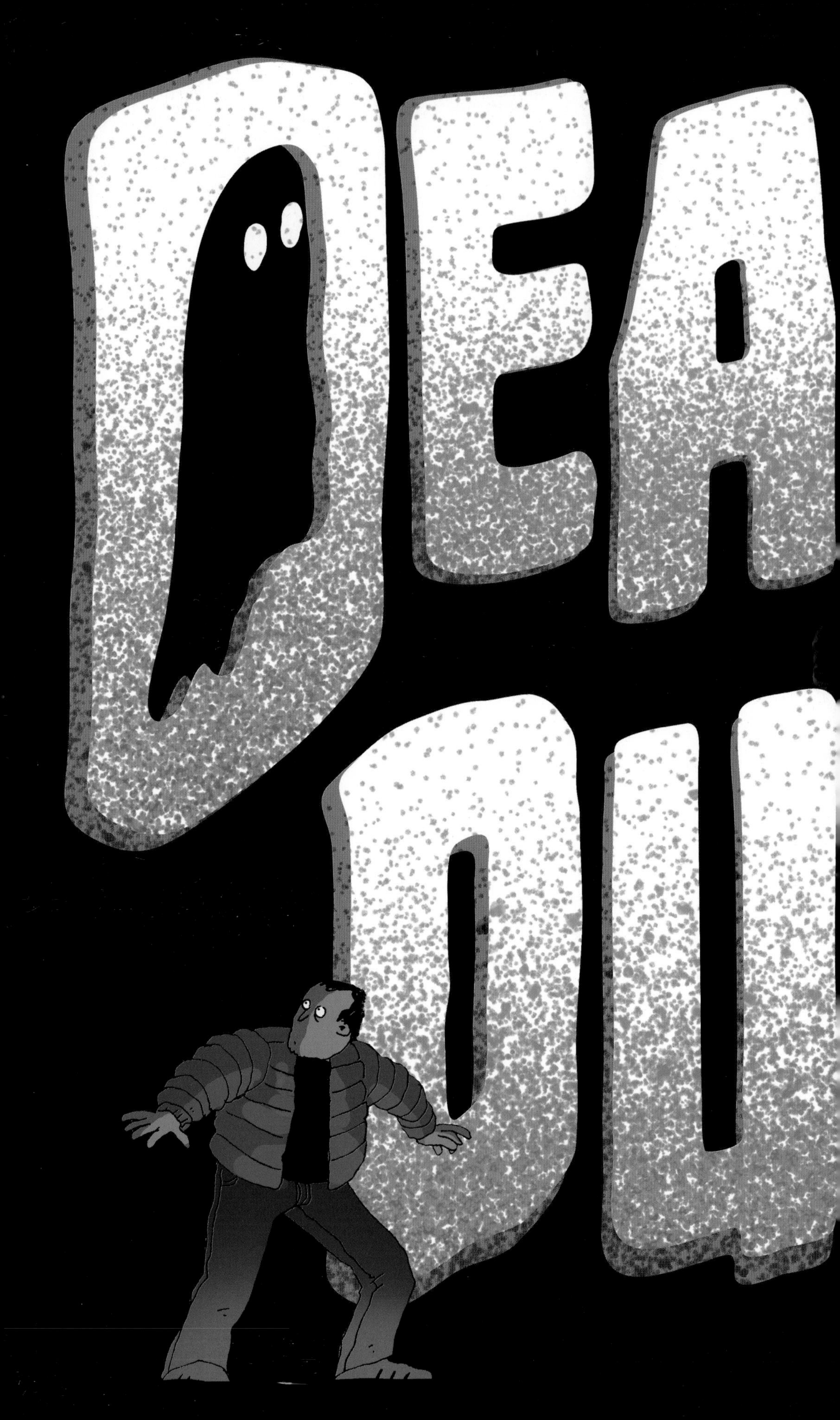

WRITTEN BY **CHRISTOPHER SEBELA**
ILLUSTRATED BY **BEN SEARS**
COLORED BY **RYAN HILL**
& **WARREN WUCINICH**
LETTERED BY **CRANK!**

PUBLISHED BY ONI-LION FORGE PUBLISHING GROUP, LLC

JAMES LUCAS JONES, president & publisher · SARAH GAYDOS, editor in chief
CHARLIE CHU, e.v.p. of creative & business development · BRAD ROOKS, director of operations
AMBER O'NEILL, special projects manager · HARRIS FISH, events manager · MARGOT WOOD, director of marketing & sales
DEVIN FUNCHES, sales & marketing manager · KATIE SAINZ, marketing manager · TARA LEHMANN, publicist
TROY LOOK, director of design & production · KATE Z. STONE, senior graphic designer · SONJA SYNAK, graphic designer
HILARY THOMPSON, graphic designer · SARAH ROCKWELL, junior graphic designer · ANGIE KNOWLES, digital prepress lead
VINCENT KUKUA, digital prepress technician · JASMINE AMIRI, senior editor · SHAWNA GORE, senior editor
AMANDA MEADOWS, senior editor · ROBERT MEYERS, senior editor, licensing · GRACE BORNHOFT, editor · ZACK SOTO, editor
CHRIS CERASI, editorial coordinator · STEVE ELLIS, vice president of games · BEN EISNER, game developer
MICHELLE NGUYEN, executive assistant · JUNG LEE, logistics coordinator · JOE NOZEMACK, publisher emeritus

Edited by **CHARLIE CHU** & **DESIREE WILSON** with **ZACK SOTO**
Designed by **KATE Z. STONE**

ONIPRESS.COM
@onipress

LIONFORGE.COM
@lionforge

FREEBENSEARS.COM / @BENSEARS
WWW.CHRISTOPHERSEBELA.COM / @XTOP

First Edition: Sept 2020

ISBN 978-1-62010-778-2
eISBN 978-1-62010-799-7

Printed in South Korea through Four Colour Print Group, Louisville, KY.

Library of Congress Control Number: 2020932166

1 2 3 4 5 6 7 8 9 10

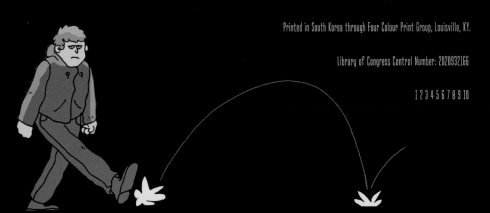

CHAPTER
ONE

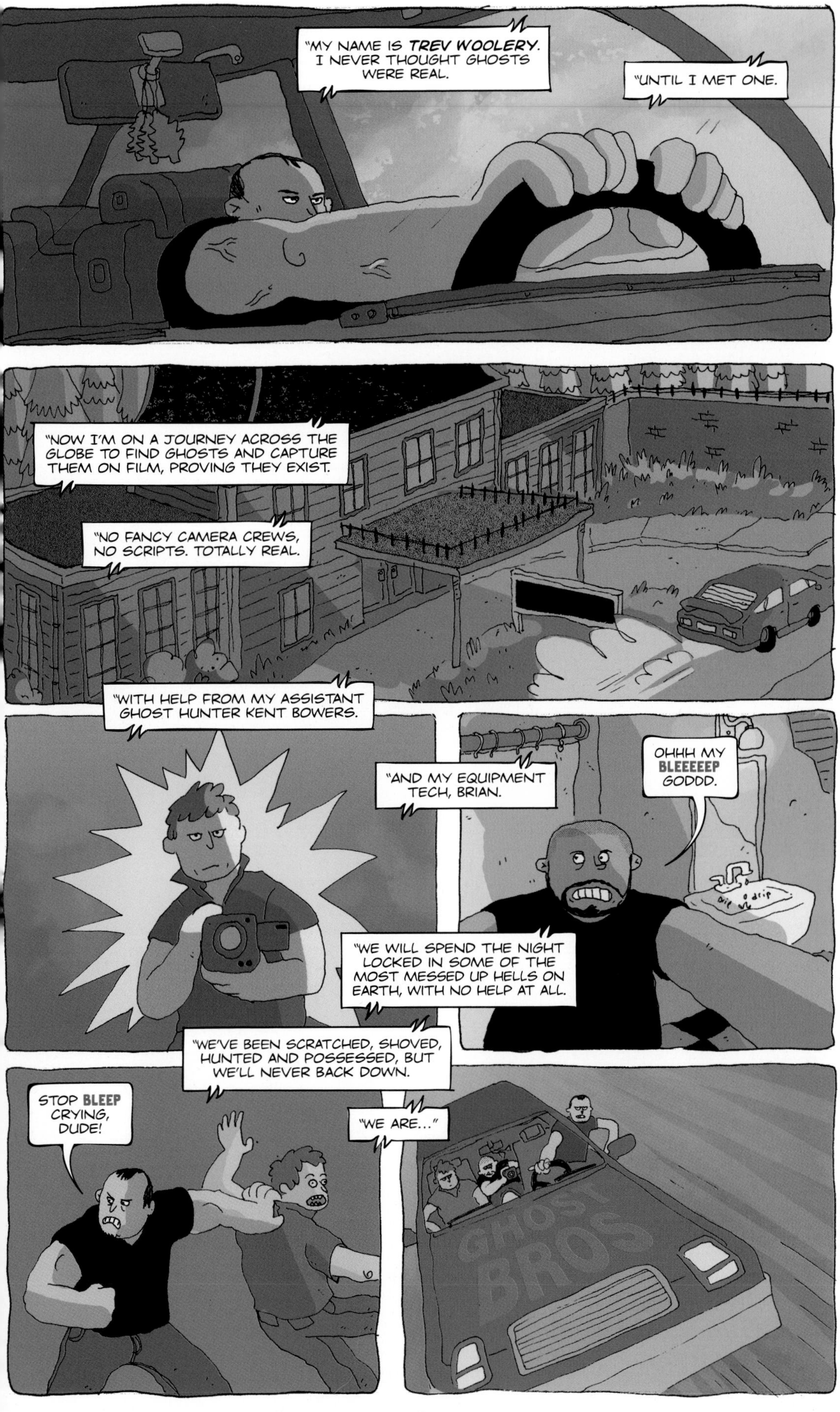
"MY NAME IS ***TREV WOOLERY***. I NEVER THOUGHT GHOSTS WERE REAL.
"UNTIL I MET ONE.
"NOW I'M ON A JOURNEY ACROSS THE GLOBE TO FIND GHOSTS AND CAPTURE THEM ON FILM, PROVING THEY EXIST.
"NO FANCY CAMERA CREWS, NO SCRIPTS. TOTALLY REAL.
"WITH HELP FROM MY ASSISTANT GHOST HUNTER KENT BOWERS.
"AND MY EQUIPMENT TECH, BRIAN.
OHHH MY **BLEEEEEP** GODDD.
drip drip
"WE WILL SPEND THE NIGHT LOCKED IN SOME OF THE MOST MESSED UP HELLS ON EARTH, WITH NO HELP AT ALL.
"WE'VE BEEN SCRATCHED, SHOVED, HUNTED AND POSSESSED, BUT WE'LL NEVER BACK DOWN.
STOP **BLEEP** CRYING, DUDE!
"WE ARE..."
GHOST BROS

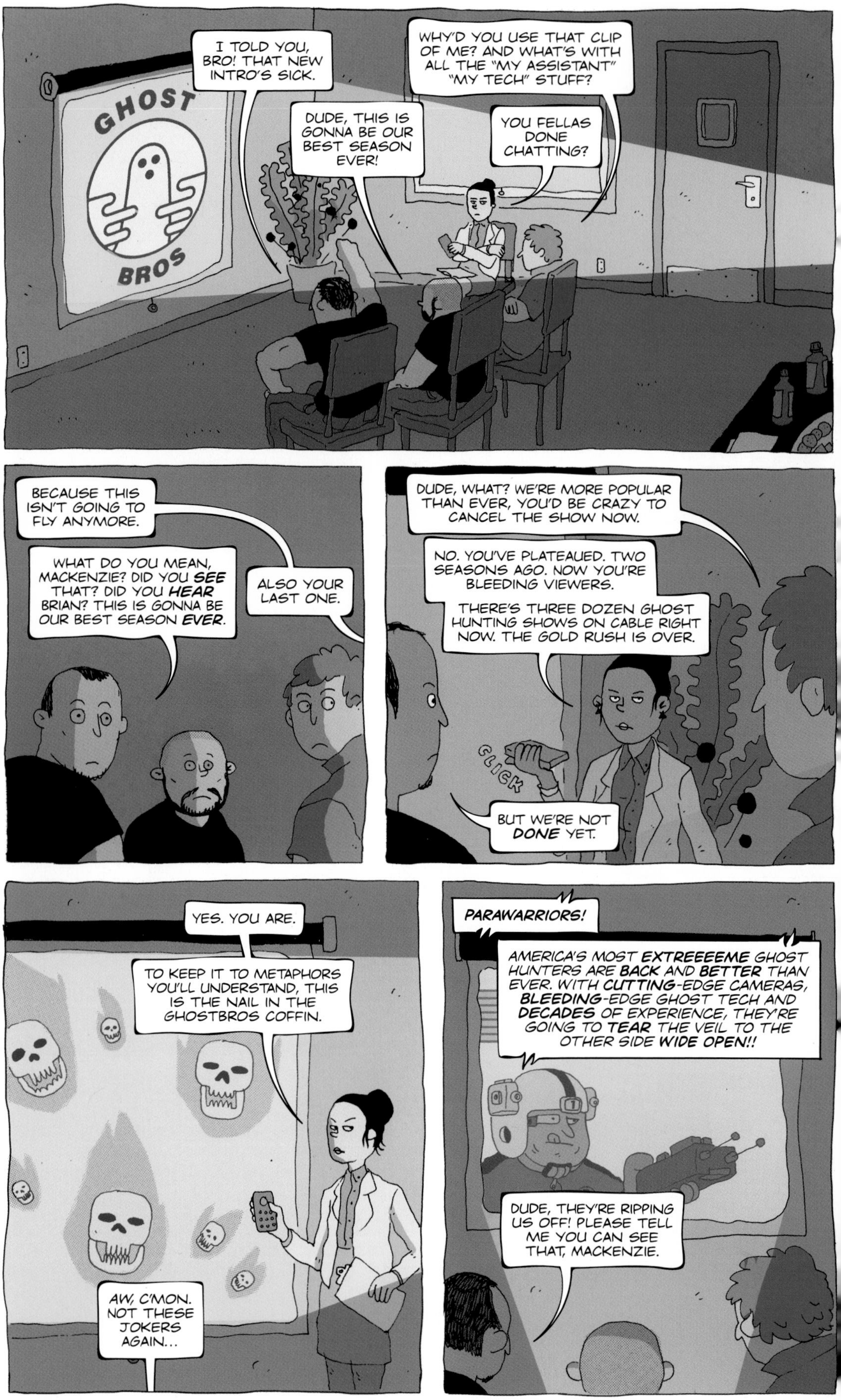
GHOST BROS
I TOLD YOU, BRO! THAT NEW INTRO'S SICK.
DUDE, THIS IS GONNA BE OUR BEST SEASON EVER!
WHY'D YOU USE THAT CLIP OF ME? AND WHAT'S WITH ALL THE "MY ASSISTANT" "MY TECH" STUFF?
YOU FELLAS DONE CHATTING?
BECAUSE THIS ISN'T GOING TO FLY ANYMORE.
WHAT DO YOU MEAN, MACKENZIE? DID YOU **SEE** THAT? DID YOU **HEAR** BRIAN? THIS IS GONNA BE OUR BEST SEASON **EVER**.
ALSO YOUR LAST ONE.
DUDE, WHAT? WE'RE MORE POPULAR THAN EVER, YOU'D BE CRAZY TO CANCEL THE SHOW NOW.
NO. YOU'VE PLATEAUED. TWO SEASONS AGO. NOW YOU'RE BLEEDING VIEWERS.
THERE'S THREE DOZEN GHOST HUNTING SHOWS ON CABLE RIGHT NOW. THE GOLD RUSH IS OVER.
CLICK
BUT WE'RE NOT **DONE** YET.
YES. YOU ARE.
TO KEEP IT TO METAPHORS YOU'LL UNDERSTAND, THIS IS THE NAIL IN THE GHOSTBROS COFFIN.
AW, C'MON. NOT THESE JOKERS AGAIN...
PARAWARRIORS!
*AMERICA'S MOST **EXTREEEEME** GHOST HUNTERS ARE **BACK** AND **BETTER** THAN EVER. WITH **CUTTING**-EDGE CAMERAS, **BLEEDING**-EDGE GHOST TECH AND **DECADES** OF EXPERIENCE, THEY'RE GOING TO **TEAR** THE VEIL TO THE OTHER SIDE **WIDE OPEN!!***
DUDE, THEY'RE RIPPING US OFF! PLEASE TELL ME YOU CAN SEE THAT, MACKENZIE.

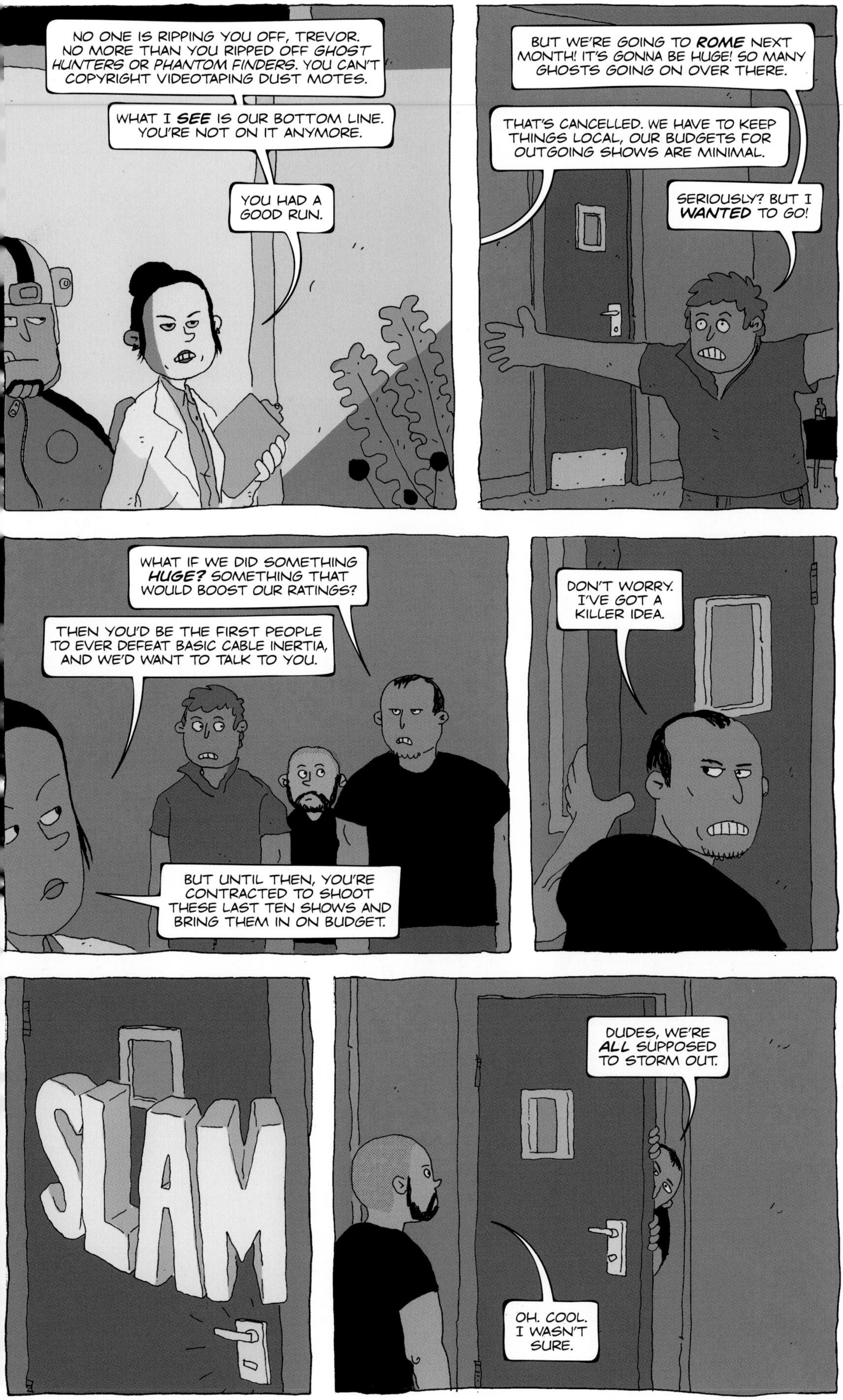
NO ONE IS RIPPING YOU OFF, TREVOR. NO MORE THAN YOU RIPPED OFF *GHOST HUNTERS* OR *PHANTOM FINDERS*. YOU CAN'T COPYRIGHT VIDEOTAPING DUST MOTES.
WHAT I **SEE** IS OUR BOTTOM LINE. YOU'RE NOT ON IT ANYMORE.
YOU HAD A GOOD RUN.
BUT WE'RE GOING TO **ROME** NEXT MONTH! IT'S GONNA BE HUGE! SO MANY GHOSTS GOING ON OVER THERE.
THAT'S CANCELLED. WE HAVE TO KEEP THINGS LOCAL, OUR BUDGETS FOR OUTGOING SHOWS ARE MINIMAL.
SERIOUSLY? BUT I **WANTED** TO GO!
WHAT IF WE DID SOMETHING ***HUGE?*** SOMETHING THAT WOULD BOOST OUR RATINGS?
THEN YOU'D BE THE FIRST PEOPLE TO EVER DEFEAT BASIC CABLE INERTIA, AND WE'D WANT TO TALK TO YOU.
BUT UNTIL THEN, YOU'RE CONTRACTED TO SHOOT THESE LAST TEN SHOWS AND BRING THEM IN ON BUDGET.
DON'T WORRY. I'VE GOT A KILLER IDEA.
SLAM
DUDES, WE'RE ***ALL*** SUPPOSED TO STORM OUT.
OH. COOL. I WASN'T SURE.

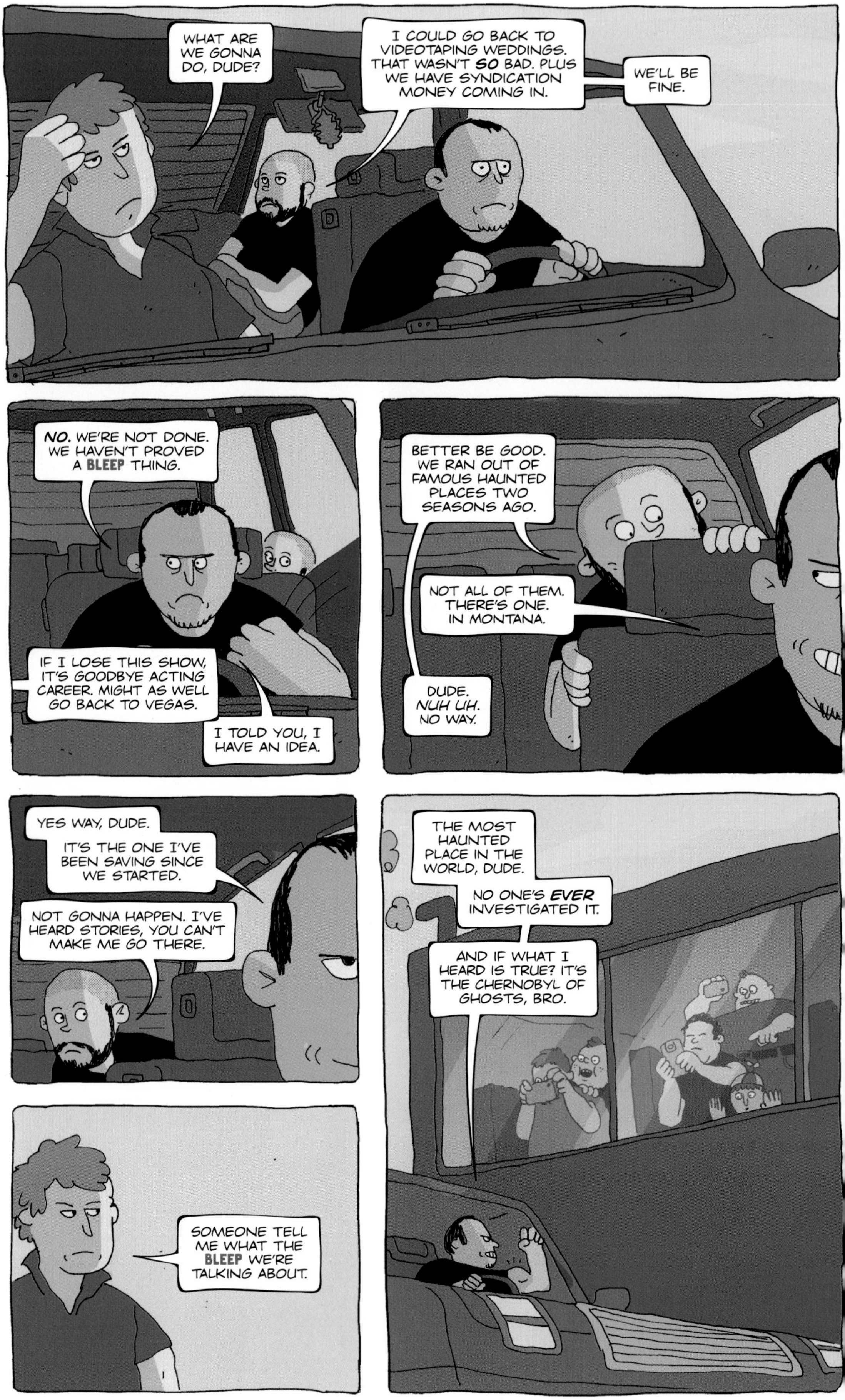
WHAT ARE WE GONNA DO, DUDE?
I COULD GO BACK TO VIDEOTAPING WEDDINGS. THAT WASN'T **SO** BAD. PLUS WE HAVE SYNDICATION MONEY COMING IN.
WE'LL BE FINE.
NO. WE'RE NOT DONE. WE HAVEN'T PROVED A **BLEEP** THING.
IF I LOSE THIS SHOW, IT'S GOODBYE ACTING CAREER. MIGHT AS WELL GO BACK TO VEGAS.
I TOLD YOU, I HAVE AN IDEA.
BETTER BE GOOD. WE RAN OUT OF FAMOUS HAUNTED PLACES TWO SEASONS AGO.
NOT ALL OF THEM. THERE'S ONE. IN MONTANA.
DUDE. *NUH UH.* NO WAY.
YES WAY, DUDE.
IT'S THE ONE I'VE BEEN SAVING SINCE WE STARTED.
NOT GONNA HAPPEN. I'VE HEARD STORIES, YOU CAN'T MAKE ME GO THERE.
SOMEONE TELL ME WHAT THE **BLEEP** WE'RE TALKING ABOUT.
THE MOST HAUNTED PLACE IN THE WORLD, DUDE.
NO ONE'S ***EVER*** INVESTIGATED IT.
AND IF WHAT I HEARD IS TRUE? IT'S THE CHERNOBYL OF GHOSTS, BRO.

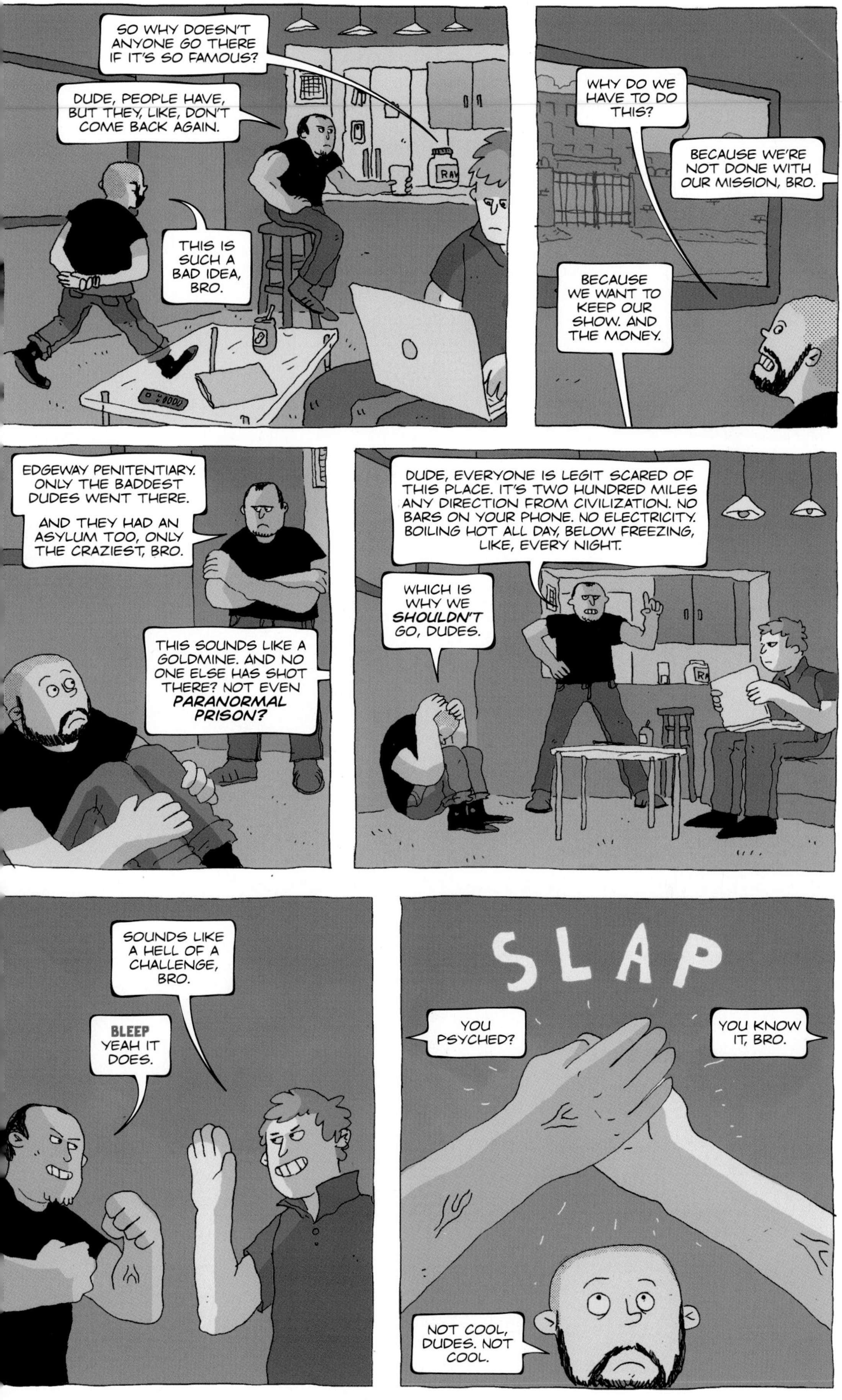
SO WHY DOESN'T ANYONE GO THERE IF IT'S SO FAMOUS?
DUDE, PEOPLE HAVE, BUT THEY, LIKE, DON'T COME BACK AGAIN.
THIS IS SUCH A BAD IDEA, BRO.
WHY DO WE HAVE TO DO THIS?
BECAUSE WE'RE NOT DONE WITH OUR MISSION, BRO.
BECAUSE WE WANT TO KEEP OUR SHOW. AND THE MONEY.
EDGEWAY PENITENTIARY. ONLY THE BADDEST DUDES WENT THERE.
AND THEY HAD AN ASYLUM TOO, ONLY THE CRAZIEST, BRO.
THIS SOUNDS LIKE A GOLDMINE. AND NO ONE ELSE HAS SHOT THERE? NOT EVEN PARANORMAL PRISON?
DUDE, EVERYONE IS LEGIT SCARED OF THIS PLACE. IT'S TWO HUNDRED MILES ANY DIRECTION FROM CIVILIZATION. NO BARS ON YOUR PHONE. NO ELECTRICITY. BOILING HOT ALL DAY, BELOW FREEZING, LIKE, EVERY NIGHT.
WHICH IS WHY WE SHOULDN'T GO, DUDES.
SOUNDS LIKE A HELL OF A CHALLENGE, BRO.
BLEEP YEAH IT DOES.
SLAP
YOU PSYCHED?
YOU KNOW IT, BRO.
NOT COOL, DUDES. NOT COOL.

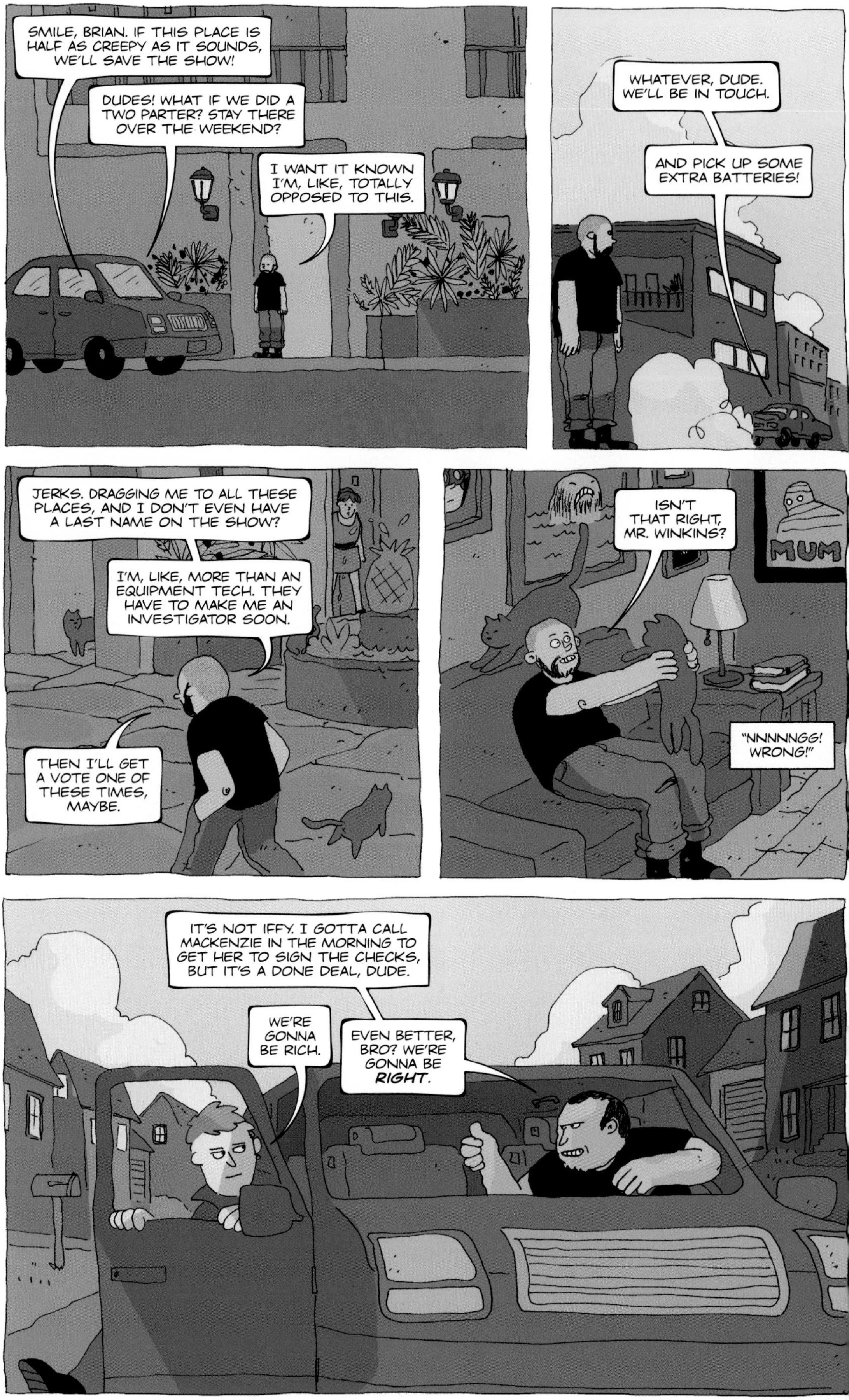
SMILE, BRIAN. IF THIS PLACE IS HALF AS CREEPY AS IT SOUNDS, WE'LL SAVE THE SHOW!
DUDES! WHAT IF WE DID A TWO PARTER? STAY THERE OVER THE WEEKEND?
I WANT IT KNOWN I'M, LIKE, TOTALLY OPPOSED TO THIS.
WHATEVER, DUDE. WE'LL BE IN TOUCH.
AND PICK UP SOME EXTRA BATTERIES!
JERKS. DRAGGING ME TO ALL THESE PLACES, AND I DON'T EVEN HAVE A LAST NAME ON THE SHOW?
I'M, LIKE, MORE THAN AN EQUIPMENT TECH. THEY HAVE TO MAKE ME AN INVESTIGATOR SOON.
THEN I'LL GET A VOTE ONE OF THESE TIMES, MAYBE.
ISN'T THAT RIGHT, MR. WINKINS?
MUM
"NNNNNGG! WRONG!"
IT'S NOT IFFY. I GOTTA CALL MACKENZIE IN THE MORNING TO GET HER TO SIGN THE CHECKS, BUT IT'S A DONE DEAL, DUDE.
WE'RE GONNA BE RICH.
EVEN BETTER, BRO? WE'RE GONNA BE ***RIGHT***.

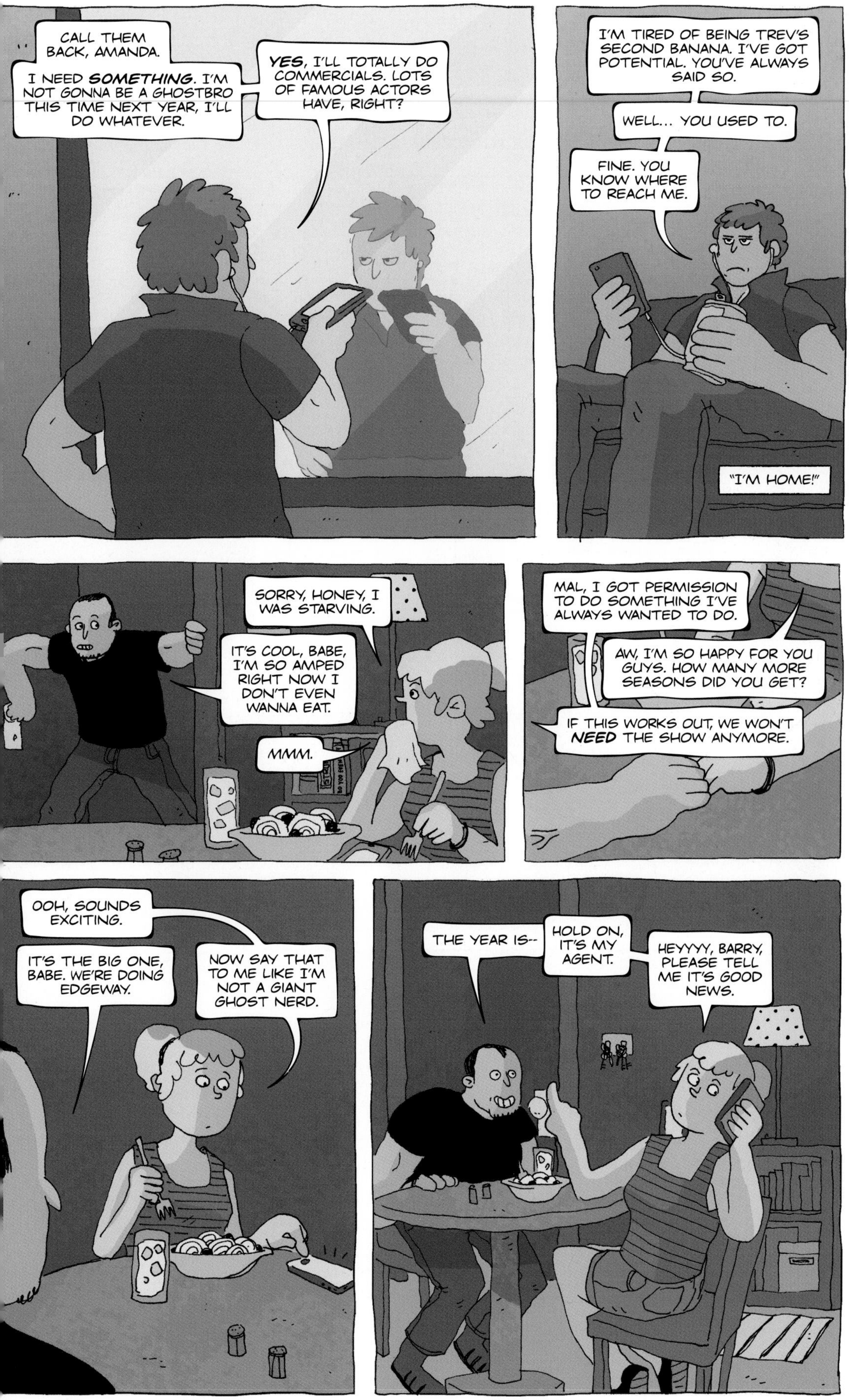
CALL THEM BACK, AMANDA.
I NEED **SOMETHING**. I'M NOT GONNA BE A GHOSTBRO THIS TIME NEXT YEAR, I'LL DO WHATEVER.
YES, I'LL TOTALLY DO COMMERCIALS. LOTS OF FAMOUS ACTORS HAVE, RIGHT?
I'M TIRED OF BEING TREV'S SECOND BANANA. I'VE GOT POTENTIAL. YOU'VE ALWAYS SAID SO.
WELL... YOU USED TO.
FINE. YOU KNOW WHERE TO REACH ME.
"I'M HOME!"
SORRY, HONEY, I WAS STARVING.
IT'S COOL, BABE, I'M SO AMPED RIGHT NOW I DON'T EVEN WANNA EAT.
MMM.
MAL, I GOT PERMISSION TO DO SOMETHING I'VE ALWAYS WANTED TO DO.
AW, I'M SO HAPPY FOR YOU GUYS. HOW MANY MORE SEASONS DID YOU GET?
IF THIS WORKS OUT, WE WON'T **NEED** THE SHOW ANYMORE.
OOH, SOUNDS EXCITING.
IT'S THE BIG ONE, BABE. WE'RE DOING EDGEWAY.
NOW SAY THAT TO ME LIKE I'M NOT A GIANT GHOST NERD.
THE YEAR IS--
HOLD ON, IT'S MY AGENT.
HEYYYY, BARRY, PLEASE TELL ME IT'S GOOD NEWS.

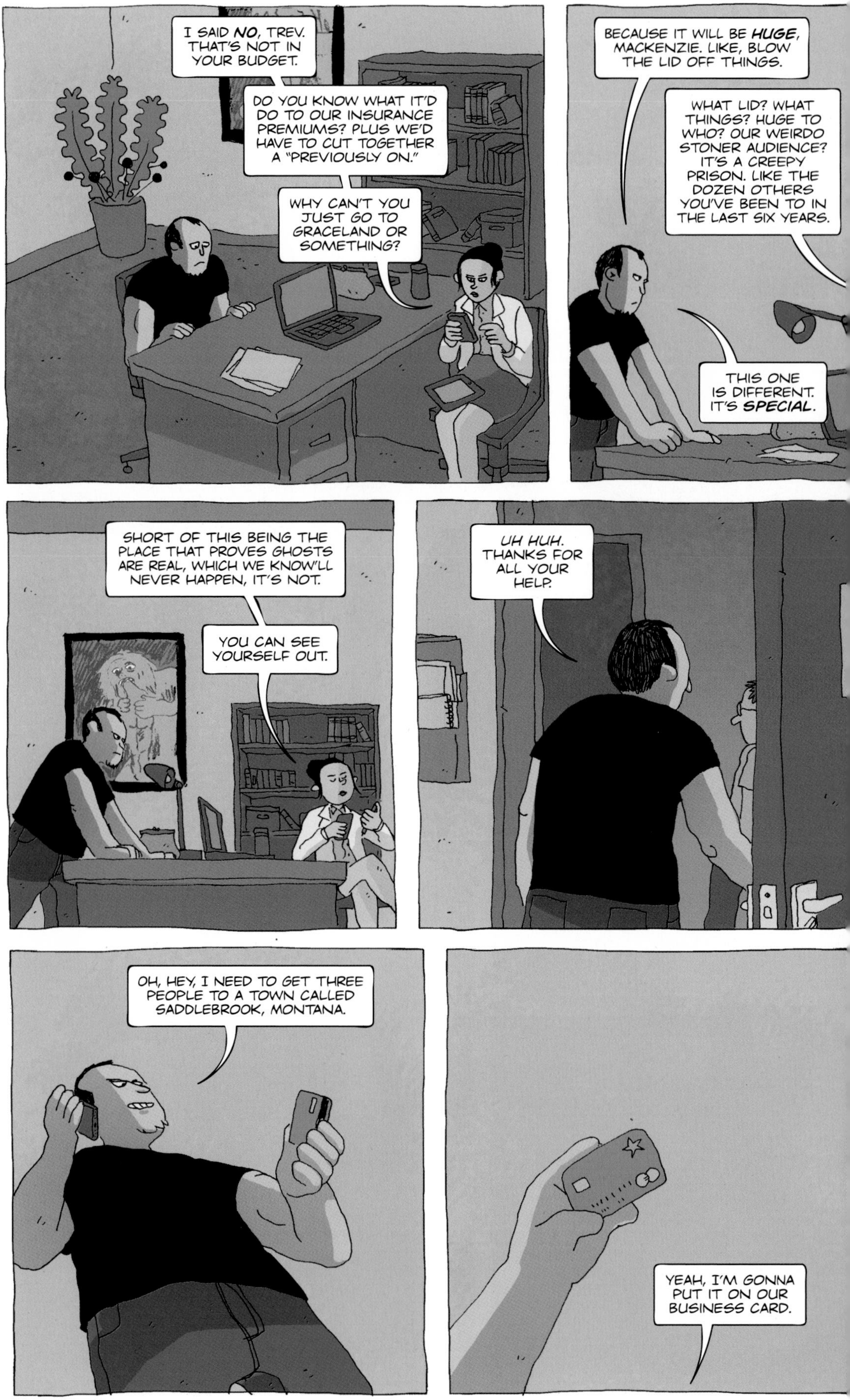
I SAID NO, TREV. THAT'S NOT IN YOUR BUDGET.
DO YOU KNOW WHAT IT'D DO TO OUR INSURANCE PREMIUMS? PLUS WE'D HAVE TO CUT TOGETHER A "PREVIOUSLY ON."
WHY CAN'T YOU JUST GO TO GRACELAND OR SOMETHING?
BECAUSE IT WILL BE HUGE, MACKENZIE. LIKE, BLOW THE LID OFF THINGS.
WHAT LID? WHAT THINGS? HUGE TO WHO? OUR WEIRDO STONER AUDIENCE? IT'S A CREEPY PRISON. LIKE THE DOZEN OTHERS YOU'VE BEEN TO IN THE LAST SIX YEARS.
THIS ONE IS DIFFERENT. IT'S SPECIAL.
SHORT OF THIS BEING THE PLACE THAT PROVES GHOSTS ARE REAL, WHICH WE KNOW'LL NEVER HAPPEN, IT'S NOT.
YOU CAN SEE YOURSELF OUT.
UH HUH. THANKS FOR ALL YOUR HELP.
OH, HEY, I NEED TO GET THREE PEOPLE TO A TOWN CALLED SADDLEBROOK, MONTANA.
YEAH, I'M GONNA PUT IT ON OUR BUSINESS CARD.

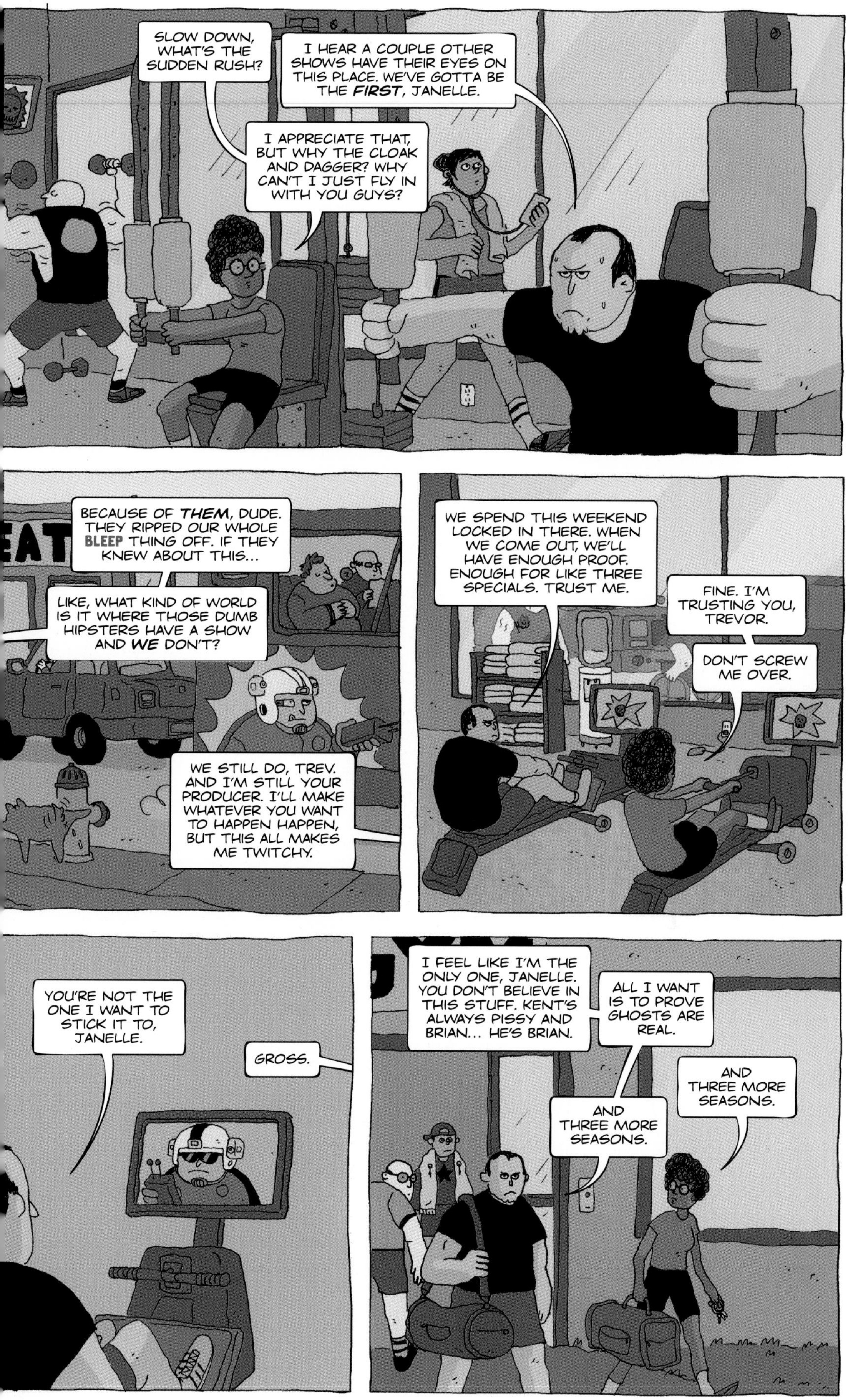
SLOW DOWN, WHAT'S THE SUDDEN RUSH?
I HEAR A COUPLE OTHER SHOWS HAVE THEIR EYES ON THIS PLACE. WE'VE GOTTA BE THE *FIRST*, JANELLE.
I APPRECIATE THAT, BUT WHY THE CLOAK AND DAGGER? WHY CAN'T I JUST FLY IN WITH YOU GUYS?
BECAUSE OF **THEM**, DUDE. THEY RIPPED OUR WHOLE BLEEP THING OFF. IF THEY KNEW ABOUT THIS...
LIKE, WHAT KIND OF WORLD IS IT WHERE THOSE DUMB HIPSTERS HAVE A SHOW AND **WE** DON'T?
WE STILL DO, TREV. AND I'M STILL YOUR PRODUCER. I'LL MAKE WHATEVER YOU WANT TO HAPPEN HAPPEN, BUT THIS ALL MAKES ME TWITCHY.
WE SPEND THIS WEEKEND LOCKED IN THERE. WHEN WE COME OUT, WE'LL HAVE ENOUGH PROOF. ENOUGH FOR LIKE THREE SPECIALS. TRUST ME.
FINE. I'M TRUSTING YOU, TREVOR.
DON'T SCREW ME OVER.
YOU'RE NOT THE ONE I WANT TO STICK IT TO, JANELLE.
GROSS.
I FEEL LIKE I'M THE ONLY ONE, JANELLE. YOU DON'T BELIEVE IN THIS STUFF. KENT'S ALWAYS PISSY AND BRIAN... HE'S BRIAN.
ALL I WANT IS TO PROVE GHOSTS ARE REAL.
AND THREE MORE SEASONS.
AND THREE MORE SEASONS.

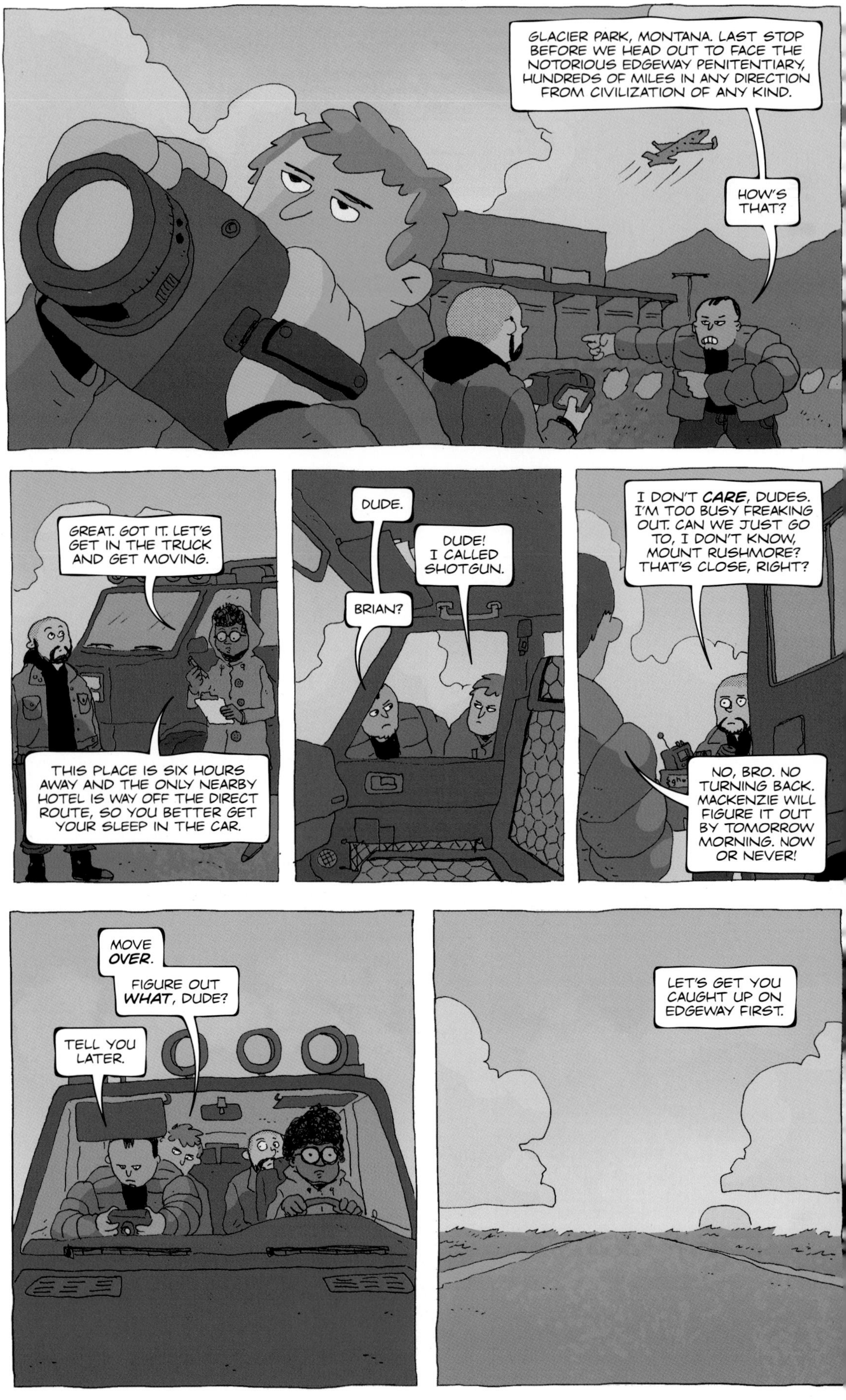
GLACIER PARK, MONTANA. LAST STOP BEFORE WE HEAD OUT TO FACE THE NOTORIOUS EDGEWAY PENITENTIARY, HUNDREDS OF MILES IN ANY DIRECTION FROM CIVILIZATION OF ANY KIND.
HOW'S THAT?
GREAT. GOT IT. LET'S GET IN THE TRUCK AND GET MOVING.
THIS PLACE IS SIX HOURS AWAY AND THE ONLY NEARBY HOTEL IS WAY OFF THE DIRECT ROUTE, SO YOU BETTER GET YOUR SLEEP IN THE CAR.
DUDE.
DUDE! I CALLED SHOTGUN.
BRIAN?
I DON'T **CARE**, DUDES. I'M TOO BUSY FREAKING OUT. CAN WE JUST GO TO, I DON'T KNOW, MOUNT RUSHMORE? THAT'S CLOSE, RIGHT?
NO, BRO. NO TURNING BACK. MACKENZIE WILL FIGURE IT OUT BY TOMORROW MORNING. NOW OR NEVER!
MOVE **OVER**.
FIGURE OUT **WHAT**, DUDE?
TELL YOU LATER.
LET'S GET YOU CAUGHT UP ON EDGEWAY FIRST.

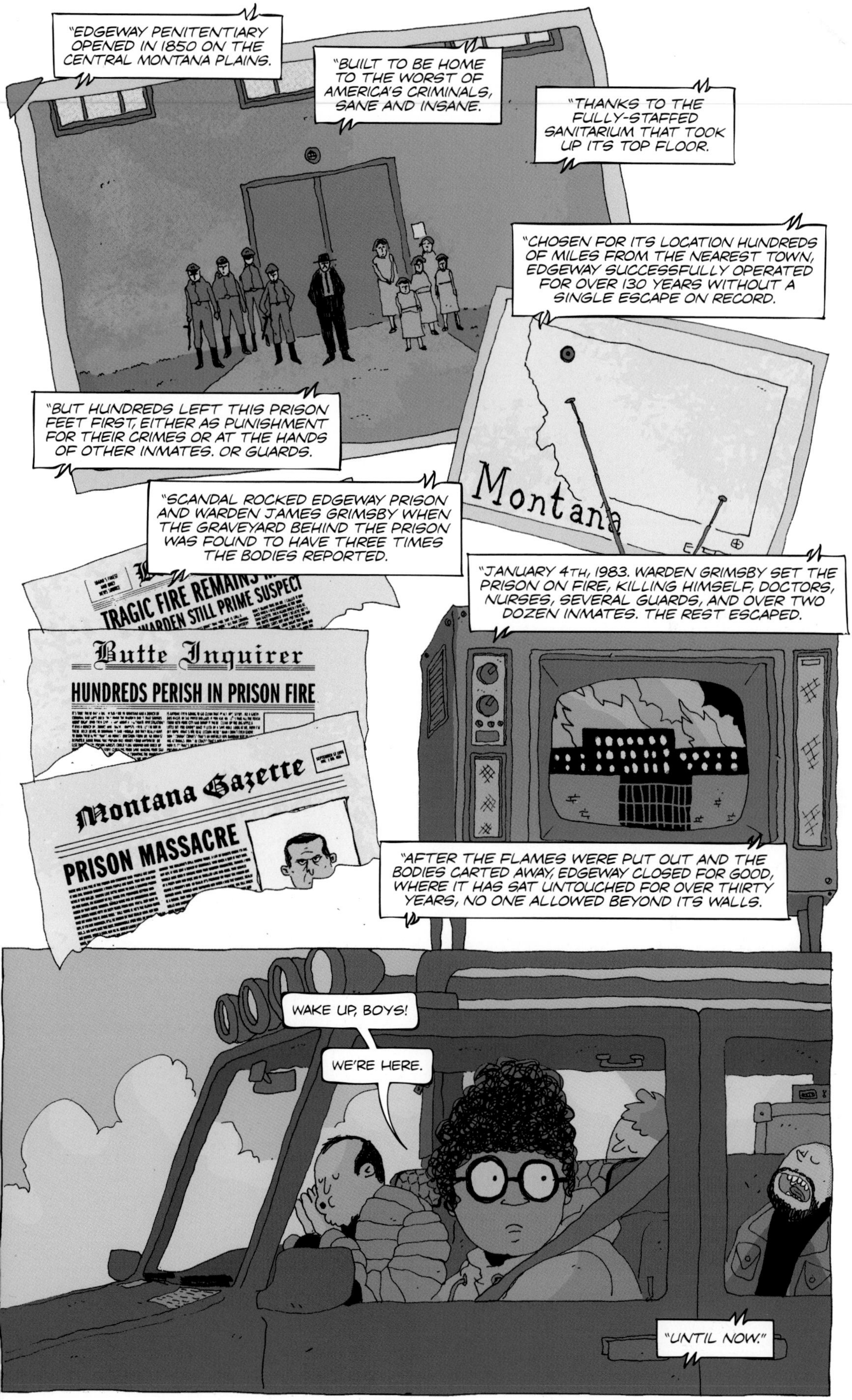
"EDGEWAY PENITENTIARY OPENED IN 1850 ON THE CENTRAL MONTANA PLAINS.
"BUILT TO BE HOME TO THE WORST OF AMERICA'S CRIMINALS, SANE AND INSANE.
"THANKS TO THE FULLY-STAFFED SANITARIUM THAT TOOK UP ITS TOP FLOOR.
"CHOSEN FOR ITS LOCATION HUNDREDS OF MILES FROM THE NEAREST TOWN, EDGEWAY SUCCESSFULLY OPERATED FOR OVER 130 YEARS WITHOUT A SINGLE ESCAPE ON RECORD.
"BUT HUNDREDS LEFT THIS PRISON FEET FIRST, EITHER AS PUNISHMENT FOR THEIR CRIMES OR AT THE HANDS OF OTHER INMATES. OR GUARDS.
Montana
"SCANDAL ROCKED EDGEWAY PRISON AND WARDEN JAMES GRIMSBY WHEN THE GRAVEYARD BEHIND THE PRISON WAS FOUND TO HAVE THREE TIMES THE BODIES REPORTED.
TRAGIC FIRE REMAINS
WARDEN STILL PRIME SUSPECT
"JANUARY 4TH, 1983. WARDEN GRIMSBY SET THE PRISON ON FIRE, KILLING HIMSELF, DOCTORS, NURSES, SEVERAL GUARDS, AND OVER TWO DOZEN INMATES. THE REST ESCAPED.
Butte Inquirer
HUNDREDS PERISH IN PRISON FIRE
Montana Gazette
PRISON MASSACRE
"AFTER THE FLAMES WERE PUT OUT AND THE BODIES CARTED AWAY, EDGEWAY CLOSED FOR GOOD, WHERE IT HAS SAT UNTOUCHED FOR OVER THIRTY YEARS, NO ONE ALLOWED BEYOND ITS WALLS.
WAKE UP, BOYS!
WE'RE HERE.
"UNTIL NOW."

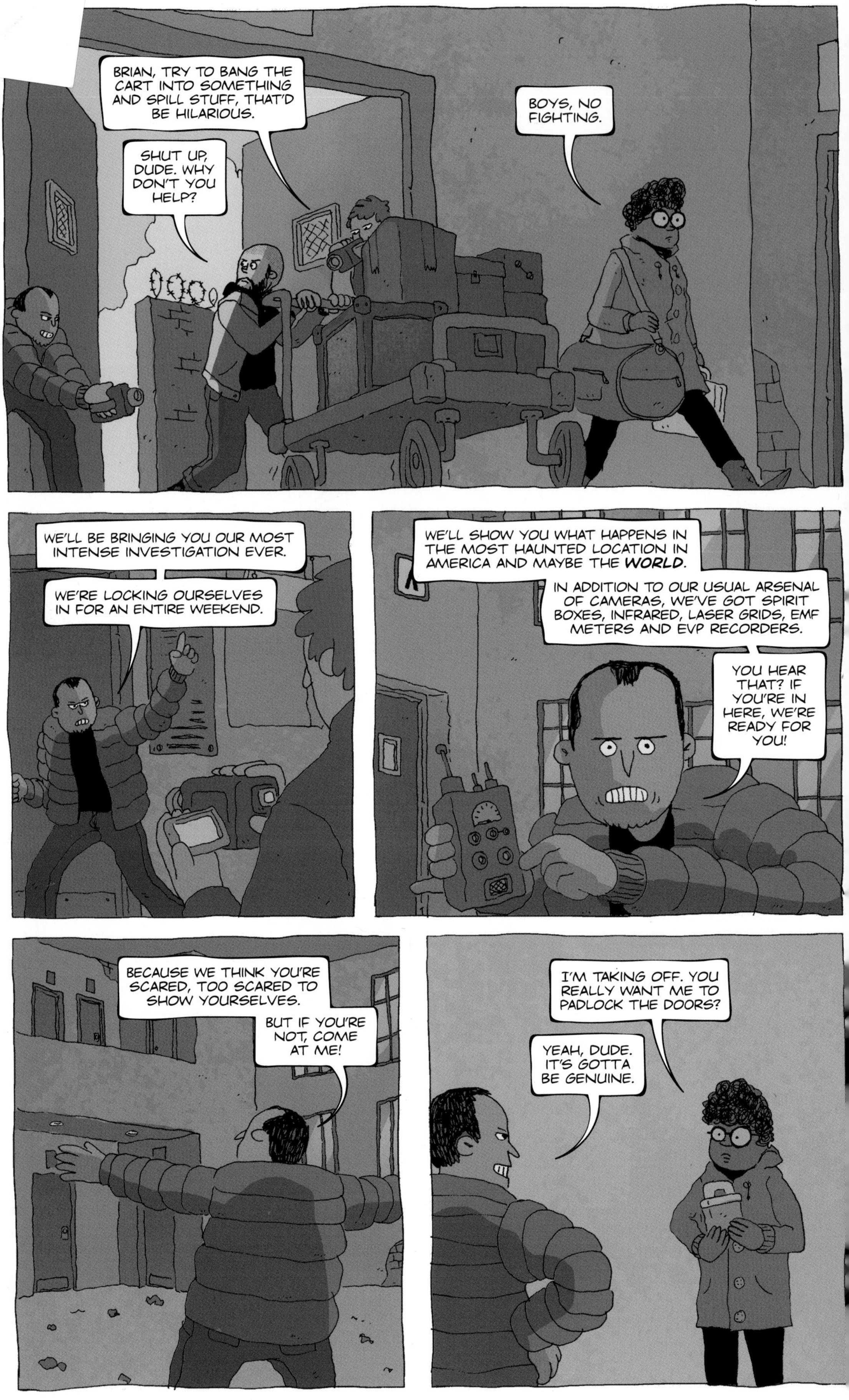
BRIAN, TRY TO BANG THE CART INTO SOMETHING AND SPILL STUFF, THAT'D BE HILARIOUS.
SHUT UP, DUDE. WHY DON'T YOU HELP?
BOYS, NO FIGHTING.
WE'LL BE BRINGING YOU OUR MOST INTENSE INVESTIGATION EVER.
WE'RE LOCKING OURSELVES IN FOR AN ENTIRE WEEKEND.
WE'LL SHOW YOU WHAT HAPPENS IN THE MOST HAUNTED LOCATION IN AMERICA AND MAYBE THE ***WORLD***.
IN ADDITION TO OUR USUAL ARSENAL OF CAMERAS, WE'VE GOT SPIRIT BOXES, INFRARED, LASER GRIDS, EMF METERS AND EVP RECORDERS.
YOU HEAR THAT? IF YOU'RE IN HERE, WE'RE READY FOR YOU!
BECAUSE WE THINK YOU'RE SCARED, TOO SCARED TO SHOW YOURSELVES.
BUT IF YOU'RE NOT, COME AT ME!
I'M TAKING OFF. YOU REALLY WANT ME TO PADLOCK THE DOORS?
YEAH, DUDE. IT'S GOTTA BE GENUINE.

THERE'S A MOTEL ABOUT A HUNDRED MILES EAST, I'M GONNA GET SOME SLEEP. BE BACK IN THE MORNING WITH BREAKFAST.

LAST CHANCE TO COME WITH.

C'MON, JANELLE, AREN'T YOU A *LITTLE* JEALOUS?

NOPE! GOOD LUCK!

TRY TO GET POSSESSED OR SOMETHING!

LET'S DO THIS.

HELL YEAH. LET'S MAKE RATINGS HISTORY.

AND NOT DIE.

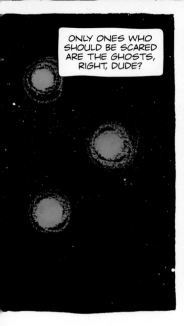

ONLY ONES WHO SHOULD BE SCARED ARE THE GHOSTS, RIGHT, DUDE?

HELL YEAH, BRO. LIKE THAT MOVIE.

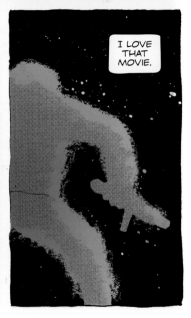

I LOVE THAT MOVIE.

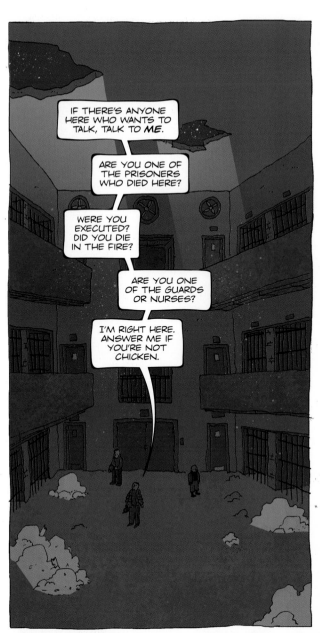

IF THERE'S ANYONE HERE WHO WANTS TO TALK, TALK TO **ME**.

ARE YOU ONE OF THE PRISONERS WHO DIED HERE?

WERE YOU EXECUTED? DID YOU DIE IN THE FIRE?

ARE YOU ONE OF THE GUARDS OR NURSES?

I'M RIGHT HERE. ANSWER ME IF YOU'RE NOT CHICKEN.

--IF YOU'RE NOT CHICKEN.

GET BACK IN YOUR CELL.

HOOOOLLLY...

WHOA, DUDE. THAT'S THE CLEAREST EVP WE EVER GOT.

I'M NOT A PRISONER. I'M FREE. ARE YOU A GUARD?

ARE YOU WARDEN GRIMSBY?

YOU'LL ALL DIE HERE.

OH MY GOD, BRO. WHAT THE **BLEEP**.

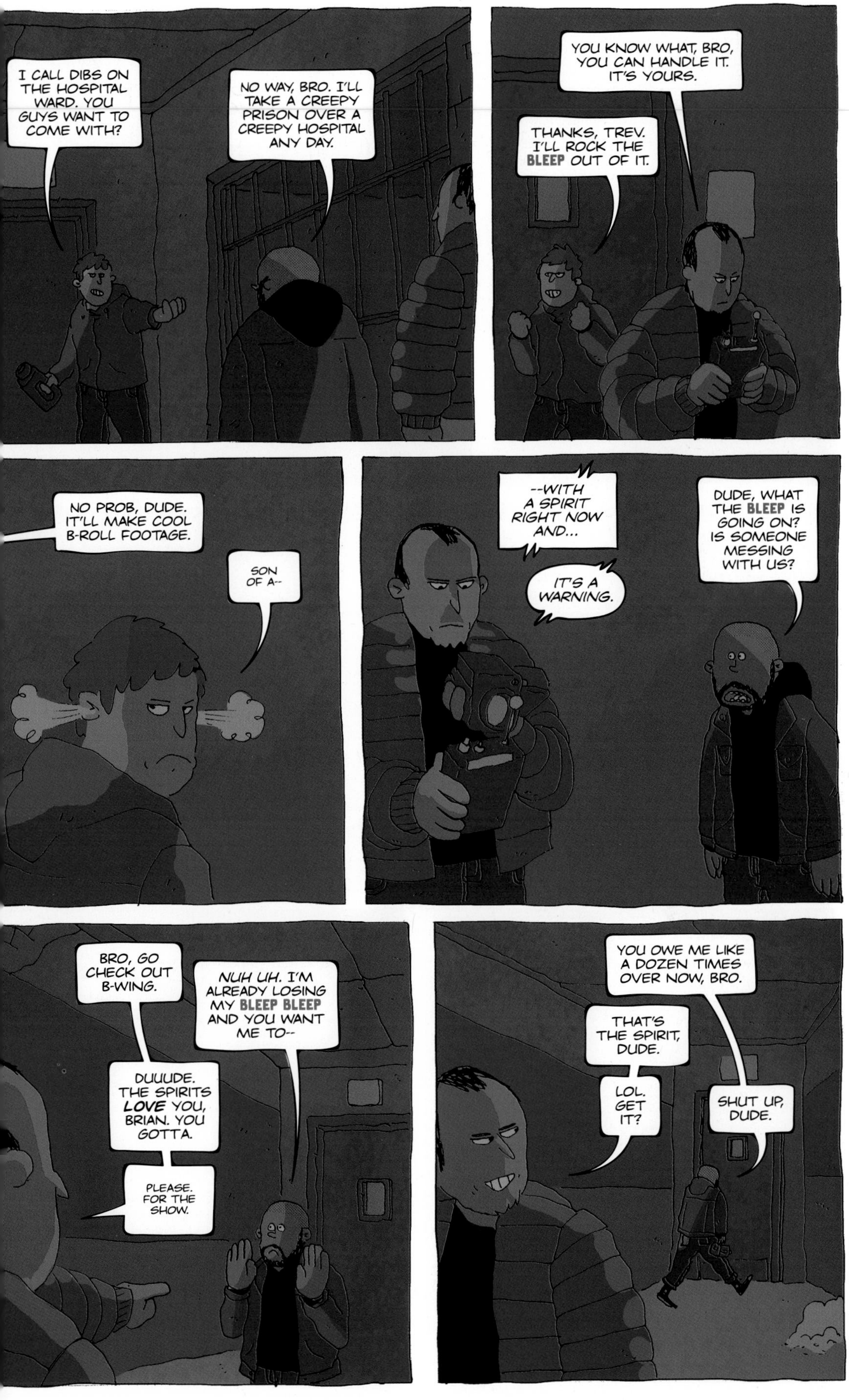
I CALL DIBS ON THE HOSPITAL WARD. YOU GUYS WANT TO COME WITH?
NO WAY, BRO. I'LL TAKE A CREEPY PRISON OVER A CREEPY HOSPITAL ANY DAY.
YOU KNOW WHAT, BRO, YOU CAN HANDLE IT. IT'S YOURS.
THANKS, TREV. I'LL ROCK THE **BLEEP** OUT OF IT.
NO PROB, DUDE. IT'LL MAKE COOL B-ROLL FOOTAGE.
SON OF A--
--WITH A SPIRIT RIGHT NOW AND...
IT'S A WARNING.
DUDE, WHAT THE **BLEEP** IS GOING ON? IS SOMEONE MESSING WITH US?
BRO, GO CHECK OUT B-WING.
NUH UH. I'M ALREADY LOSING MY **BLEEP BLEEP** AND YOU WANT ME TO--
DUUUDE. THE SPIRITS ***LOVE*** YOU, BRIAN. YOU GOTTA.
PLEASE. FOR THE SHOW.
YOU OWE ME LIKE A DOZEN TIMES OVER NOW, BRO.
THAT'S THE SPIRIT, DUDE.
LOL. GET IT?
SHUT UP, DUDE.

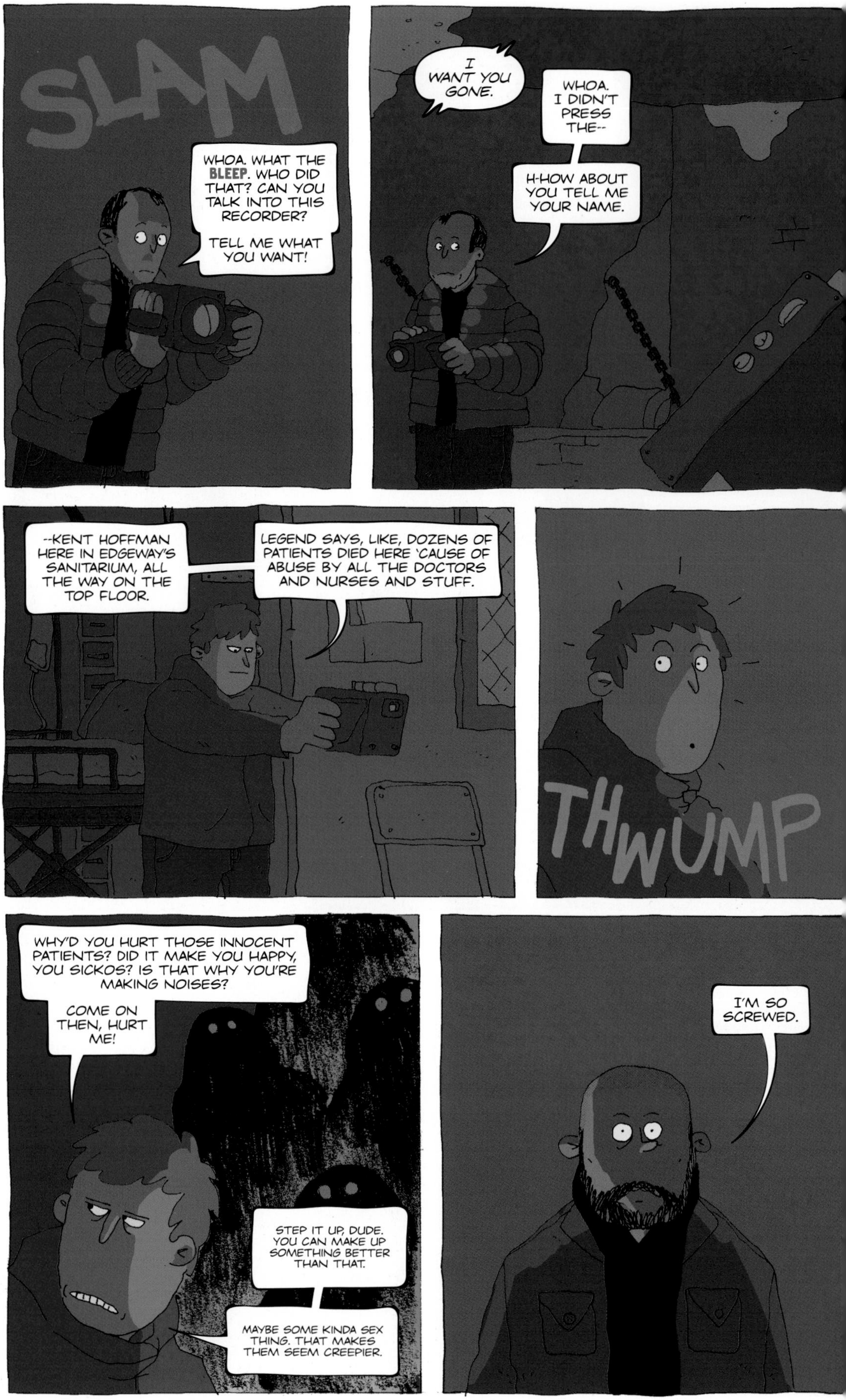
SLAM
WHOA. WHAT THE BLEEP. WHO DID THAT? CAN YOU TALK INTO THIS RECORDER?
TELL ME WHAT YOU WANT!
I WANT YOU GONE.
WHOA. I DIDN'T PRESS THE--
H-HOW ABOUT YOU TELL ME YOUR NAME.
--KENT HOFFMAN HERE IN EDGEWAY'S SANITARIUM, ALL THE WAY ON THE TOP FLOOR.
LEGEND SAYS, LIKE, DOZENS OF PATIENTS DIED HERE 'CAUSE OF ABUSE BY ALL THE DOCTORS AND NURSES AND STUFF.
THWUMP
WHY'D YOU HURT THOSE INNOCENT PATIENTS? DID IT MAKE YOU HAPPY, YOU SICKOS? IS THAT WHY YOU'RE MAKING NOISES?
COME ON THEN, HURT ME!
STEP IT UP, DUDE. YOU CAN MAKE UP SOMETHING BETTER THAN THAT.
MAYBE SOME KINDA SEX THING. THAT MAKES THEM SEEM CREEPIER.
I'M SO SCREWED.

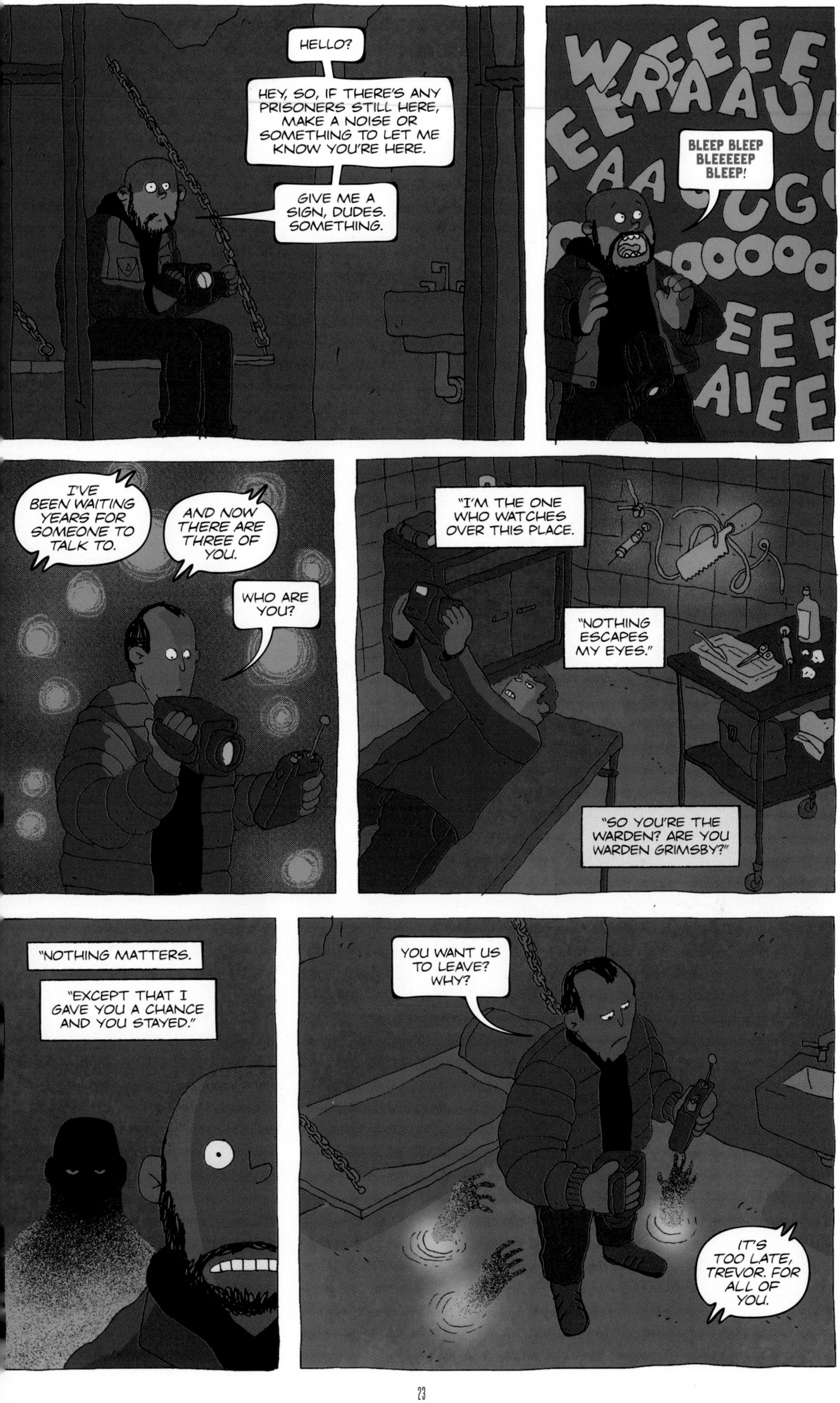

HELLO?
HEY, SO, IF THERE'S ANY PRISONERS STILL HERE, MAKE A NOISE OR SOMETHING TO LET ME KNOW YOU'RE HERE.
GIVE ME A SIGN, DUDES. SOMETHING.
WEEEEE EEE RAAAU AAUGG OOOOOOO EEE AIEEE
BLEEP BLEEP BLEEEEEP BLEEP!
I'VE BEEN WAITING YEARS FOR SOMEONE TO TALK TO.
AND NOW THERE ARE THREE OF YOU.
WHO ARE YOU?
"I'M THE ONE WHO WATCHES OVER THIS PLACE.
"NOTHING ESCAPES MY EYES."
"SO YOU'RE THE WARDEN? ARE YOU WARDEN GRIMSBY?"
"NOTHING MATTERS.
"EXCEPT THAT I GAVE YOU A CHANCE AND YOU STAYED."
YOU WANT US TO LEAVE? WHY?
IT'S TOO LATE, TREVOR. FOR ALL OF YOU.

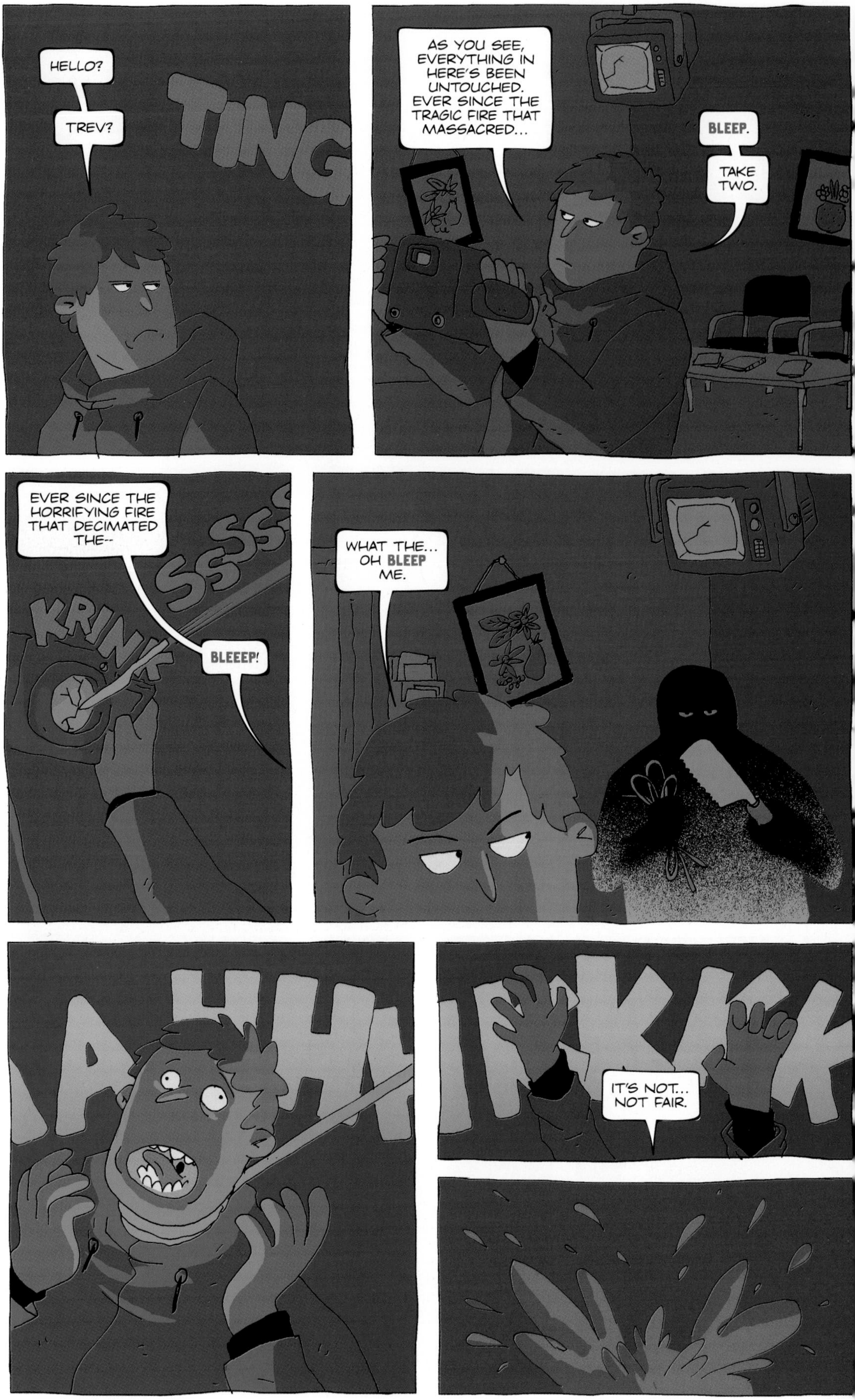
HELLO?
TREV?
TING
AS YOU SEE, EVERYTHING IN HERE'S BEEN UNTOUCHED. EVER SINCE THE TRAGIC FIRE THAT MASSACRED...
BLEEP.
TAKE TWO.
EVER SINCE THE HORRIFYING FIRE THAT DECIMATED THE--
KRINK
SSSSS
BLEEEP!
WHAT THE... OH BLEEP ME.
AHHH
IT'S NOT... NOT FAIR.

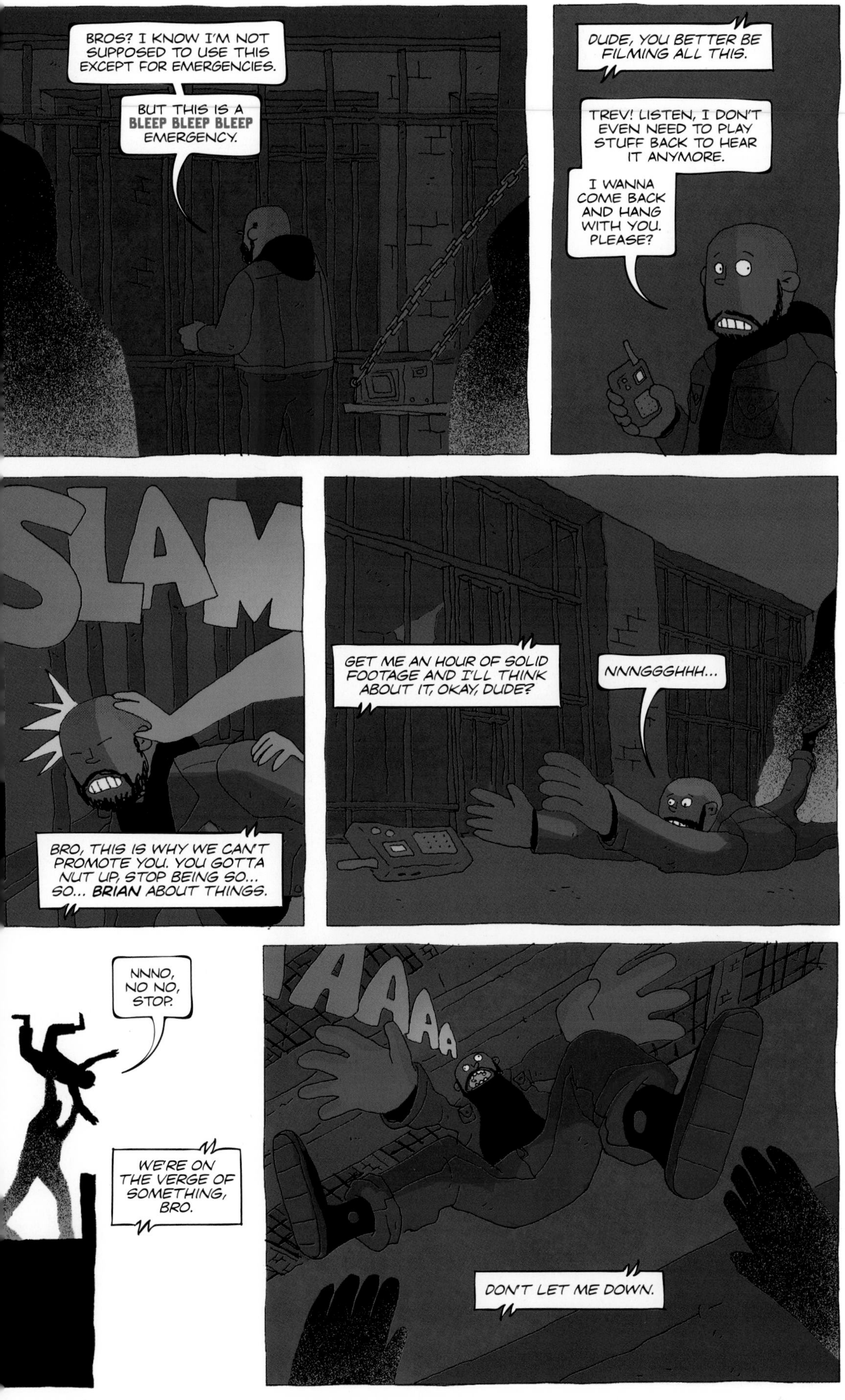
BROS? I KNOW I'M NOT SUPPOSED TO USE THIS EXCEPT FOR EMERGENCIES.
BUT THIS IS A BLEEP BLEEP BLEEP EMERGENCY.
DUDE, YOU BETTER BE FILMING ALL THIS.
TREV! LISTEN, I DON'T EVEN NEED TO PLAY STUFF BACK TO HEAR IT ANYMORE.
I WANNA COME BACK AND HANG WITH YOU. PLEASE?
SLAM
BRO, THIS IS WHY WE CAN'T PROMOTE YOU. YOU GOTTA NUT UP, STOP BEING SO... SO... BRIAN ABOUT THINGS.
GET ME AN HOUR OF SOLID FOOTAGE AND I'LL THINK ABOUT IT, OKAY, DUDE?
NNNGGGHHH...
NNNO, NO NO, STOP.
WE'RE ON THE VERGE OF SOMETHING, BRO.
AAAAA
DON'T LET ME DOWN.

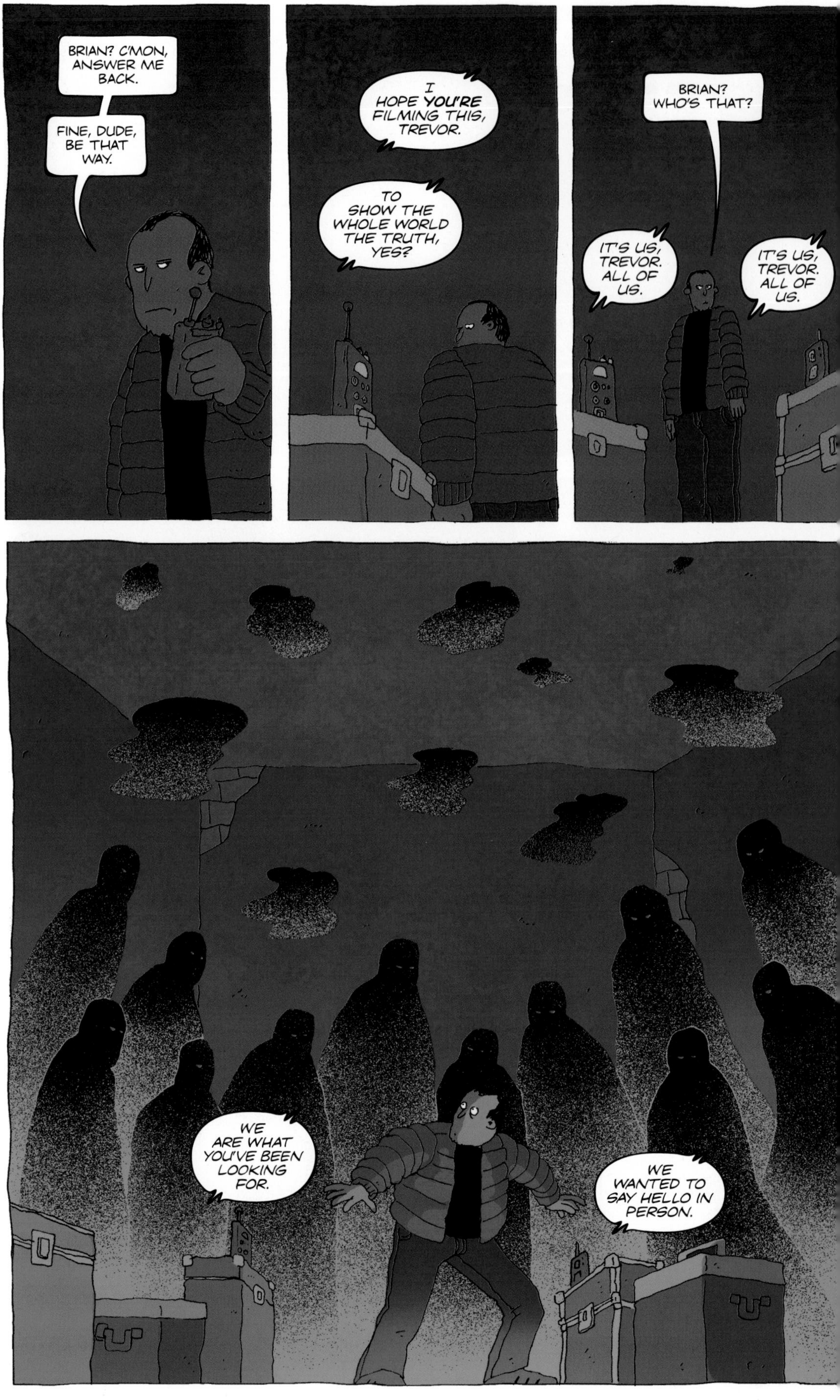
BRIAN? C'MON, ANSWER ME BACK.
FINE, DUDE, BE THAT WAY.
I HOPE **YOU'RE** FILMING THIS, TREVOR.
TO SHOW THE WHOLE WORLD THE TRUTH, YES?
BRIAN? WHO'S THAT?
IT'S US, TREVOR. ALL OF US.
IT'S US, TREVOR. ALL OF US.
WE ARE WHAT YOU'VE BEEN LOOKING FOR.
WE WANTED TO SAY HELLO IN PERSON.

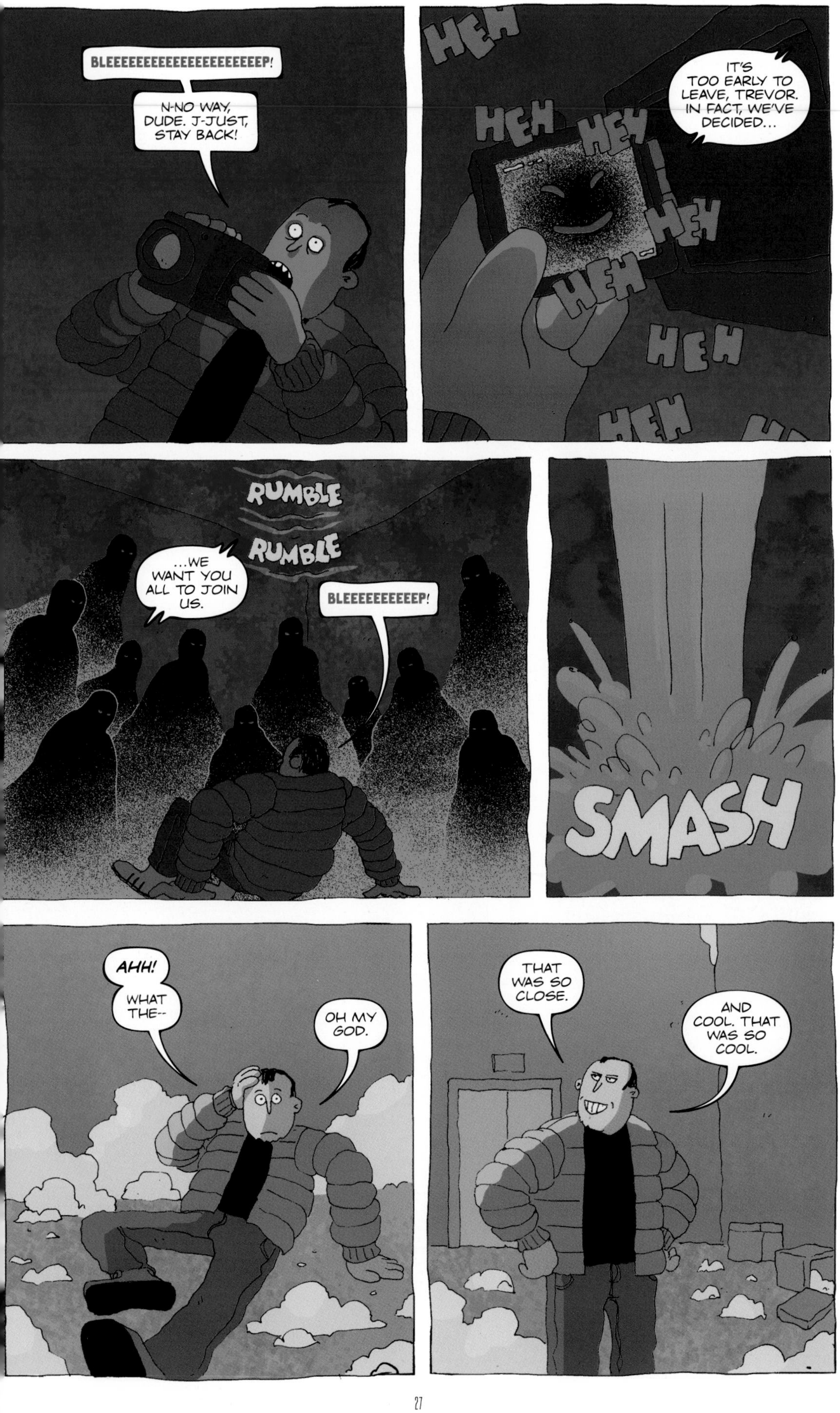
BLEEEEEEEEEEEEEEEEEEEEEP!
N-NO WAY, DUDE. J-JUST, STAY BACK!
HEH
IT'S TOO EARLY TO LEAVE, TREVOR. IN FACT, WE'VE DECIDED...
HEH
HEH
HEH
HEH
HEH
HEH
RUMBLE
RUMBLE
...WE WANT YOU ALL TO JOIN US.
BLEEEEEEEEEEEP!
SMASH
AHH!
WHAT THE--
OH MY GOD.
THAT WAS SO CLOSE.
AND COOL. THAT WAS SO COOL.

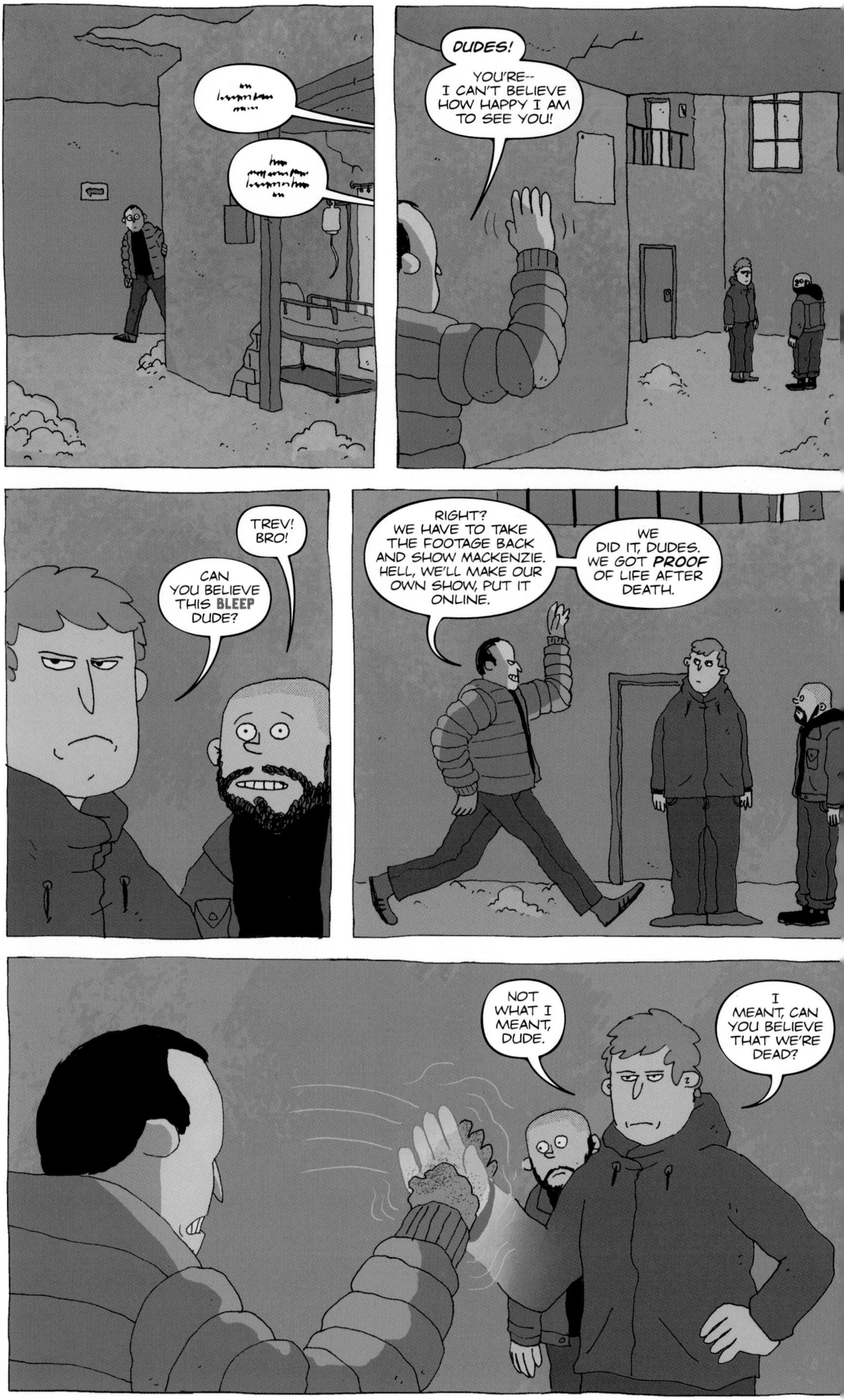
DUDES!
YOU'RE-- I CAN'T BELIEVE HOW HAPPY I AM TO SEE YOU!
TREV! BRO!
CAN YOU BELIEVE THIS BLEEP DUDE?
RIGHT? WE HAVE TO TAKE THE FOOTAGE BACK AND SHOW MACKENZIE. HELL, WE'LL MAKE OUR OWN SHOW, PUT IT ONLINE.
WE DID IT, DUDES. WE GOT PROOF OF LIFE AFTER DEATH.
NOT WHAT I MEANT, DUDE.
I MEANT, CAN YOU BELIEVE THAT WE'RE DEAD?

CHAPTER TWO

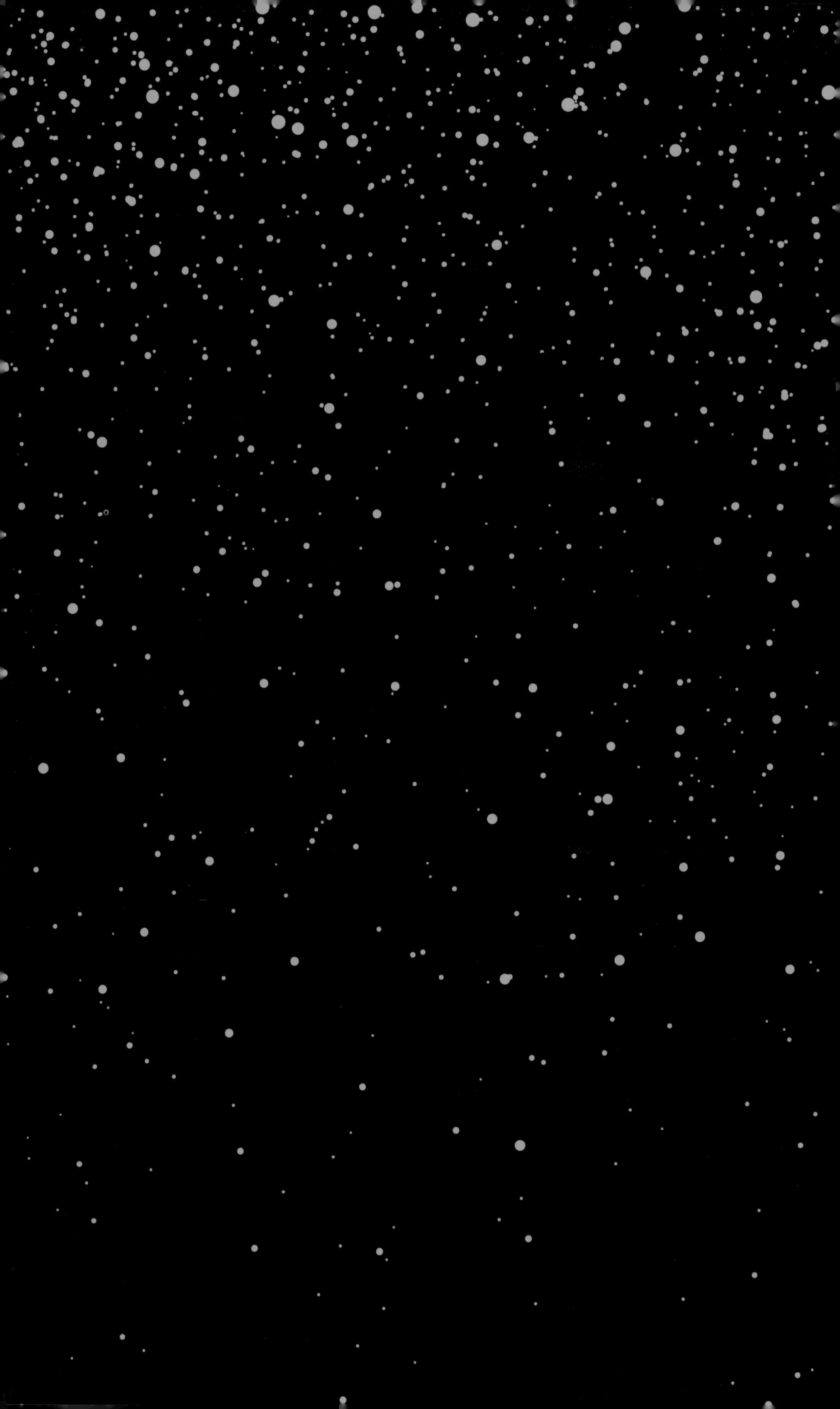

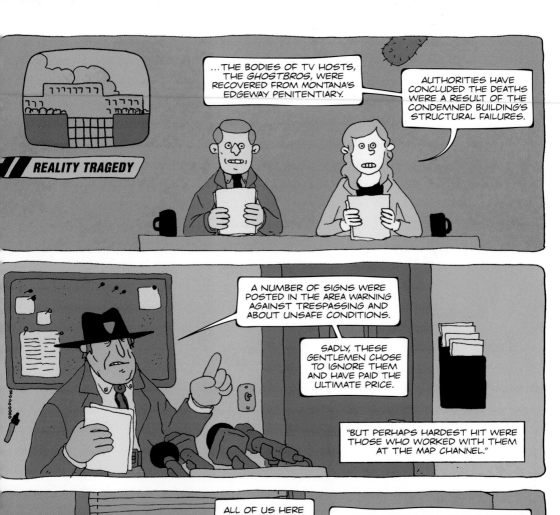

REALITY TRAGEDY

...THE BODIES OF TV HOSTS, THE *GHOSTBROS*, WERE RECOVERED FROM MONTANA'S EDGEWAY PENITENTIARY.

AUTHORITIES HAVE CONCLUDED THE DEATHS WERE A RESULT OF THE CONDEMNED BUILDING'S STRUCTURAL FAILURES.

A NUMBER OF SIGNS WERE POSTED IN THE AREA WARNING AGAINST TRESPASSING AND ABOUT UNSAFE CONDITIONS.

SADLY, THESE GENTLEMEN CHOSE TO IGNORE THEM AND HAVE PAID THE ULTIMATE PRICE.

"BUT PERHAPS HARDEST HIT WERE THOSE WHO WORKED WITH THEM AT THE MAP CHANNEL."

ALL OF US HERE ARE DEVASTATED.

TREVOR, KENT AND BRIAN WERE PART OF OUR FAMILY. WE WILL MISS THEM AS DEARLY AS ANY LOVED ONE. WE TAKE COMFORT KNOWING THEY DIED DOING WHAT THEY LOVED.

TO HONOR OUR LOST FAMILY MEMBERS, WE WILL BE AIRING ALL EIGHT SEASONS OF *GHOSTBROS* AND RELEASING EXCLUSIVE, NEW COMMEMORATIVE MERCHANDISE IN THE MAP CHANNEL STORE.

"THEIR FANS, HOWEVER, ARE LEFT TO ASK 'WHY?' AND WONDER."

I DON'T KNOW WHAT I'M GONNA DO NOW. THEY WEREN'T JUST PEOPLE ON TV, THEY WERE LIKE MY *FRIENDS*.

DUDE, THEY FINALLY DISCOVERED WHAT HAPPENS WHEN YOU DIE. JUST, Y'KNOW, IT SUCKS THAT THEY'LL NEVER BE ABLE TO TELL US.

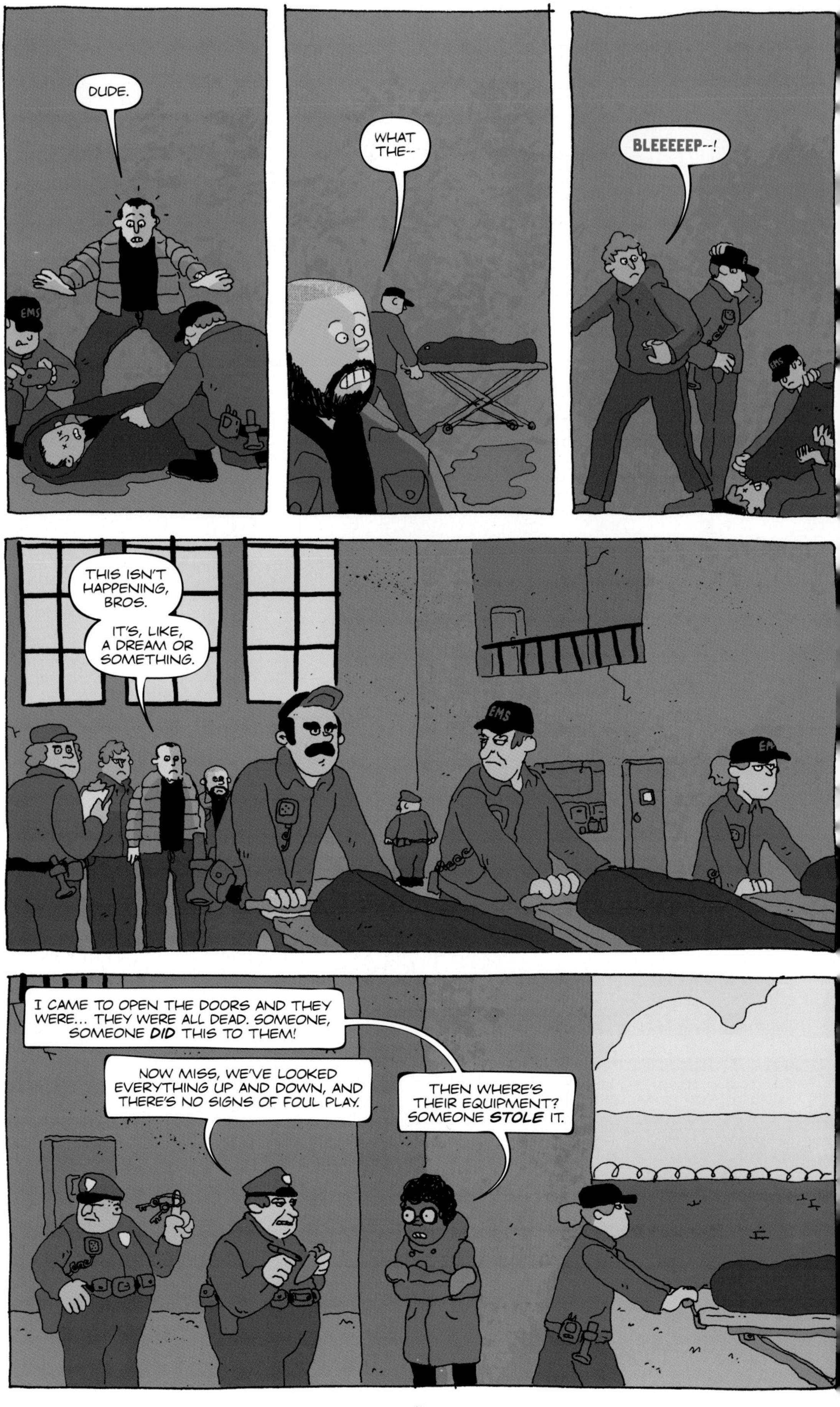

DUDE.
WHAT THE--
BLEEEEEP--!
THIS ISN'T HAPPENING, BROS.
IT'S, LIKE, A DREAM OR SOMETHING.
EMS
I CAME TO OPEN THE DOORS AND THEY WERE... THEY WERE ALL DEAD. SOMEONE, SOMEONE ***DID*** THIS TO THEM!
NOW MISS, WE'VE LOOKED EVERYTHING UP AND DOWN, AND THERE'S NO SIGNS OF FOUL PLAY.
THEN WHERE'S THEIR EQUIPMENT? SOMEONE ***STOLE*** IT.

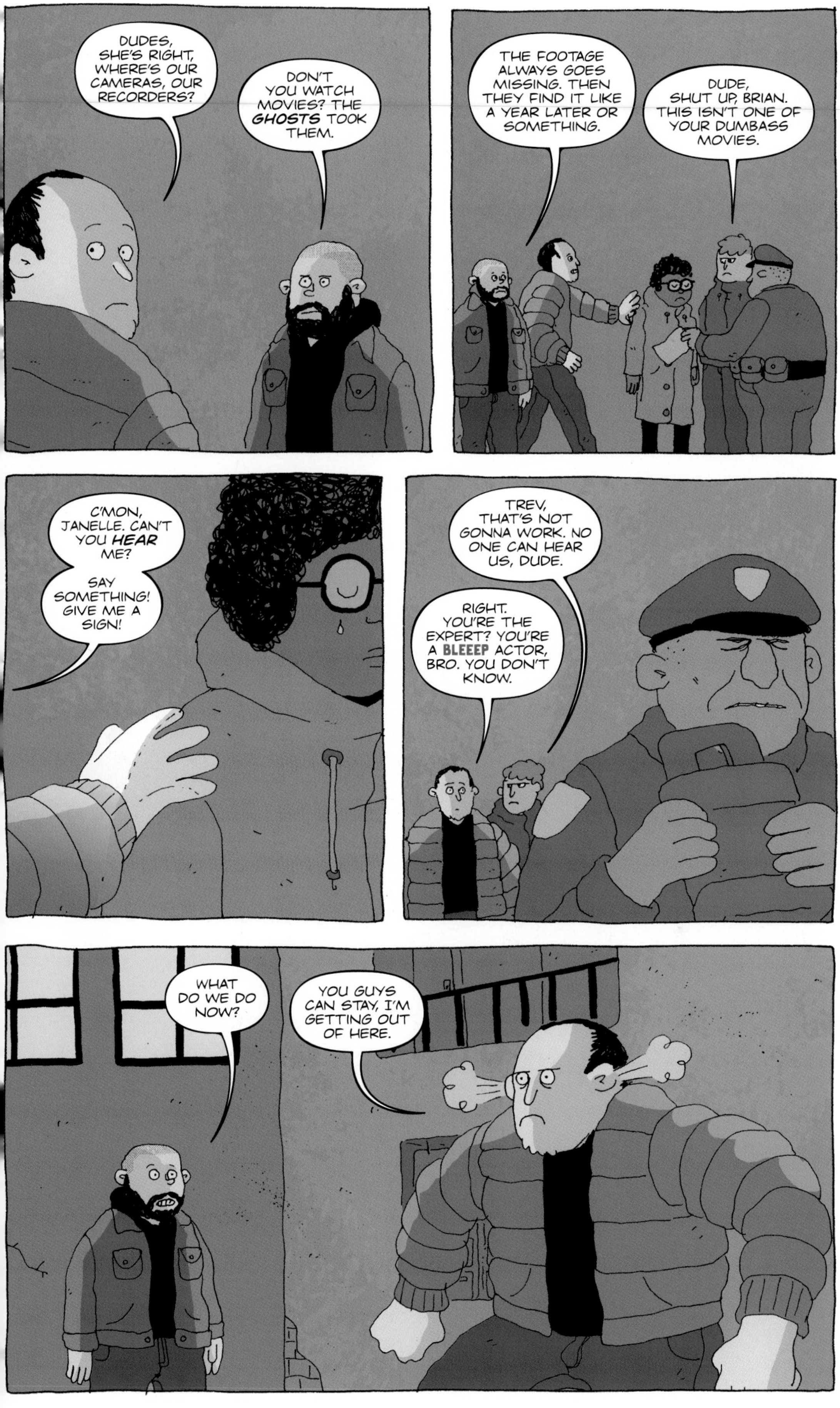
DUDES, SHE'S RIGHT, WHERE'S OUR CAMERAS, OUR RECORDERS?
DON'T YOU WATCH MOVIES? THE GHOSTS TOOK THEM.
THE FOOTAGE ALWAYS GOES MISSING. THEN THEY FIND IT LIKE A YEAR LATER OR SOMETHING.
DUDE, SHUT UP, BRIAN. THIS ISN'T ONE OF YOUR DUMBASS MOVIES.
C'MON, JANELLE. CAN'T YOU HEAR ME?
SAY SOMETHING! GIVE ME A SIGN!
TREV, THAT'S NOT GONNA WORK. NO ONE CAN HEAR US, DUDE.
RIGHT. YOU'RE THE EXPERT? YOU'RE A BLEEEP ACTOR, BRO. YOU DON'T KNOW.
WHAT DO WE DO NOW?
YOU GUYS CAN STAY, I'M GETTING OUT OF HERE.

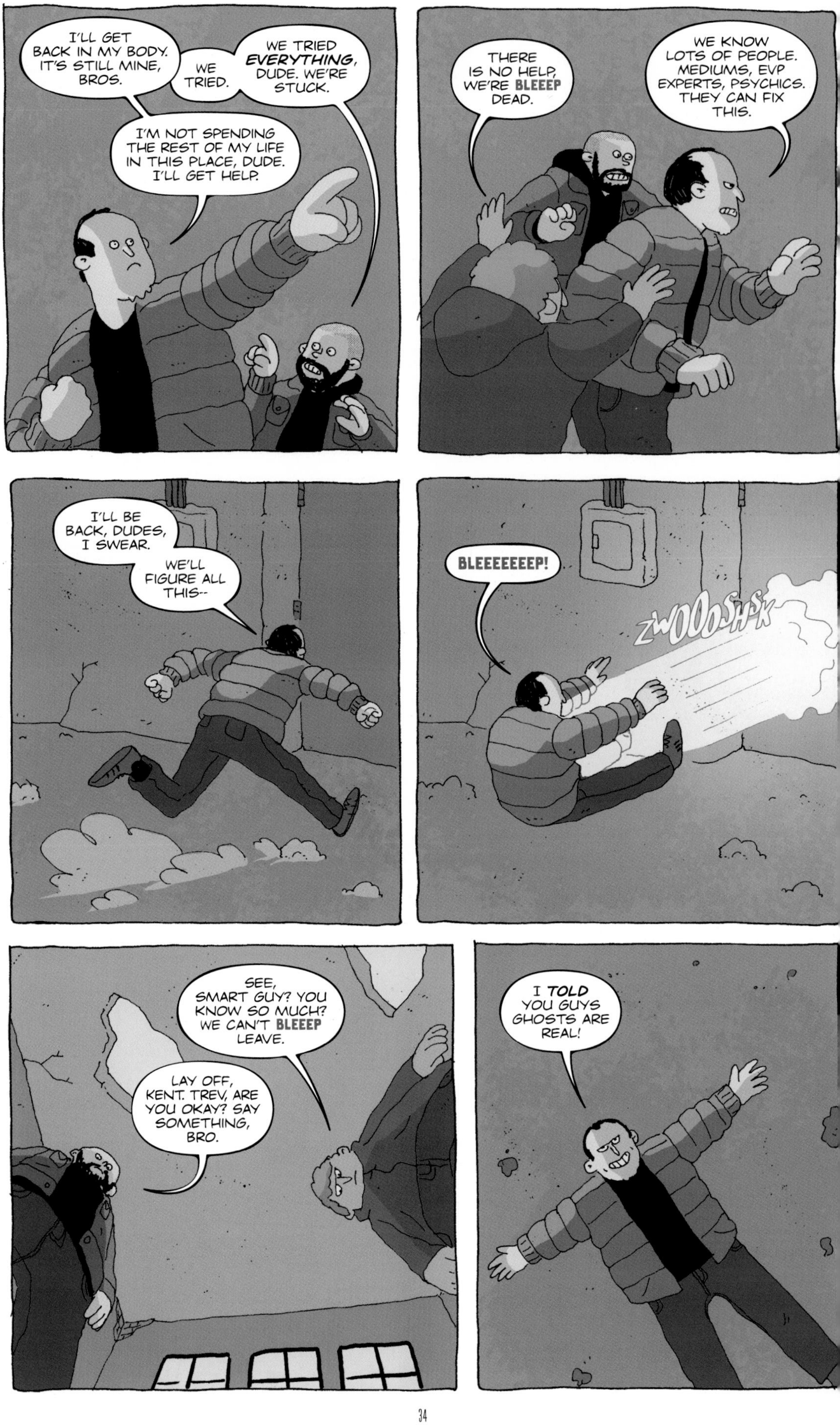
I'LL GET BACK IN MY BODY. IT'S STILL MINE, BROS.
WE TRIED.
WE TRIED *EVERYTHING*, DUDE. WE'RE STUCK.
I'M NOT SPENDING THE REST OF MY LIFE IN THIS PLACE, DUDE. I'LL GET HELP.
THERE IS NO HELP, WE'RE BLEEEP DEAD.
WE KNOW LOTS OF PEOPLE. MEDIUMS, EVP EXPERTS, PSYCHICS. THEY CAN FIX THIS.
I'LL BE BACK, DUDES, I SWEAR.
WE'LL FIGURE ALL THIS--
BLEEEEEEEP!
ZWOOOSHSK
SEE, SMART GUY? YOU KNOW SO MUCH? WE CAN'T BLEEEP LEAVE.
LAY OFF, KENT. TREV, ARE YOU OKAY? SAY SOMETHING, BRO.
I *TOLD* YOU GUYS GHOSTS ARE REAL!

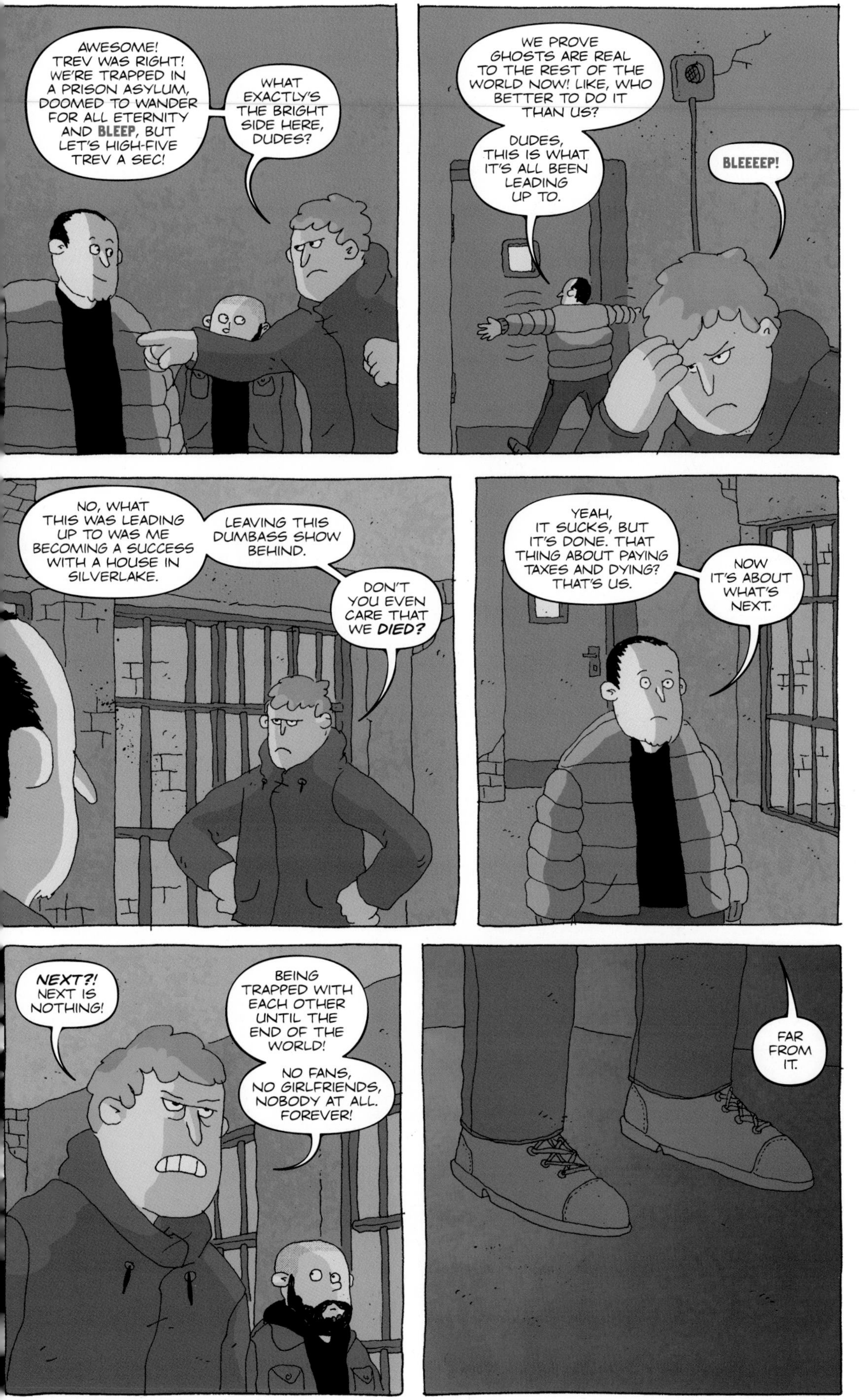
AWESOME! TREV WAS RIGHT! WE'RE TRAPPED IN A PRISON ASYLUM, DOOMED TO WANDER FOR ALL ETERNITY AND BLEEP, BUT LET'S HIGH-FIVE TREV A SEC!
WHAT EXACTLY'S THE BRIGHT SIDE HERE, DUDES?
WE PROVE GHOSTS ARE REAL TO THE REST OF THE WORLD NOW! LIKE, WHO BETTER TO DO IT THAN US?
DUDES, THIS IS WHAT IT'S ALL BEEN LEADING UP TO.
BLEEEEP!
NO, WHAT THIS WAS LEADING UP TO WAS ME BECOMING A SUCCESS WITH A HOUSE IN SILVERLAKE.
LEAVING THIS DUMBASS SHOW BEHIND.
DON'T YOU EVEN CARE THAT WE *DIED?*
YEAH, IT SUCKS, BUT IT'S DONE. THAT THING ABOUT PAYING TAXES AND DYING? THAT'S US.
NOW IT'S ABOUT WHAT'S NEXT.
NEXT?! NEXT IS NOTHING!
BEING TRAPPED WITH EACH OTHER UNTIL THE END OF THE WORLD!
NO FANS, NO GIRLFRIENDS, NOBODY AT ALL. FOREVER!
FAR FROM IT.

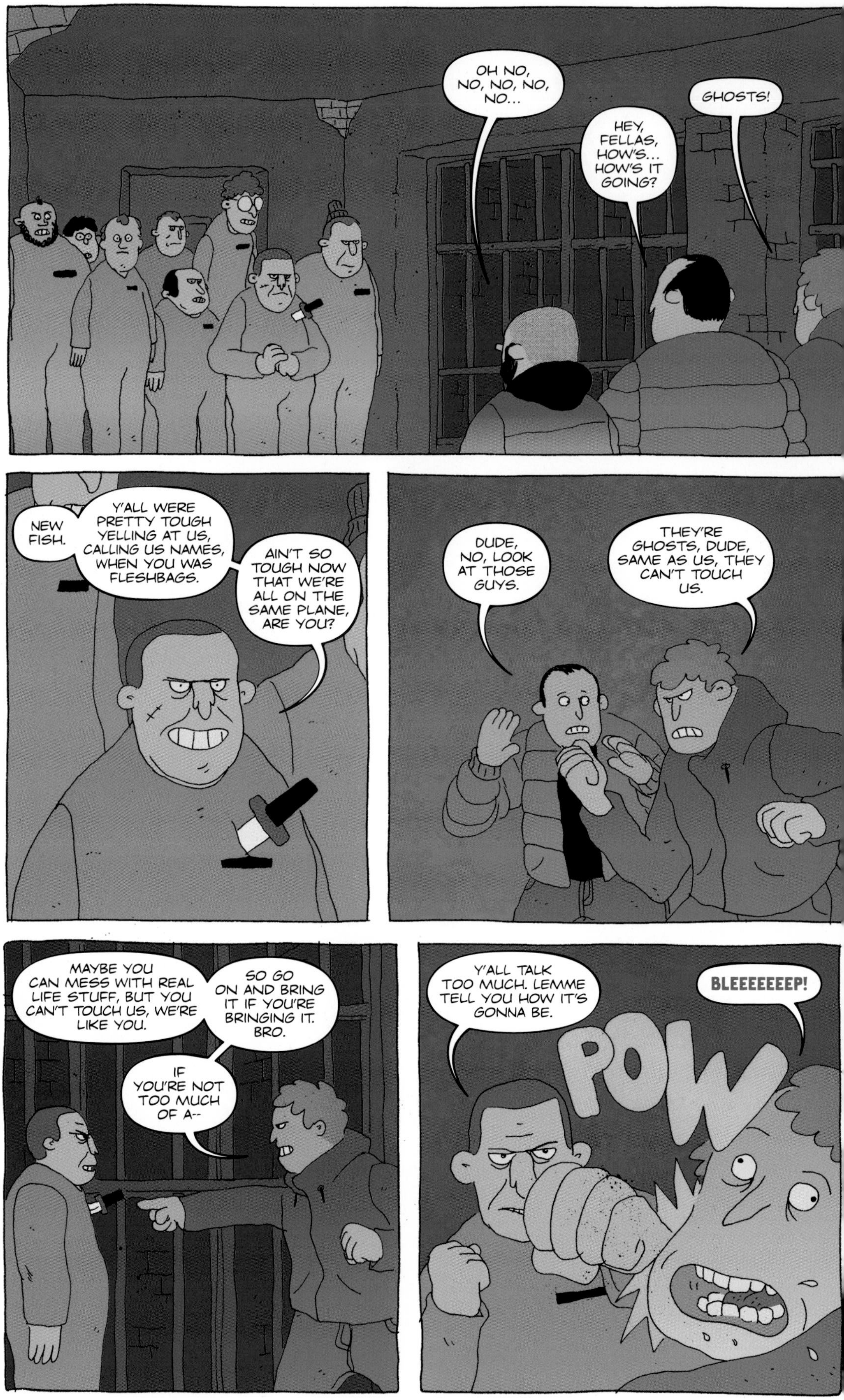
OH NO, NO, NO, NO, NO...
HEY, FELLAS, HOW'S... HOW'S IT GOING?
GHOSTS!
NEW FISH.
Y'ALL WERE PRETTY TOUGH YELLING AT US, CALLING US NAMES, WHEN YOU WAS FLESHBAGS.
AIN'T SO TOUGH NOW THAT WE'RE ALL ON THE SAME PLANE, ARE YOU?
DUDE, NO, LOOK AT THOSE GUYS.
THEY'RE GHOSTS, DUDE, SAME AS US, THEY CAN'T TOUCH US.
MAYBE YOU CAN MESS WITH REAL LIFE STUFF, BUT YOU CAN'T TOUCH US, WE'RE LIKE YOU.
SO GO ON AND BRING IT IF YOU'RE BRINGING IT. BRO.
IF YOU'RE NOT TOO MUCH OF A--
Y'ALL TALK TOO MUCH. LEMME TELL YOU HOW IT'S GONNA BE.
BLEEEEEEEP!
POW

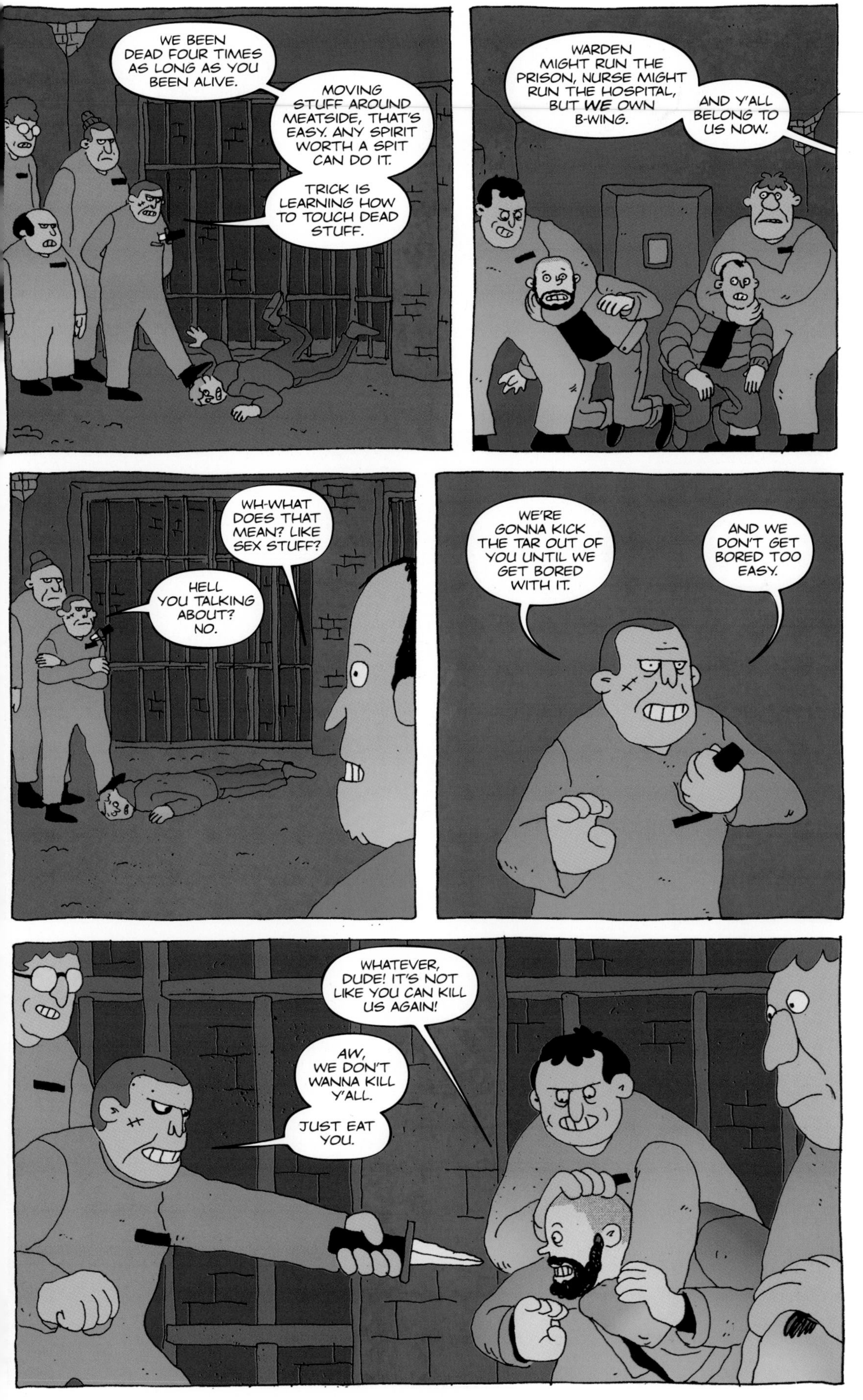
WE BEEN DEAD FOUR TIMES AS LONG AS YOU BEEN ALIVE.
MOVING STUFF AROUND MEATSIDE, THAT'S EASY. ANY SPIRIT WORTH A SPIT CAN DO IT.
TRICK IS LEARNING HOW TO TOUCH DEAD STUFF.
WARDEN MIGHT RUN THE PRISON, NURSE MIGHT RUN THE HOSPITAL, BUT WE OWN B-WING.
AND Y'ALL BELONG TO US NOW.
WH-WHAT DOES THAT MEAN? LIKE SEX STUFF?
HELL YOU TALKING ABOUT? NO.
WE'RE GONNA KICK THE TAR OUT OF YOU UNTIL WE GET BORED WITH IT.
AND WE DON'T GET BORED TOO EASY.
WHATEVER, DUDE! IT'S NOT LIKE YOU CAN KILL US AGAIN!
AW, WE DON'T WANNA KILL Y'ALL.
JUST EAT YOU.

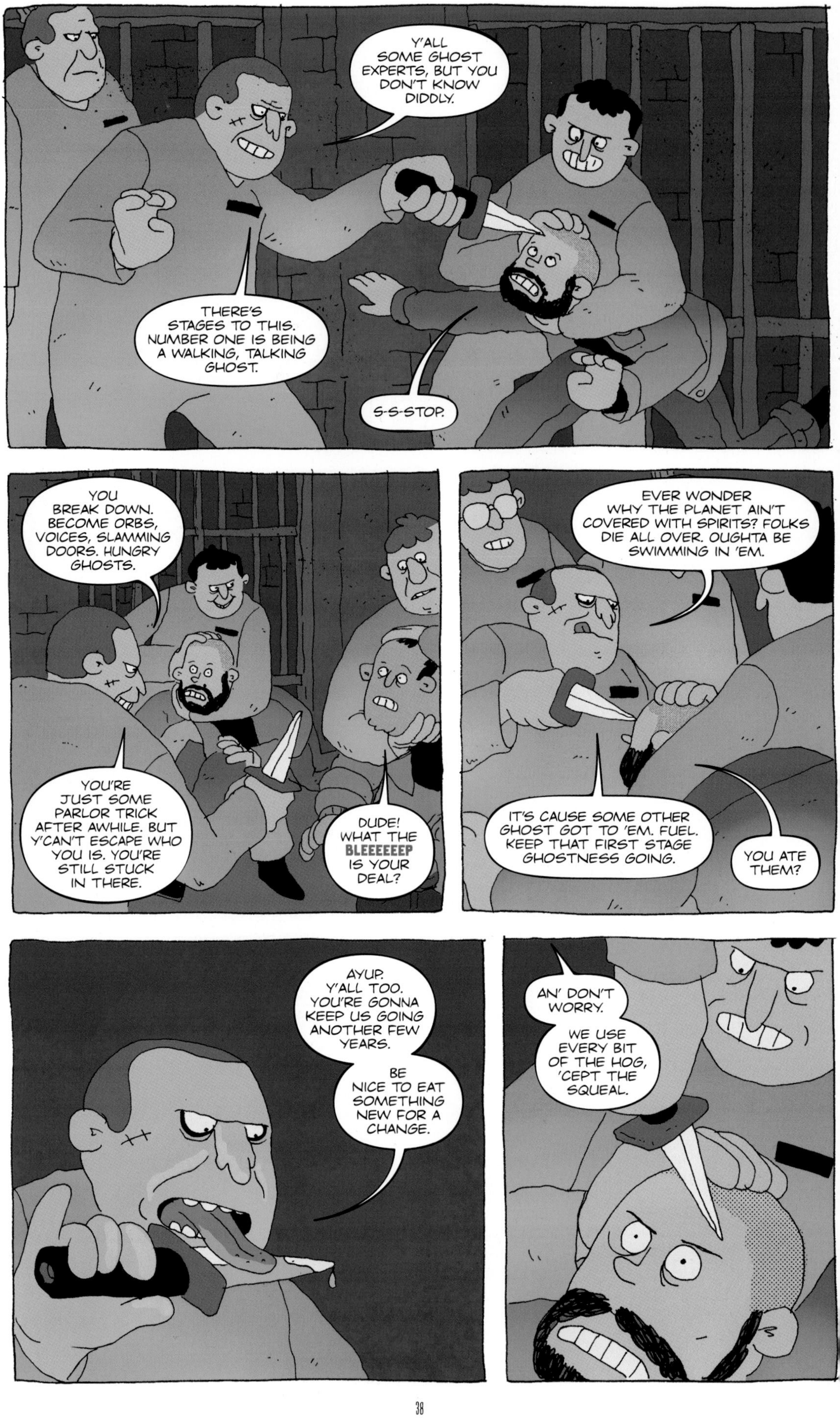

Y'ALL SOME GHOST EXPERTS, BUT YOU DON'T KNOW DIDDLY.
THERE'S STAGES TO THIS. NUMBER ONE IS BEING A WALKING, TALKING GHOST.
S-S-STOP.
YOU BREAK DOWN. BECOME ORBS, VOICES, SLAMMING DOORS. HUNGRY GHOSTS.
YOU'RE JUST SOME PARLOR TRICK AFTER AWHILE. BUT Y'CAN'T ESCAPE WHO YOU IS. YOU'RE STILL STUCK IN THERE.
DUDE! WHAT THE BLEEEEEEP IS YOUR DEAL?
EVER WONDER WHY THE PLANET AIN'T COVERED WITH SPIRITS? FOLKS DIE ALL OVER. OUGHTA BE SWIMMING IN 'EM.
IT'S CAUSE SOME OTHER GHOST GOT TO 'EM. FUEL. KEEP THAT FIRST STAGE GHOSTNESS GOING.
YOU ATE THEM?
AYUP. Y'ALL TOO. YOU'RE GONNA KEEP US GOING ANOTHER FEW YEARS.
BE NICE TO EAT SOMETHING NEW FOR A CHANGE.
AN' DON'T WORRY.
WE USE EVERY BIT OF THE HOG, 'CEPT THE SQUEAL.

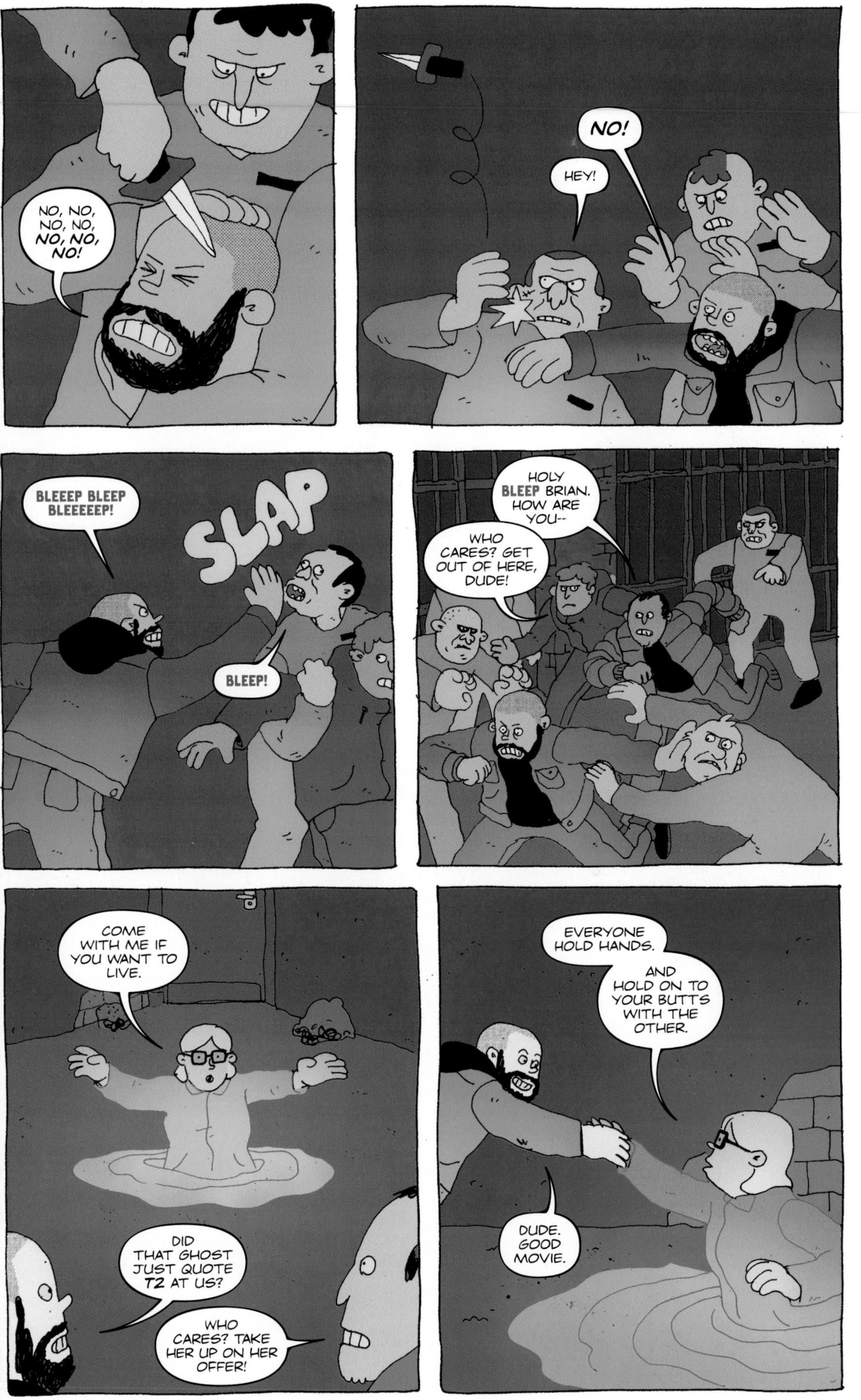
NO, NO, NO, NO, NO, NO, NO!
NO!
HEY!
BLEEEP BLEEP BLEEEEEP!
SLAP
BLEEP!
HOLY BLEEP BRIAN. HOW ARE YOU--
WHO CARES? GET OUT OF HERE, DUDE!
COME WITH ME IF YOU WANT TO LIVE.
DID THAT GHOST JUST QUOTE T2 AT US?
WHO CARES? TAKE HER UP ON HER OFFER!
EVERYONE HOLD HANDS.
AND HOLD ON TO YOUR BUTTS WITH THE OTHER.
DUDE. GOOD MOVIE.

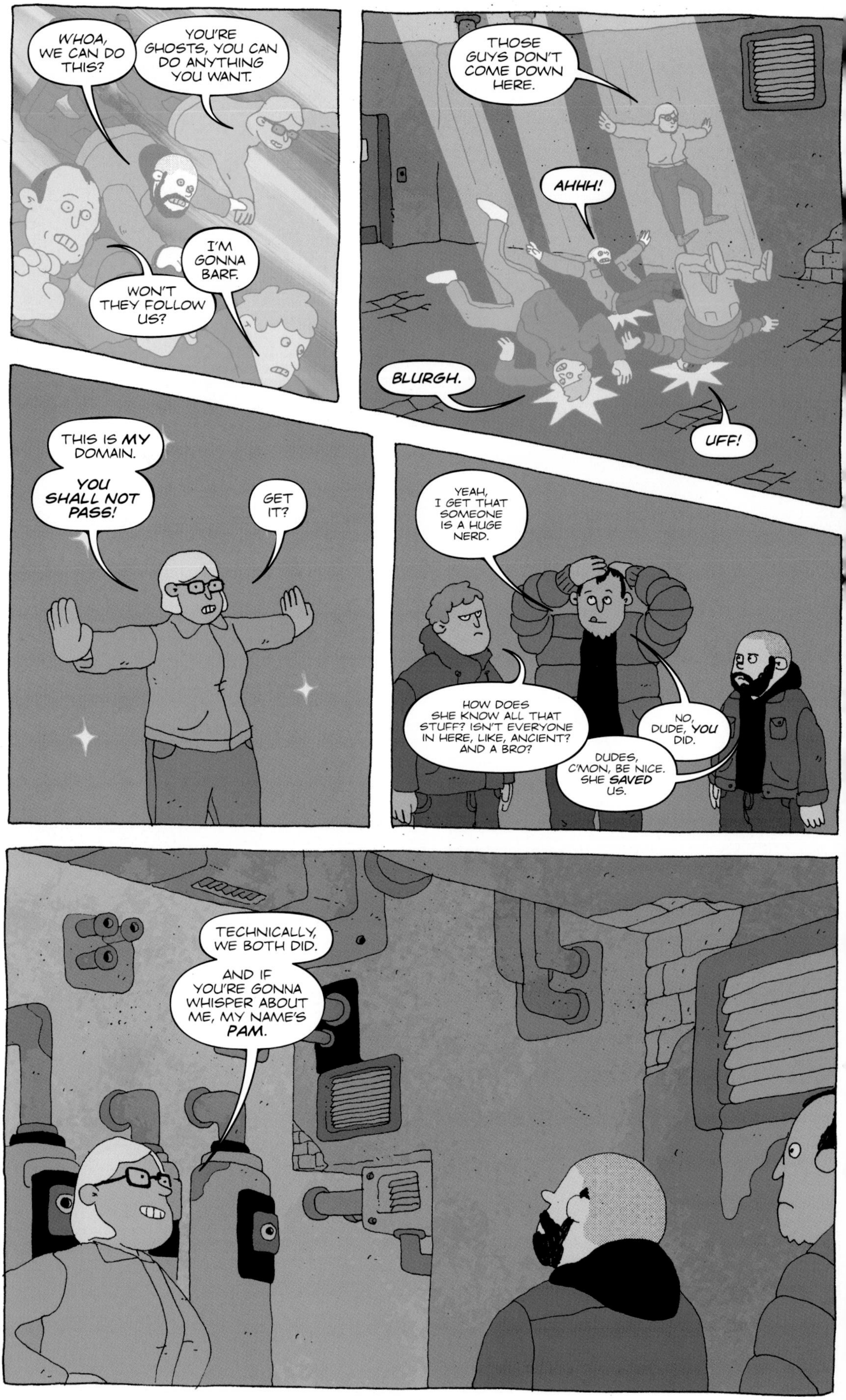

WHOA, WE CAN DO THIS?
YOU'RE GHOSTS, YOU CAN DO ANYTHING YOU WANT.
I'M GONNA BARF.
WON'T THEY FOLLOW US?
THOSE GUYS DON'T COME DOWN HERE.
AHHH!
BLURGH.
UFF!
THIS IS **MY** DOMAIN.
YOU SHALL NOT PASS!
GET IT?
YEAH, I GET THAT SOMEONE IS A HUGE NERD.
HOW DOES SHE KNOW ALL THAT STUFF? ISN'T EVERYONE IN HERE, LIKE, ANCIENT? AND A BRO?
NO, DUDE, ***YOU*** DID.
DUDES, C'MON, BE NICE. SHE ***SAVED*** US.
TECHNICALLY, WE BOTH DID.
AND IF YOU'RE GONNA WHISPER ABOUT ME, MY NAME'S ***PAM***.

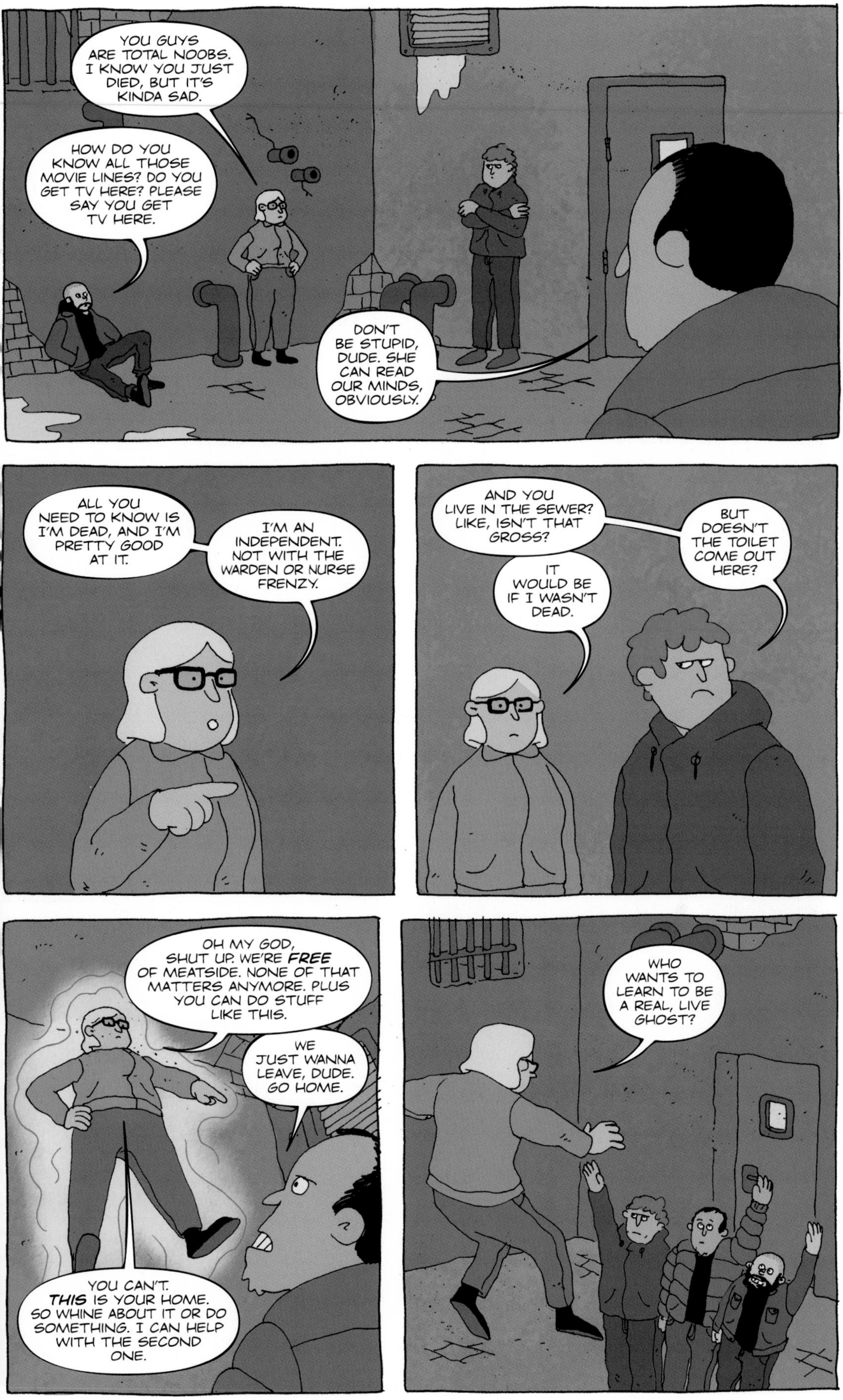
YOU GUYS ARE TOTAL NOOBS. I KNOW YOU JUST DIED, BUT IT'S KINDA SAD.
HOW DO YOU KNOW ALL THOSE MOVIE LINES? DO YOU GET TV HERE? PLEASE SAY YOU GET TV HERE.
DON'T BE STUPID, DUDE. SHE CAN READ OUR MINDS, OBVIOUSLY.
ALL YOU NEED TO KNOW IS I'M DEAD, AND I'M PRETTY GOOD AT IT.
I'M AN INDEPENDENT. NOT WITH THE WARDEN OR NURSE FRENZY.
AND YOU LIVE IN THE SEWER? LIKE, ISN'T THAT GROSS?
IT WOULD BE IF I WASN'T DEAD.
BUT DOESN'T THE TOILET COME OUT HERE?
OH MY GOD, SHUT UP. WE'RE ***FREE*** OF MEATSIDE. NONE OF THAT MATTERS ANYMORE. PLUS YOU CAN DO STUFF LIKE THIS.
WE JUST WANNA LEAVE, DUDE. GO HOME.
YOU CAN'T. ***THIS*** IS YOUR HOME. SO WHINE ABOUT IT OR DO SOMETHING. I CAN HELP WITH THE SECOND ONE.
WHO WANTS TO LEARN TO BE A REAL, LIVE GHOST?

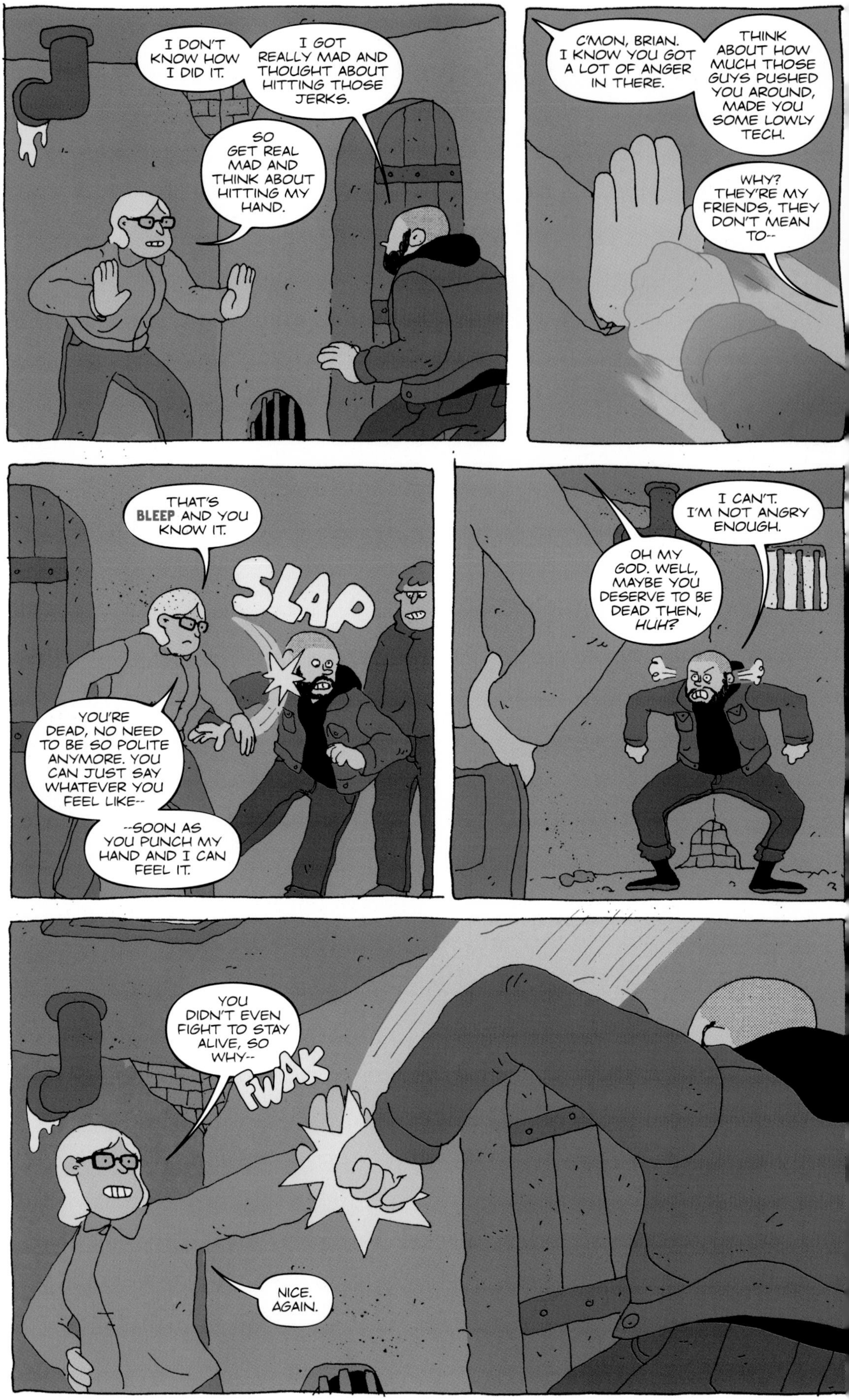
I DON'T KNOW HOW I DID IT.
I GOT REALLY MAD AND THOUGHT ABOUT HITTING THOSE JERKS.
SO GET REAL MAD AND THINK ABOUT HITTING MY HAND.
C'MON, BRIAN. I KNOW YOU GOT A LOT OF ANGER IN THERE.
THINK ABOUT HOW MUCH THOSE GUYS PUSHED YOU AROUND, MADE YOU SOME LOWLY TECH.
WHY? THEY'RE MY FRIENDS, THEY DON'T MEAN TO--
THAT'S **BLEEP** AND YOU KNOW IT.
SLAP
YOU'RE DEAD, NO NEED TO BE SO POLITE ANYMORE. YOU CAN JUST SAY WHATEVER YOU FEEL LIKE--
--SOON AS YOU PUNCH MY HAND AND I CAN FEEL IT.
I CAN'T. I'M NOT ANGRY ENOUGH.
OH MY GOD. WELL, MAYBE YOU DESERVE TO BE DEAD THEN, *HUH?*
YOU DIDN'T EVEN FIGHT TO STAY ALIVE, SO WHY--
FWAK
NICE. AGAIN.

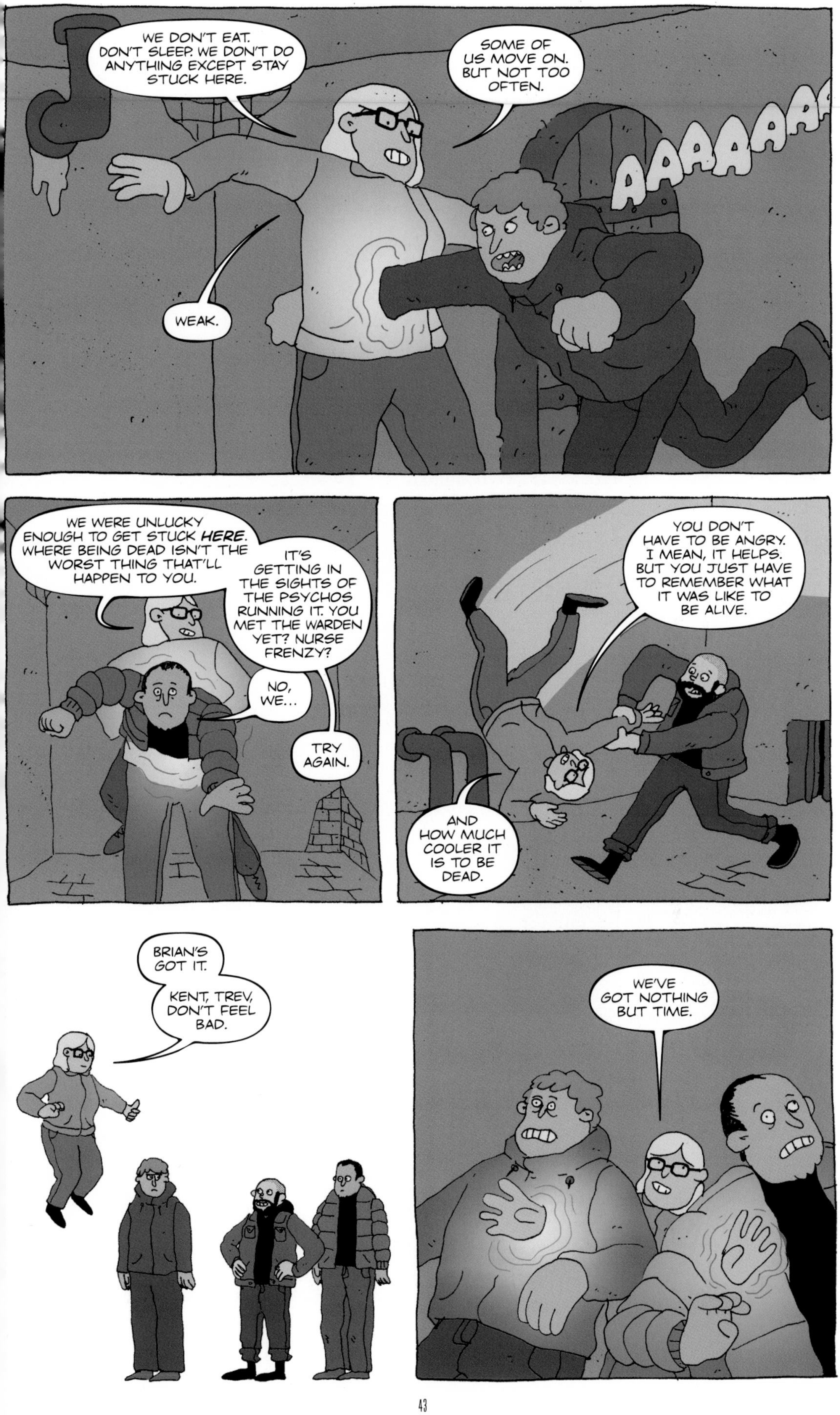
WE DON'T EAT. DON'T SLEEP. WE DON'T DO ANYTHING EXCEPT STAY STUCK HERE.
SOME OF US MOVE ON. BUT NOT TOO OFTEN.
AAAAAAA
WEAK.
WE WERE UNLUCKY ENOUGH TO GET STUCK ***HERE***. WHERE BEING DEAD ISN'T THE WORST THING THAT'LL HAPPEN TO YOU.
IT'S GETTING IN THE SIGHTS OF THE PSYCHOS RUNNING IT. YOU MET THE WARDEN YET? NURSE FRENZY?
NO, WE...
TRY AGAIN.
YOU DON'T HAVE TO BE ANGRY. I MEAN, IT HELPS. BUT YOU JUST HAVE TO REMEMBER WHAT IT WAS LIKE TO BE ALIVE.
AND HOW MUCH COOLER IT IS TO BE DEAD.
BRIAN'S GOT IT.
KENT, TREV, DON'T FEEL BAD.
WE'VE GOT NOTHING BUT TIME.

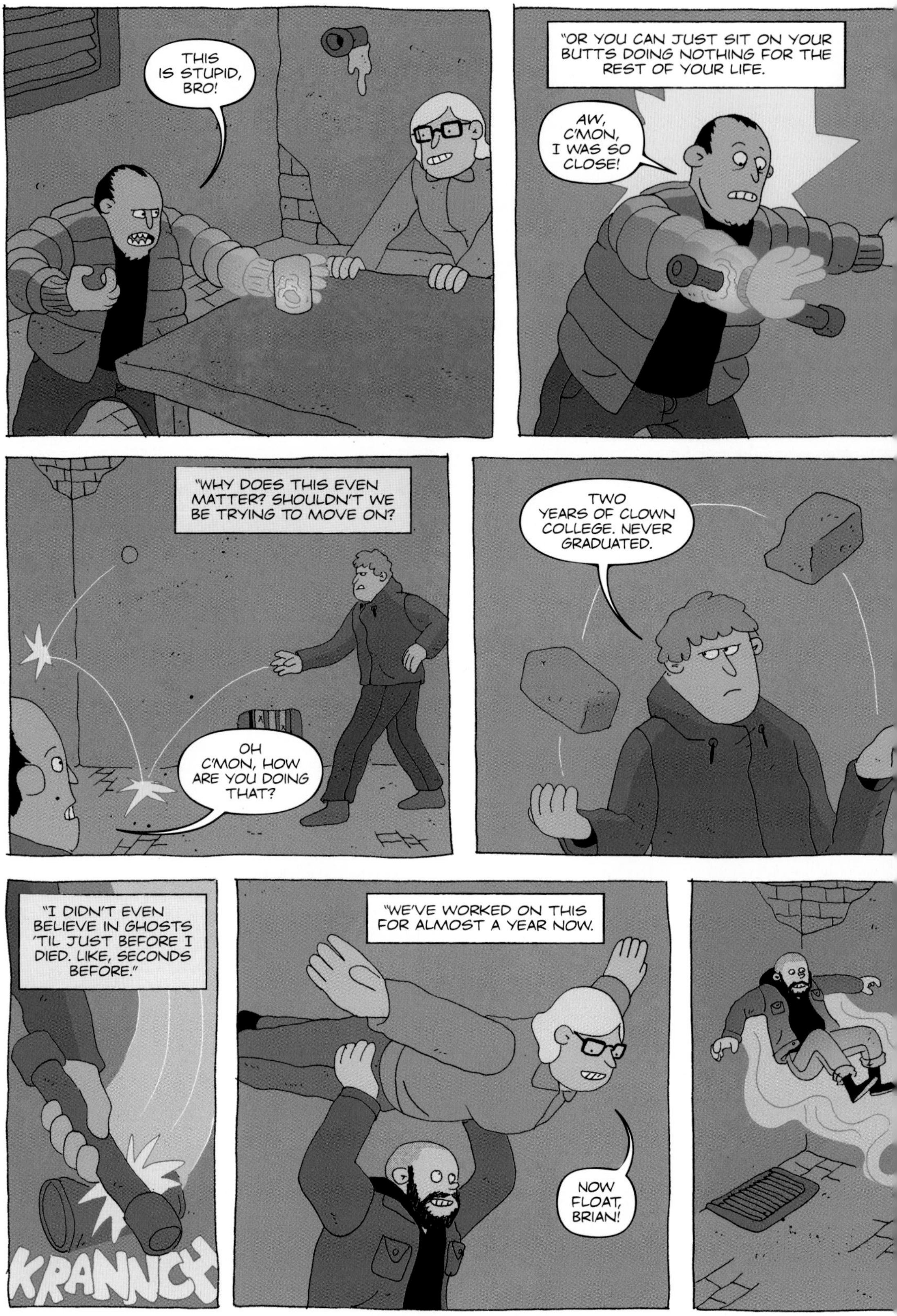
THIS IS STUPID, BRO!
"OR YOU CAN JUST SIT ON YOUR BUTTS DOING NOTHING FOR THE REST OF YOUR LIFE.
AW, C'MON, I WAS SO CLOSE!
"WHY DOES THIS EVEN MATTER? SHOULDN'T WE BE TRYING TO MOVE ON?
OH C'MON, HOW ARE YOU DOING THAT?
TWO YEARS OF CLOWN COLLEGE. NEVER GRADUATED.
"I DIDN'T EVEN BELIEVE IN GHOSTS 'TIL JUST BEFORE I DIED. LIKE, SECONDS BEFORE."
KRANNCK
"WE'VE WORKED ON THIS FOR ALMOST A YEAR NOW.
NOW FLOAT, BRIAN!

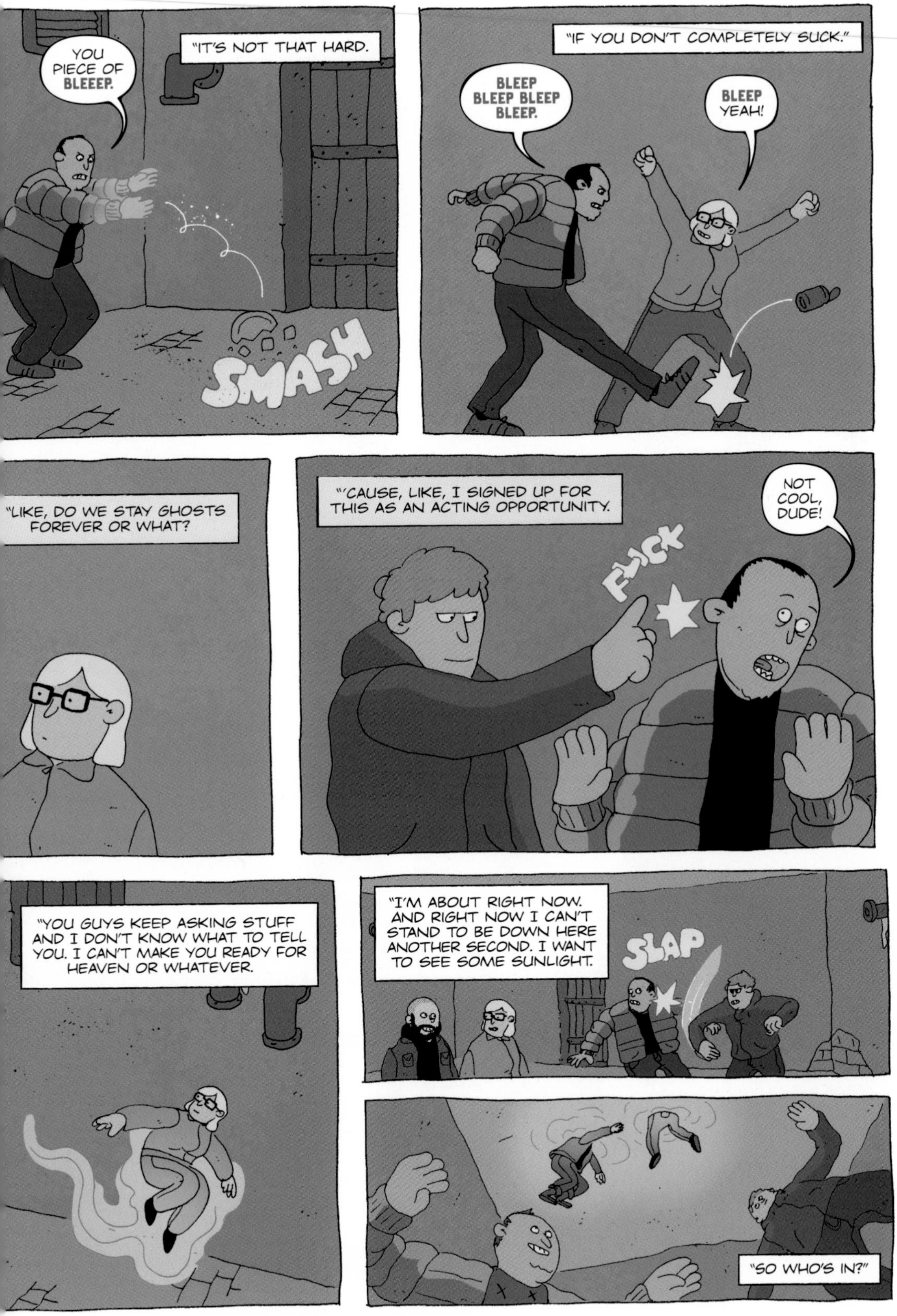
YOU PIECE OF BLEEEP.
"IT'S NOT THAT HARD.
SMASH
"IF YOU DON'T COMPLETELY SUCK."
BLEEP BLEEP BLEEP BLEEP.
BLEEP YEAH!
"LIKE, DO WE STAY GHOSTS FOREVER OR WHAT?
"'CAUSE, LIKE, I SIGNED UP FOR THIS AS AN ACTING OPPORTUNITY.
FLICK
NOT COOL, DUDE!
"YOU GUYS KEEP ASKING STUFF AND I DON'T KNOW WHAT TO TELL YOU. I CAN'T MAKE YOU READY FOR HEAVEN OR WHATEVER.
"I'M ABOUT RIGHT NOW. AND RIGHT NOW I CAN'T STAND TO BE DOWN HERE ANOTHER SECOND. I WANT TO SEE SOME SUNLIGHT.
SLAP
"SO WHO'S IN?"

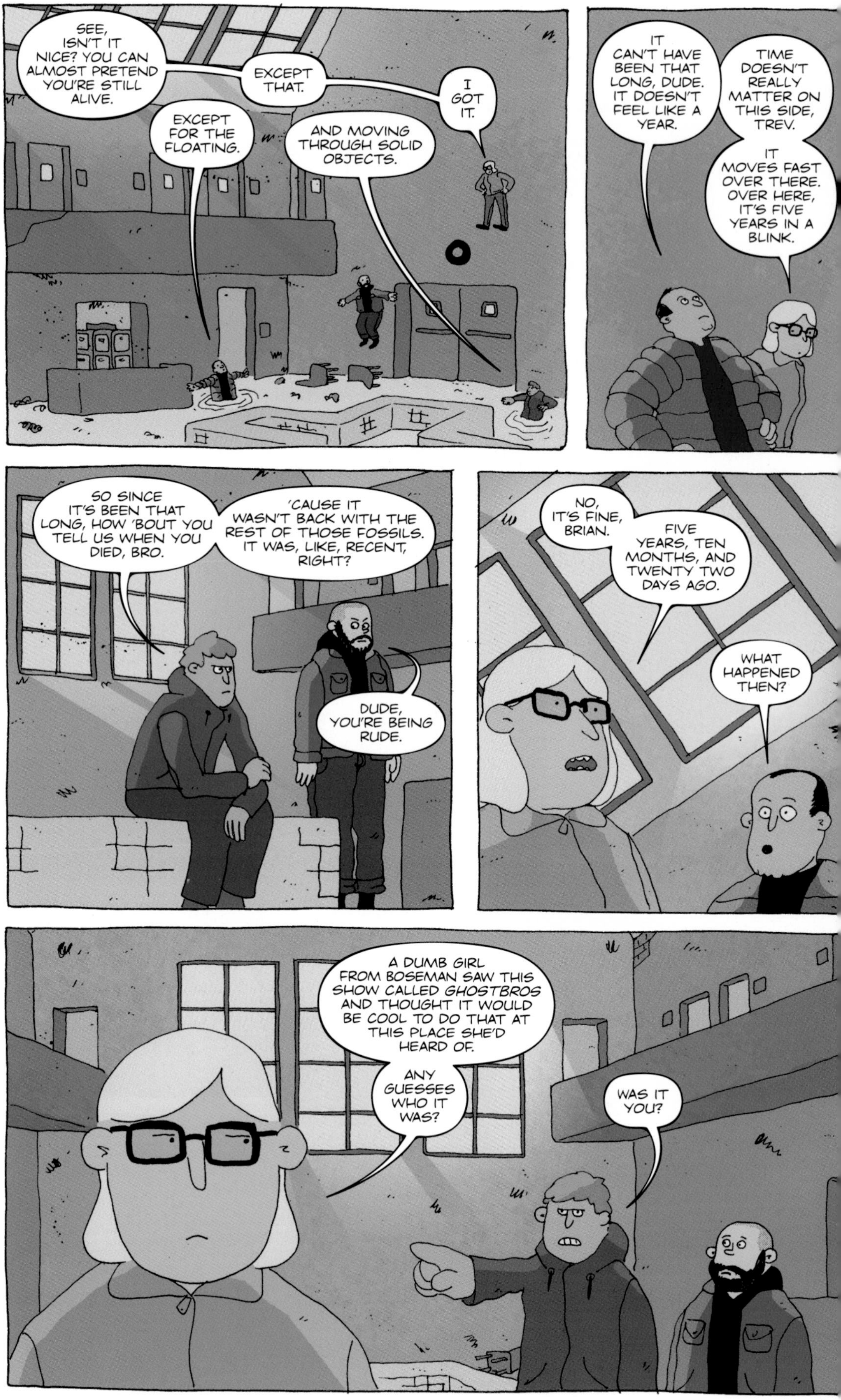
SEE, ISN'T IT NICE? YOU CAN ALMOST PRETEND YOU'RE STILL ALIVE.
EXCEPT FOR THE FLOATING.
EXCEPT THAT.
AND MOVING THROUGH SOLID OBJECTS.
I GOT IT.
IT CAN'T HAVE BEEN THAT LONG, DUDE. IT DOESN'T FEEL LIKE A YEAR.
TIME DOESN'T REALLY MATTER ON THIS SIDE, TREV.
IT MOVES FAST OVER THERE. OVER HERE, IT'S FIVE YEARS IN A BLINK.
SO SINCE IT'S BEEN THAT LONG, HOW 'BOUT YOU TELL US WHEN YOU DIED, BRO.
'CAUSE IT WASN'T BACK WITH THE REST OF THOSE FOSSILS. IT WAS, LIKE, RECENT, RIGHT?
DUDE, YOU'RE BEING RUDE.
NO, IT'S FINE, BRIAN.
FIVE YEARS, TEN MONTHS, AND TWENTY TWO DAYS AGO.
WHAT HAPPENED THEN?
A DUMB GIRL FROM BOSEMAN SAW THIS SHOW CALLED *GHOSTBROS* AND THOUGHT IT WOULD BE COOL TO DO THAT AT THIS PLACE SHE'D HEARD OF.
ANY GUESSES WHO IT WAS?
WAS IT YOU?

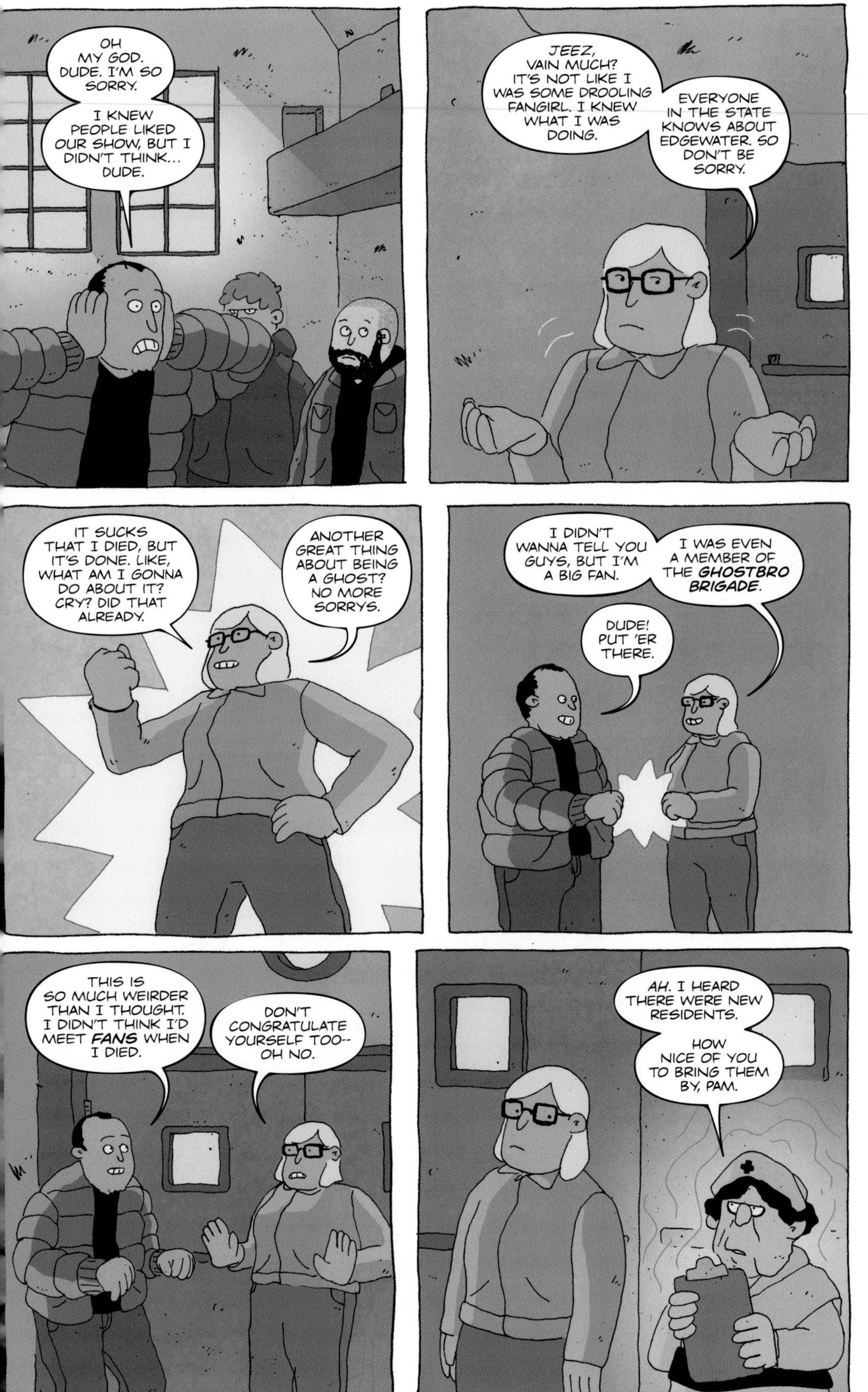
OH MY GOD. DUDE. I'M SO SORRY.
I KNEW PEOPLE LIKED OUR SHOW, BUT I DIDN'T THINK... DUDE.
JEEZ, VAIN MUCH? IT'S NOT LIKE I WAS SOME DROOLING FANGIRL. I KNEW WHAT I WAS DOING.
EVERYONE IN THE STATE KNOWS ABOUT EDGEWATER. SO DON'T BE SORRY.
IT SUCKS THAT I DIED, BUT IT'S DONE. LIKE, WHAT AM I GONNA DO ABOUT IT? CRY? DID THAT ALREADY.
ANOTHER GREAT THING ABOUT BEING A GHOST? NO MORE SORRYS.
I DIDN'T WANNA TELL YOU GUYS, BUT I'M A BIG FAN.
I WAS EVEN A MEMBER OF THE ***GHOSTBRO BRIGADE***.
DUDE! PUT 'ER THERE.
THIS IS SO MUCH WEIRDER THAN I THOUGHT. I DIDN'T THINK I'D MEET ***FANS*** WHEN I DIED.
DON'T CONGRATULATE YOURSELF TOO-- OH NO.
AH. I HEARD THERE WERE NEW RESIDENTS.
HOW NICE OF YOU TO BRING THEM BY, PAM.

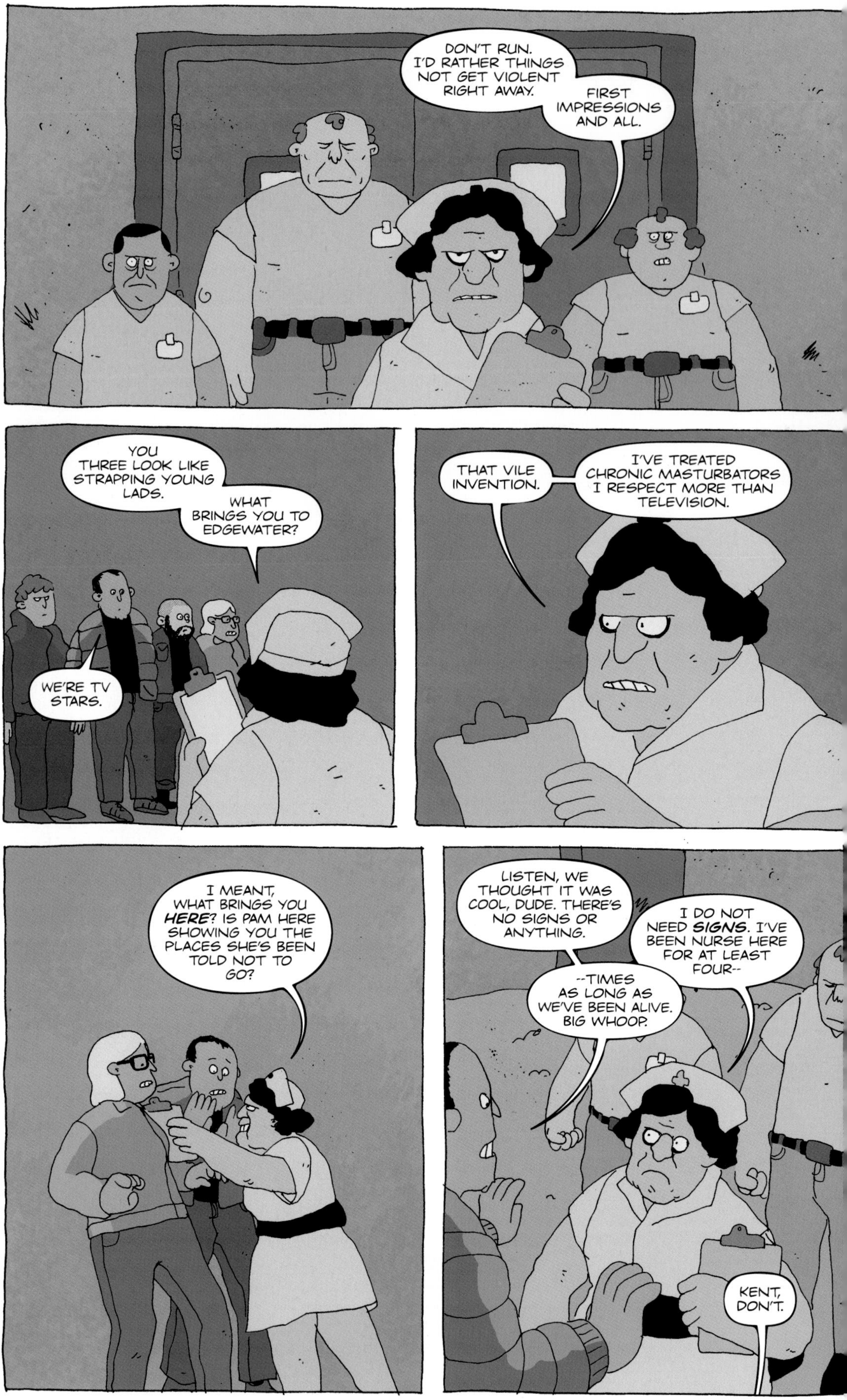
DON'T RUN. I'D RATHER THINGS NOT GET VIOLENT RIGHT AWAY.
FIRST IMPRESSIONS AND ALL.
YOU THREE LOOK LIKE STRAPPING YOUNG LADS.
WHAT BRINGS YOU TO EDGEWATER?
WE'RE TV STARS.
THAT VILE INVENTION.
I'VE TREATED CHRONIC MASTURBATORS I RESPECT MORE THAN TELEVISION.
I MEANT, WHAT BRINGS YOU ***HERE***? IS PAM HERE SHOWING YOU THE PLACES SHE'S BEEN TOLD NOT TO GO?
LISTEN, WE THOUGHT IT WAS COOL, DUDE. THERE'S NO SIGNS OR ANYTHING.
I DO NOT NEED ***SIGNS***. I'VE BEEN NURSE HERE FOR AT LEAST FOUR--
--TIMES AS LONG AS WE'VE BEEN ALIVE. BIG WHOOP.
KENT, DON'T.

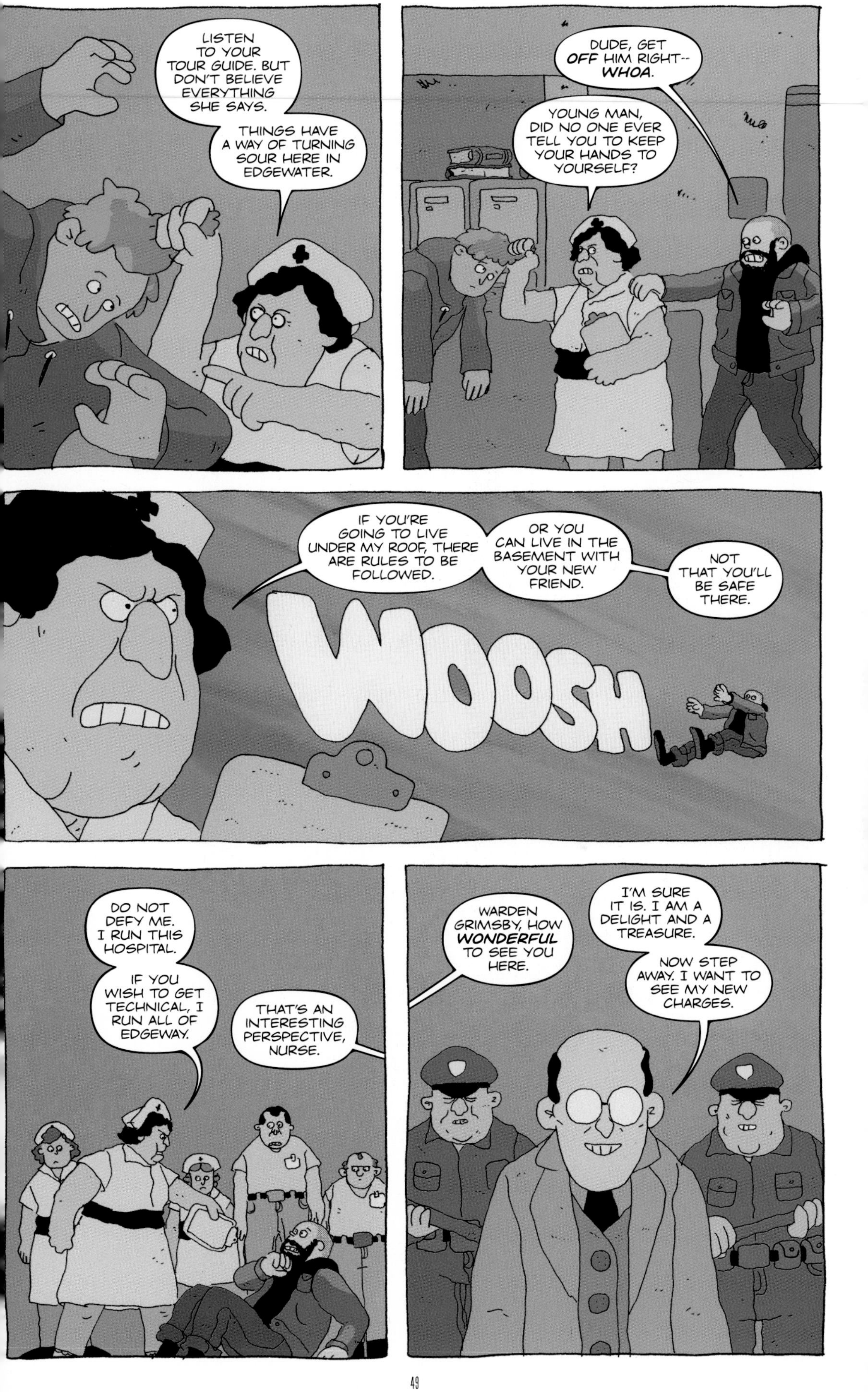
LISTEN TO YOUR TOUR GUIDE. BUT DON'T BELIEVE EVERYTHING SHE SAYS.
THINGS HAVE A WAY OF TURNING SOUR HERE IN EDGEWATER.
DUDE, GET **OFF** HIM RIGHT-- ***WHOA***.
YOUNG MAN, DID NO ONE EVER TELL YOU TO KEEP YOUR HANDS TO YOURSELF?
IF YOU'RE GOING TO LIVE UNDER MY ROOF, THERE ARE RULES TO BE FOLLOWED.
OR YOU CAN LIVE IN THE BASEMENT WITH YOUR NEW FRIEND.
NOT THAT YOU'LL BE SAFE THERE.
WOOSH
DO NOT DEFY ME. I RUN THIS HOSPITAL.
IF YOU WISH TO GET TECHNICAL, I RUN ALL OF EDGEWAY.
THAT'S AN INTERESTING PERSPECTIVE, NURSE.
WARDEN GRIMSBY, HOW **WONDERFUL** TO SEE YOU HERE.
I'M SURE IT IS. I AM A DELIGHT AND A TREASURE.
NOW STEP AWAY. I WANT TO SEE MY NEW CHARGES.

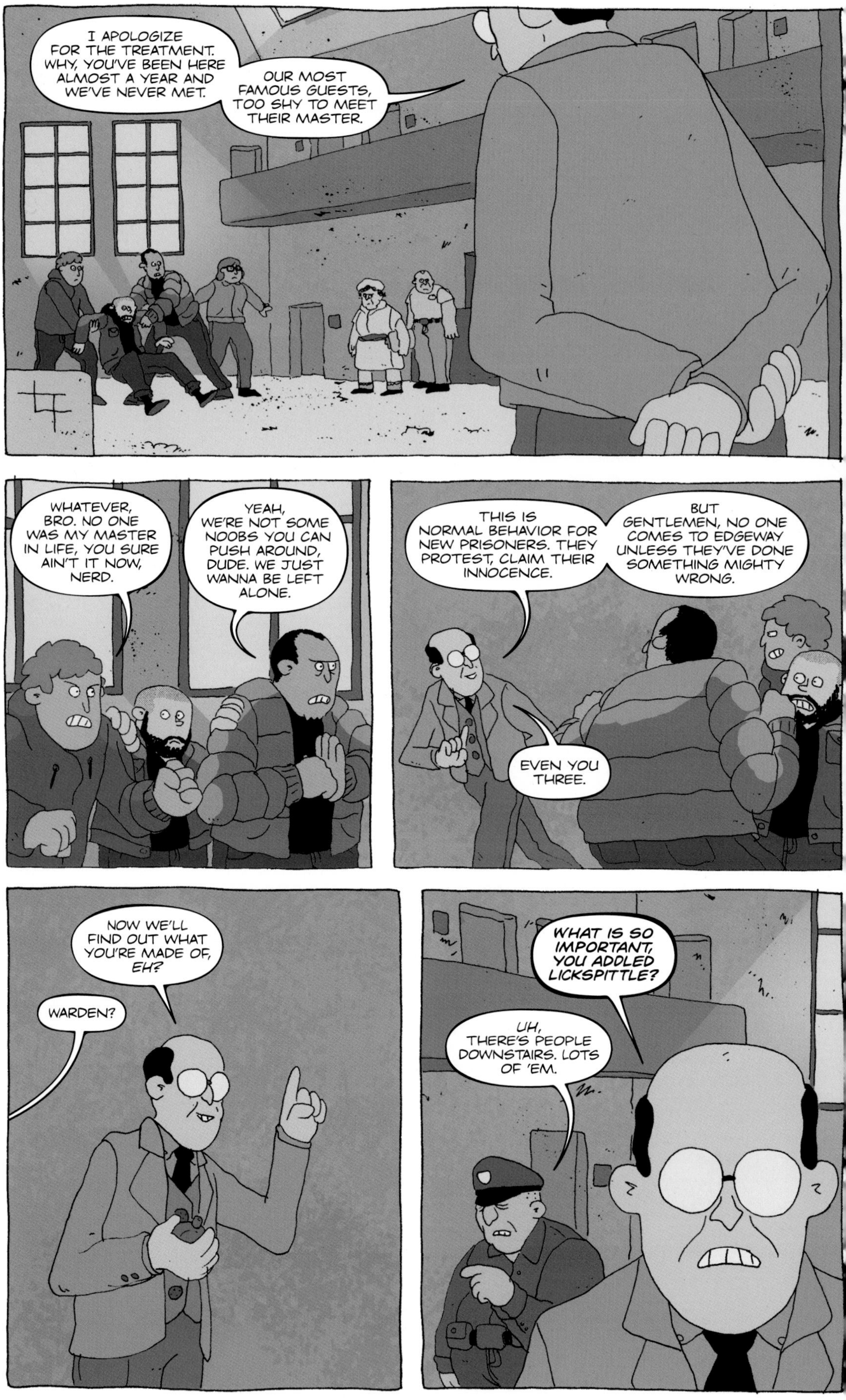
I APOLOGIZE FOR THE TREATMENT. WHY, YOU'VE BEEN HERE ALMOST A YEAR AND WE'VE NEVER MET.
OUR MOST FAMOUS GUESTS, TOO SHY TO MEET THEIR MASTER.
WHATEVER, BRO. NO ONE WAS MY MASTER IN LIFE, YOU SURE AIN'T IT NOW, NERD.
YEAH, WE'RE NOT SOME NOOBS YOU CAN PUSH AROUND, DUDE. WE JUST WANNA BE LEFT ALONE.
THIS IS NORMAL BEHAVIOR FOR NEW PRISONERS. THEY PROTEST, CLAIM THEIR INNOCENCE.
BUT GENTLEMEN, NO ONE COMES TO EDGEWAY UNLESS THEY'VE DONE SOMETHING MIGHTY WRONG.
EVEN YOU THREE.
NOW WE'LL FIND OUT WHAT YOU'RE MADE OF, EH?
WARDEN?
WHAT IS SO IMPORTANT, YOU ADDLED LICKSPITTLE?
UH, THERE'S PEOPLE DOWNSTAIRS. LOTS OF 'EM.

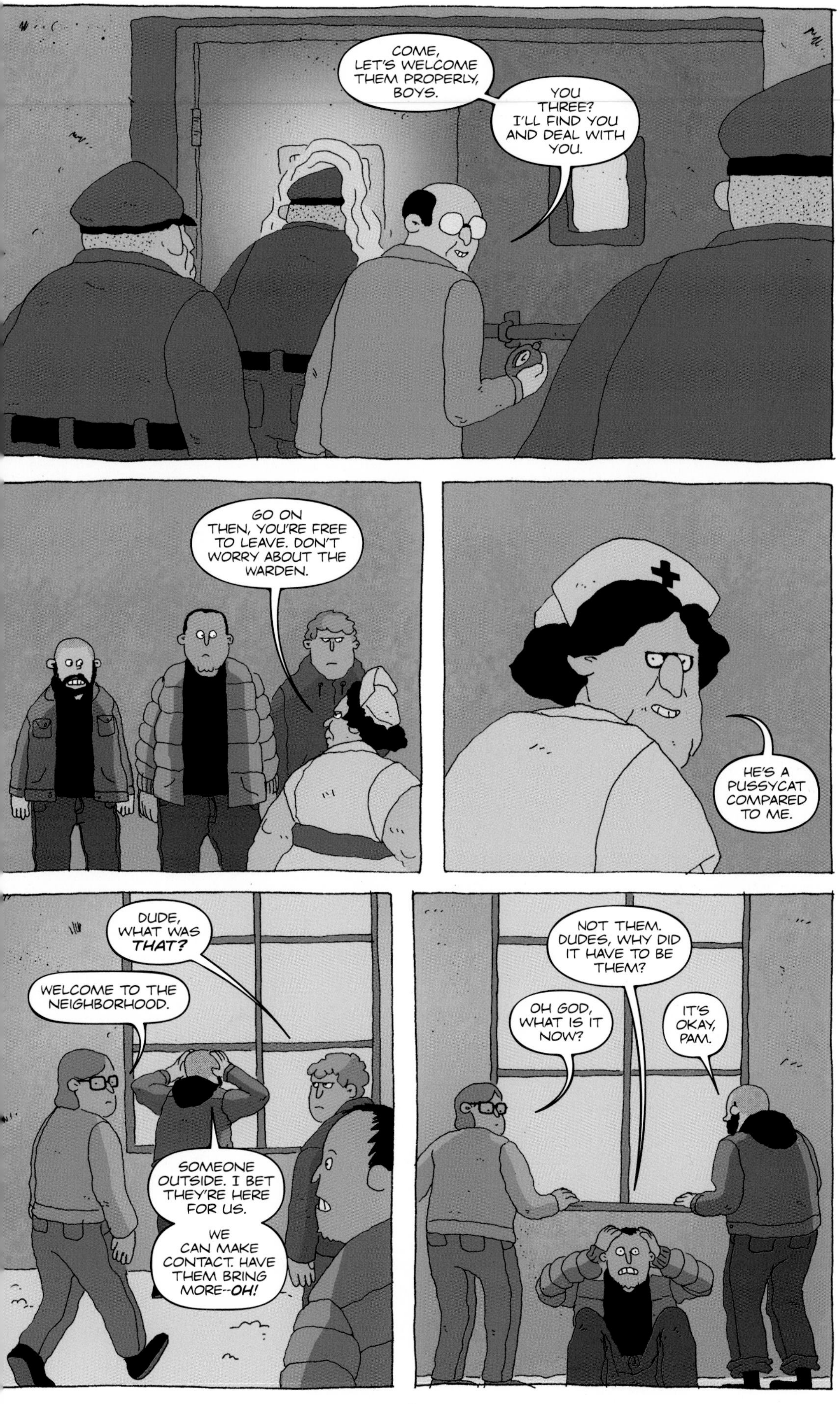
COME, LET'S WELCOME THEM PROPERLY, BOYS.
YOU THREE? I'LL FIND YOU AND DEAL WITH YOU.
GO ON THEN, YOU'RE FREE TO LEAVE. DON'T WORRY ABOUT THE WARDEN.
HE'S A PUSSYCAT COMPARED TO ME.
DUDE, WHAT WAS *THAT?*
WELCOME TO THE NEIGHBORHOOD.
SOMEONE OUTSIDE. I BET THEY'RE HERE FOR US.
WE CAN MAKE CONTACT. HAVE THEM BRING MORE--*OH!*
NOT THEM. DUDES, WHY DID IT HAVE TO BE THEM?
OH GOD, WHAT IS IT NOW?
IT'S OKAY, PAM.

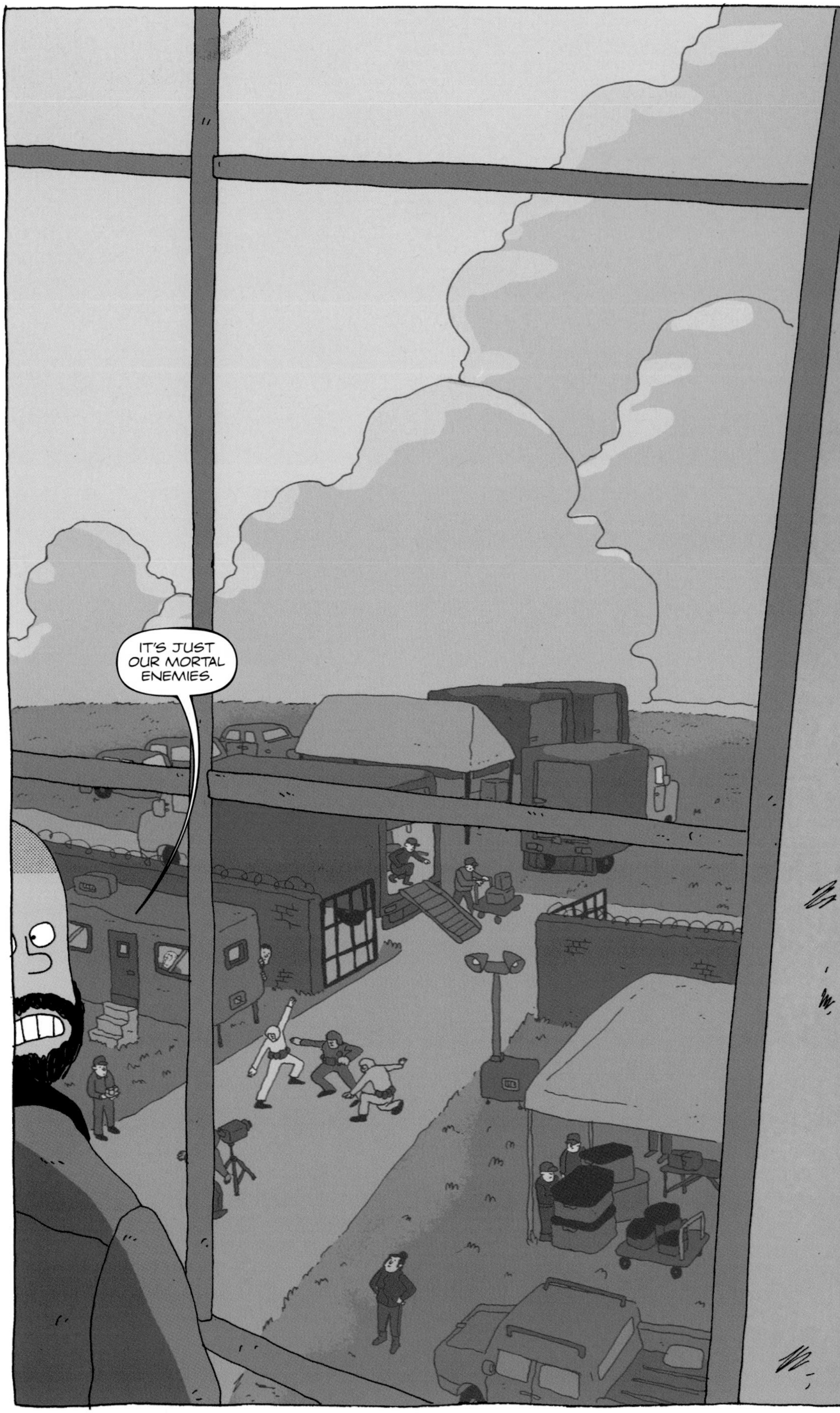
IT'S JUST OUR MORTAL ENEMIES.

CHAPTER THREE

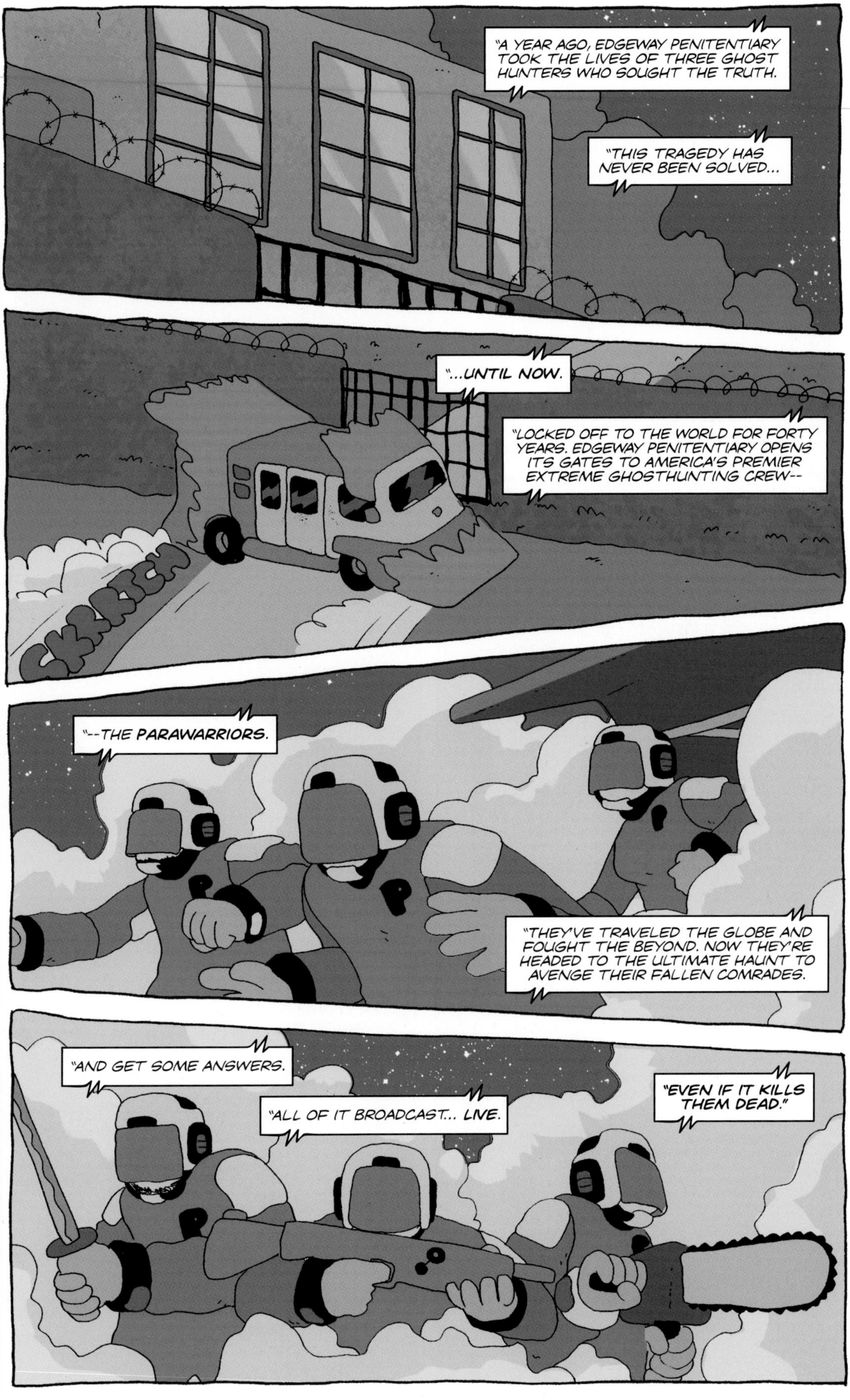
"A YEAR AGO, EDGEWAY PENITENTIARY TOOK THE LIVES OF THREE GHOST HUNTERS WHO SOUGHT THE TRUTH.
"THIS TRAGEDY HAS NEVER BEEN SOLVED...
"...UNTIL NOW.
"LOCKED OFF TO THE WORLD FOR FORTY YEARS. EDGEWAY PENITENTIARY OPENS ITS GATES TO AMERICA'S PREMIER EXTREME GHOSTHUNTING CREW--
SKRRTCH
"--THE PARAWARRIORS.
"THEY'VE TRAVELED THE GLOBE AND FOUGHT THE BEYOND. NOW THEY'RE HEADED TO THE ULTIMATE HAUNT TO AVENGE THEIR FALLEN COMRADES.
"AND GET SOME ANSWERS.
"ALL OF IT BROADCAST... LIVE.
"EVEN IF IT KILLS THEM DEAD."

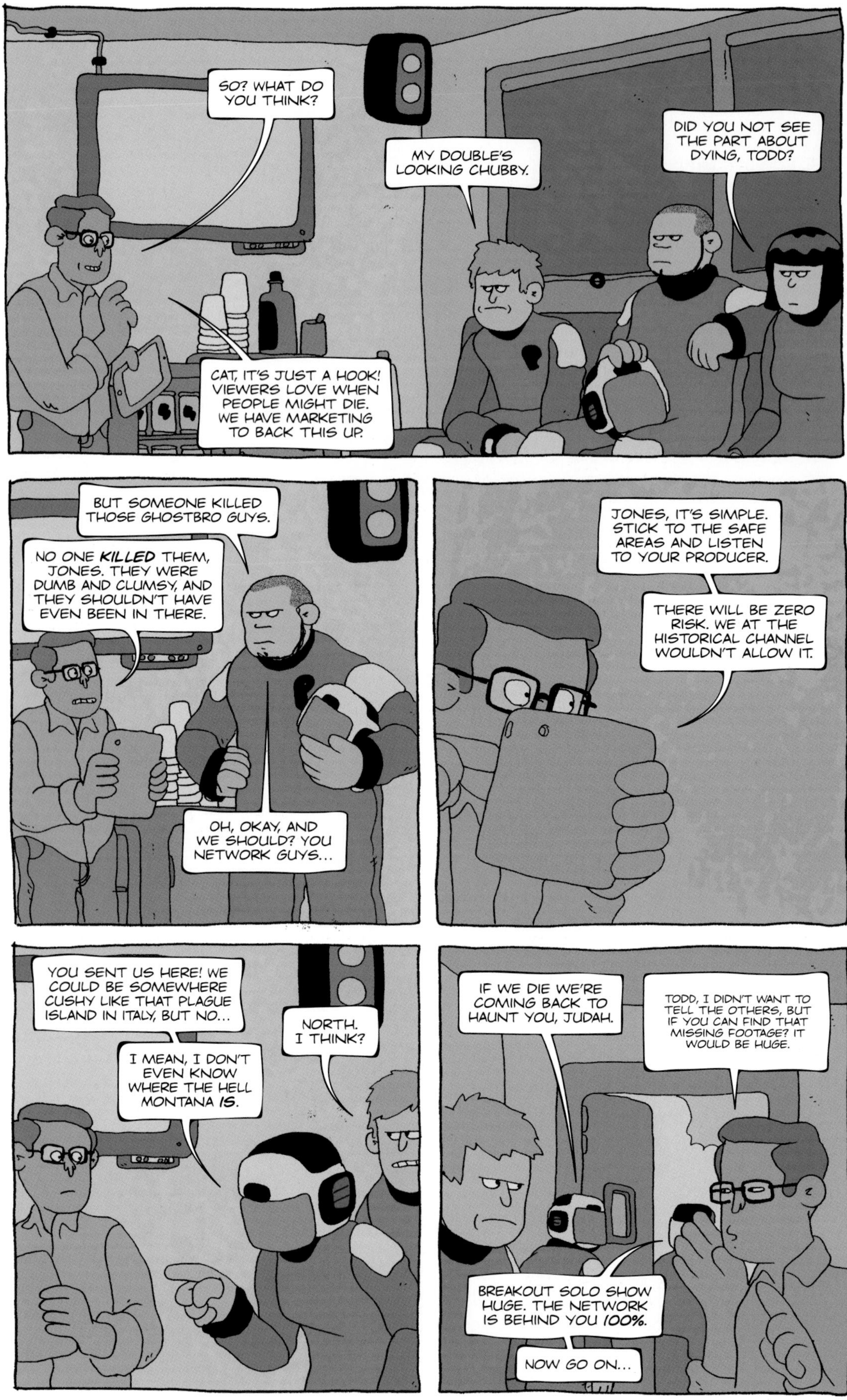
SO? WHAT DO YOU THINK?
MY DOUBLE'S LOOKING CHUBBY.
DID YOU NOT SEE THE PART ABOUT DYING, TODD?
CAT, IT'S JUST A HOOK! VIEWERS LOVE WHEN PEOPLE MIGHT DIE. WE HAVE MARKETING TO BACK THIS UP.
BUT SOMEONE KILLED THOSE GHOSTBRO GUYS.
NO ONE **KILLED** THEM, JONES. THEY WERE DUMB AND CLUMSY, AND THEY SHOULDN'T HAVE EVEN BEEN IN THERE.
OH, OKAY, AND WE SHOULD? YOU NETWORK GUYS...
JONES, IT'S SIMPLE. STICK TO THE SAFE AREAS AND LISTEN TO YOUR PRODUCER.
THERE WILL BE ZERO RISK. WE AT THE HISTORICAL CHANNEL WOULDN'T ALLOW IT.
YOU SENT US HERE! WE COULD BE SOMEWHERE CUSHY LIKE THAT PLAGUE ISLAND IN ITALY, BUT NO...
I MEAN, I DON'T EVEN KNOW WHERE THE HELL MONTANA ***IS***.
NORTH. I THINK?
IF WE DIE WE'RE COMING BACK TO HAUNT YOU, JUDAH.
TODD, I DIDN'T WANT TO TELL THE OTHERS, BUT IF YOU CAN FIND THAT MISSING FOOTAGE? IT WOULD BE HUGE.
BREAKOUT SOLO SHOW HUGE. THE NETWORK IS BEHIND YOU ***100%***.
NOW GO ON...

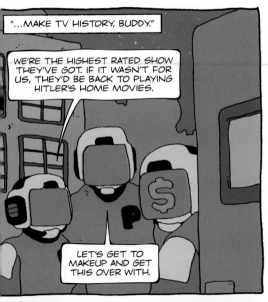

"...MAKE TV HISTORY, BUDDY."

WE'RE THE HIGHEST RATED SHOW THEY'VE GOT. IF IT WASN'T FOR US, THEY'D BE BACK TO PLAYING HITLER'S HOME MOVIES.

LET'S GET TO MAKEUP AND GET THIS OVER WITH.

BUT, YOU GUYS...

WHAT IF--WHAT IF WE FIND PROOF OF LIFE AFTER DEATH?

HAHAHA

HAHAH

BUT SERIOUSLY, THIS COULD BE COOL, YO.

ALL THOSE PSYCHOS DIED BACK IN OLDEN TIMES FROM THAT FIRE. AND THEN THOSE D-LISTERS? IMAGINE HOW MESSED UP IT IS IN THERE.

IT'S NOT LIKE **THIS** IS GOING TO BE THE ONE WITH ACTUAL GHOSTS IN IT. WE GOTTA FILL TWO HOURS WITH SOMETHING INTERESTING.

DR. NERD HERE CAN MAKE SOMETHING UP IF WE NEED HER TO.

CAN'T BELIEVE I WENT TO GRAD SCHOOL FOR THIS.

LOOSEN **UP**, SHANNON. YOU'RE GONNA BE A STAR. **ALL** OF US ARE.

SO EXCITED.

PRODUCER'S YELLING. WE GOTTA GET INSIDE, START GETTING COVERAGE BEFORE WE GO LIVE.

WHO'D THEY STICK US WITH THIS TIME?

SOME HOTSHOT WITH A SHORT TEMPER, SOUNDS LIKE.

THIS IS GONNA BLOW.

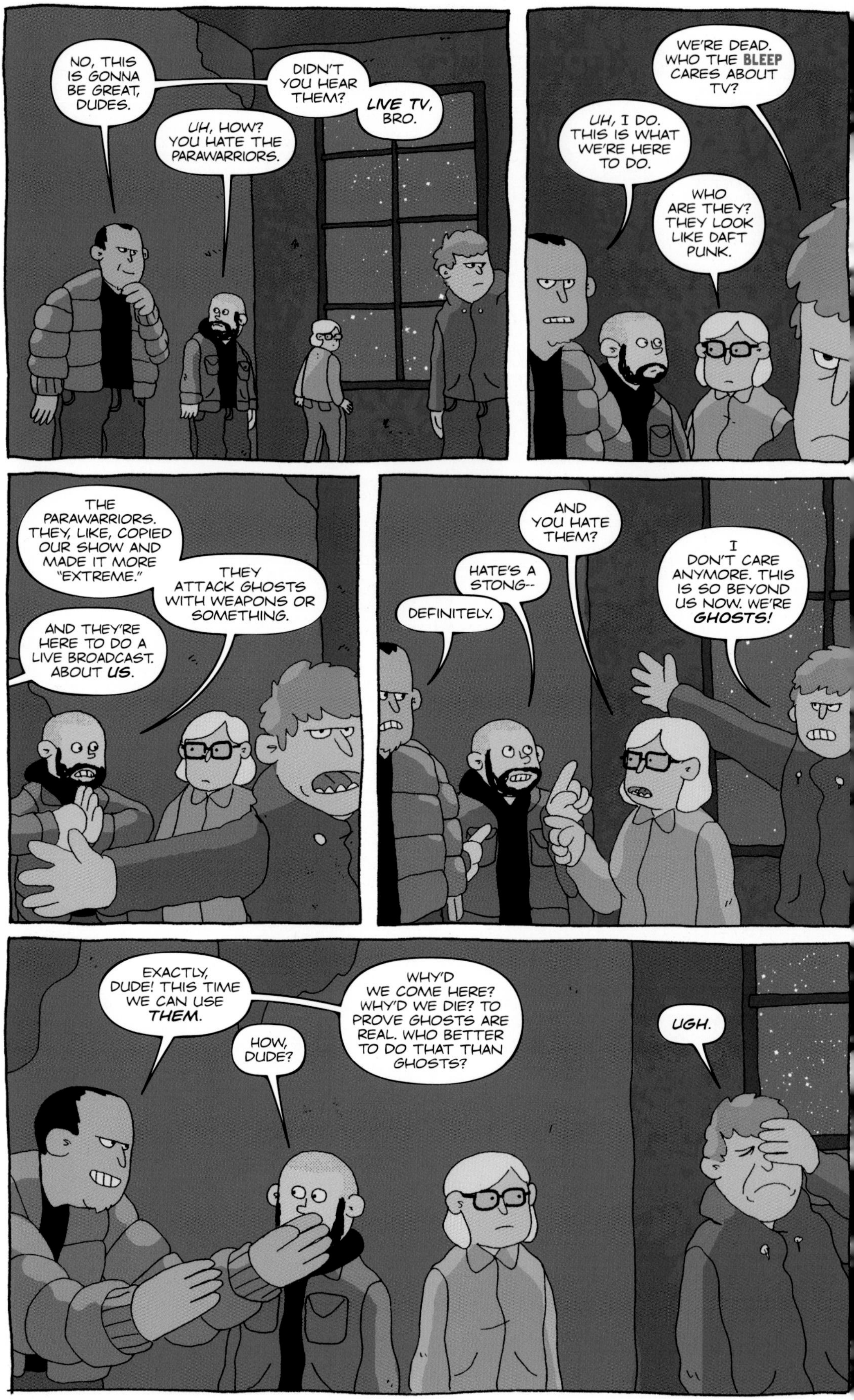
NO, THIS IS GONNA BE GREAT, DUDES.
UH, HOW? YOU HATE THE PARAWARRIORS.
DIDN'T YOU HEAR THEM?
LIVE TV, BRO.
WE'RE DEAD. WHO THE BLEEP CARES ABOUT TV?
UH, I DO. THIS IS WHAT WE'RE HERE TO DO.
WHO ARE THEY? THEY LOOK LIKE DAFT PUNK.
THE PARAWARRIORS. THEY, LIKE, COPIED OUR SHOW AND MADE IT MORE "EXTREME."
THEY ATTACK GHOSTS WITH WEAPONS OR SOMETHING.
AND THEY'RE HERE TO DO A LIVE BROADCAST. ABOUT US.
AND YOU HATE THEM?
HATE'S A STONG--
DEFINITELY.
I DON'T CARE ANYMORE. THIS IS SO BEYOND US NOW. WE'RE GHOSTS!
EXACTLY, DUDE! THIS TIME WE CAN USE THEM.
HOW, DUDE?
WHY'D WE COME HERE? WHY'D WE DIE? TO PROVE GHOSTS ARE REAL. WHO BETTER TO DO THAT THAN GHOSTS?
UGH.

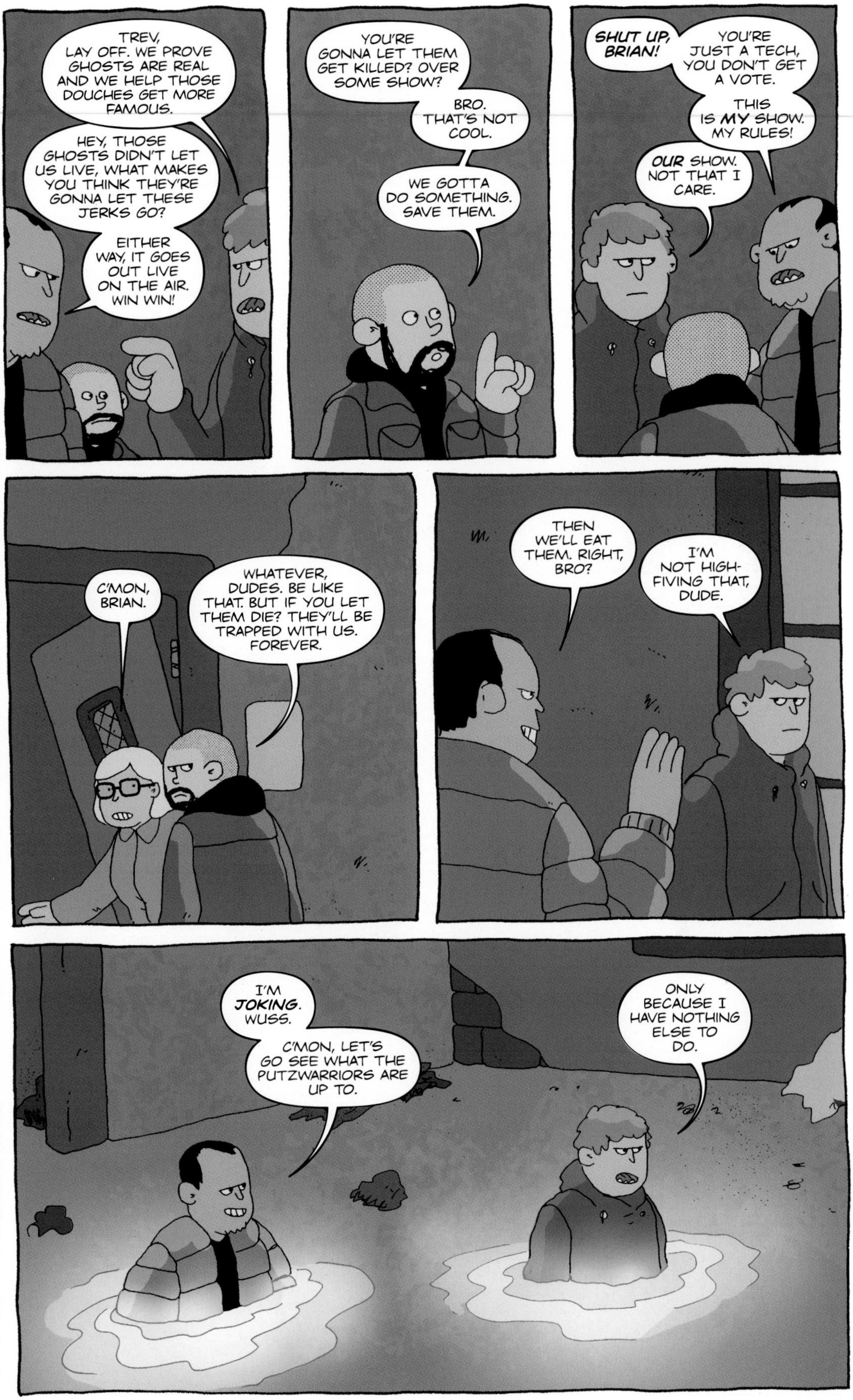
TREV, LAY OFF. WE PROVE GHOSTS ARE REAL AND WE HELP THOSE DOUCHES GET MORE FAMOUS.
HEY, THOSE GHOSTS DIDN'T LET US LIVE, WHAT MAKES YOU THINK THEY'RE GONNA LET THESE JERKS GO?
EITHER WAY, IT GOES OUT LIVE ON THE AIR. WIN WIN!
YOU'RE GONNA LET THEM GET KILLED? OVER SOME SHOW?
BRO. THAT'S NOT COOL.
WE GOTTA DO SOMETHING. SAVE THEM.
SHUT UP, BRIAN!
YOU'RE JUST A TECH, YOU DON'T GET A VOTE.
THIS IS MY SHOW. MY RULES!
OUR SHOW. NOT THAT I CARE.
C'MON, BRIAN.
WHATEVER, DUDES. BE LIKE THAT. BUT IF YOU LET THEM DIE? THEY'LL BE TRAPPED WITH US. FOREVER.
THEN WE'LL EAT THEM. RIGHT, BRO?
I'M NOT HIGH-FIVING THAT, DUDE.
I'M JOKING. WUSS.
C'MON, LET'S GO SEE WHAT THE PUTZWARRIORS ARE UP TO.
ONLY BECAUSE I HAVE NOTHING ELSE TO DO.

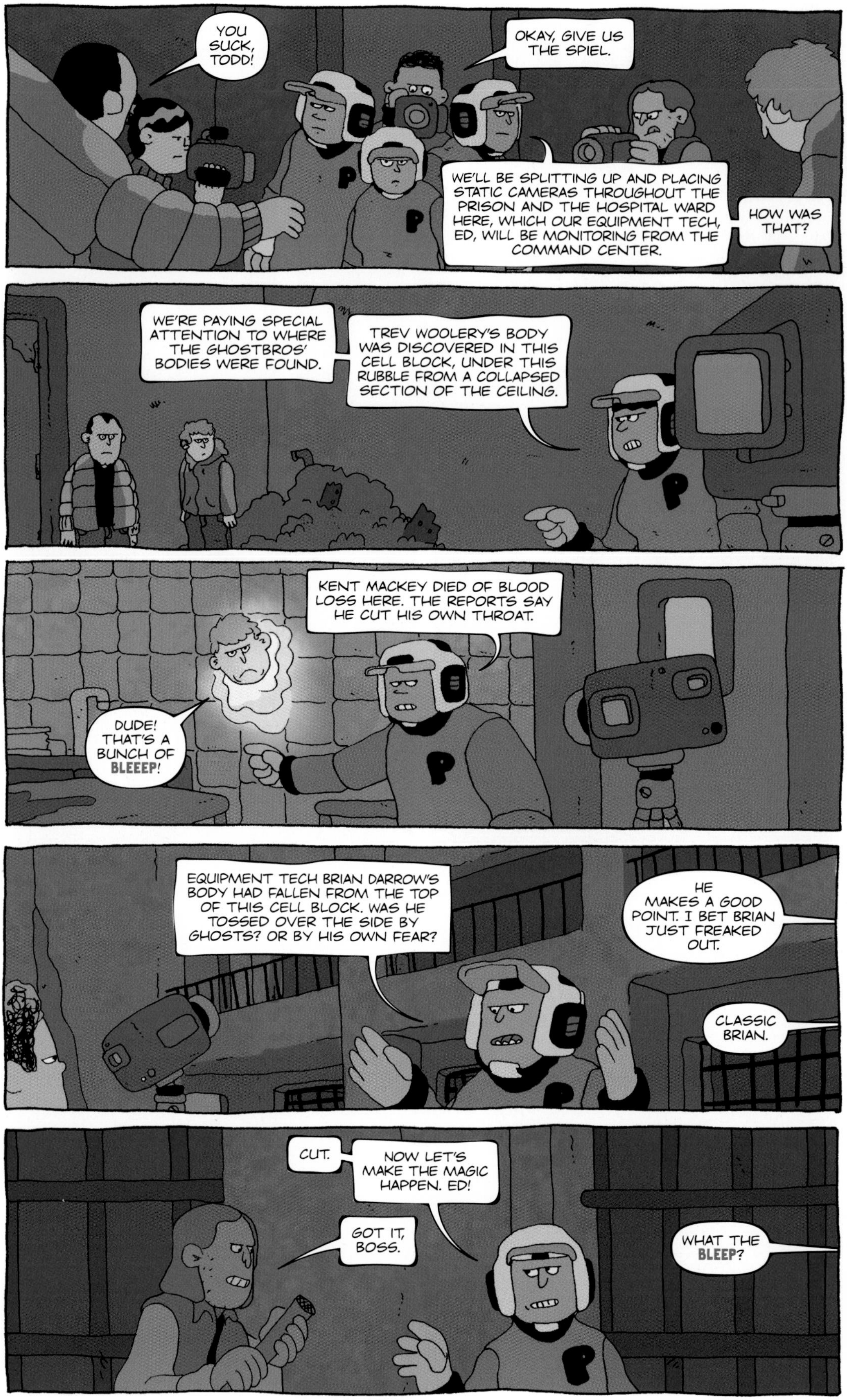
YOU SUCK, TODD!
OKAY, GIVE US THE SPIEL.
WE'LL BE SPLITTING UP AND PLACING STATIC CAMERAS THROUGHOUT THE PRISON AND THE HOSPITAL WARD HERE, WHICH OUR EQUIPMENT TECH, ED, WILL BE MONITORING FROM THE COMMAND CENTER.
HOW WAS THAT?
WE'RE PAYING SPECIAL ATTENTION TO WHERE THE GHOSTBROS' BODIES WERE FOUND.
TREV WOOLERY'S BODY WAS DISCOVERED IN THIS CELL BLOCK, UNDER THIS RUBBLE FROM A COLLAPSED SECTION OF THE CEILING.
KENT MACKEY DIED OF BLOOD LOSS HERE. THE REPORTS SAY HE CUT HIS OWN THROAT.
DUDE! THAT'S A BUNCH OF BLEEEP!
EQUIPMENT TECH BRIAN DARROW'S BODY HAD FALLEN FROM THE TOP OF THIS CELL BLOCK. WAS HE TOSSED OVER THE SIDE BY GHOSTS? OR BY HIS OWN FEAR?
HE MAKES A GOOD POINT. I BET BRIAN JUST FREAKED OUT.
CLASSIC BRIAN.
CUT.
NOW LET'S MAKE THE MAGIC HAPPEN. ED!
GOT IT, BOSS.
WHAT THE BLEEP?

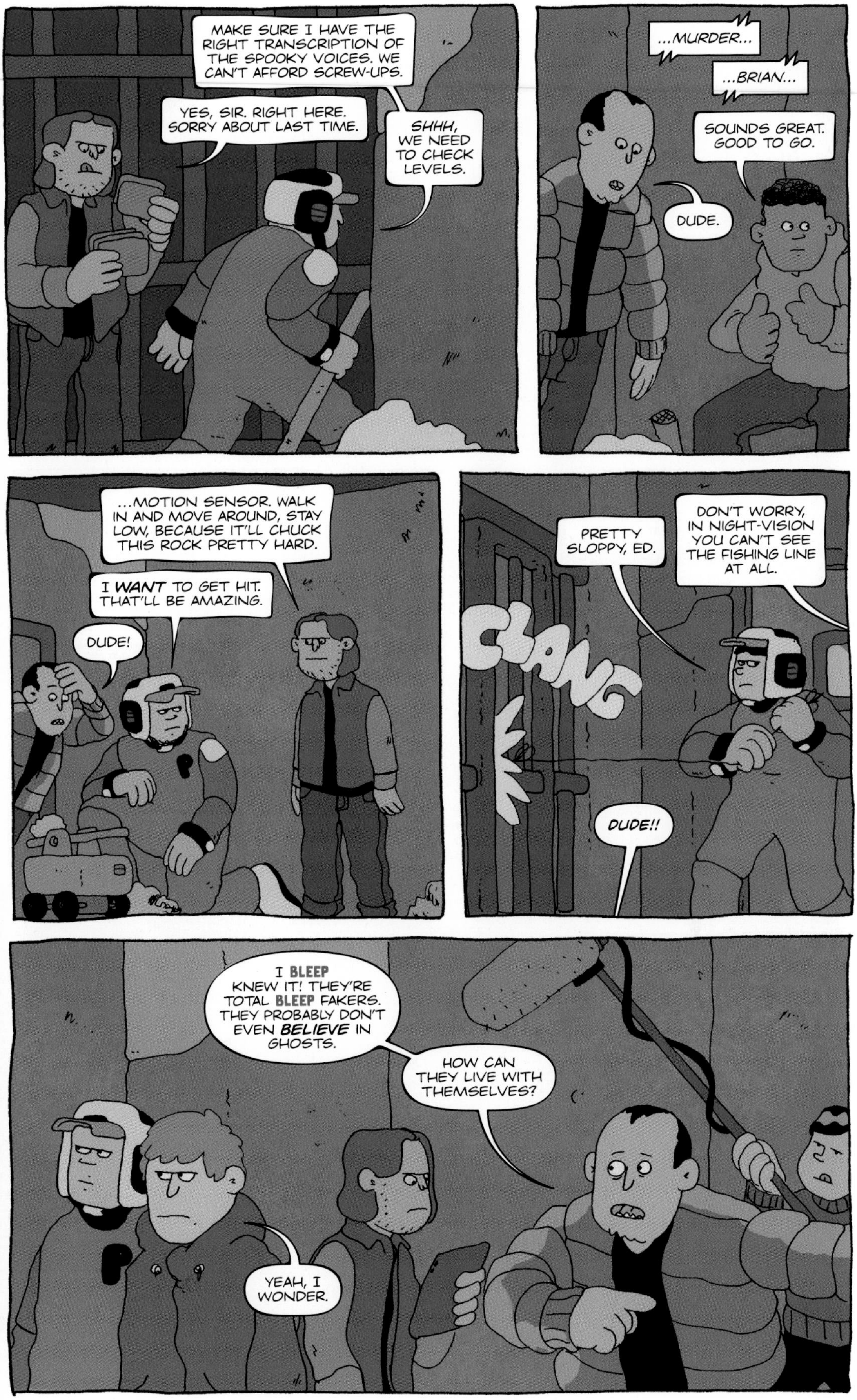
MAKE SURE I HAVE THE RIGHT TRANSCRIPTION OF THE SPOOKY VOICES. WE CAN'T AFFORD SCREW-UPS.
YES, SIR. RIGHT HERE. SORRY ABOUT LAST TIME.
SHHH, WE NEED TO CHECK LEVELS.
...MURDER...
...BRIAN...
SOUNDS GREAT. GOOD TO GO.
DUDE.
...MOTION SENSOR. WALK IN AND MOVE AROUND, STAY LOW, BECAUSE IT'LL CHUCK THIS ROCK PRETTY HARD.
I *WANT* TO GET HIT. THAT'LL BE AMAZING.
DUDE!
PRETTY SLOPPY, ED.
DON'T WORRY, IN NIGHT-VISION YOU CAN'T SEE THE FISHING LINE AT ALL.
CLANG
DUDE!!
I BLEEP KNEW IT! THEY'RE TOTAL BLEEP FAKERS. THEY PROBABLY DON'T EVEN *BELIEVE* IN GHOSTS.
HOW CAN THEY LIVE WITH THEMSELVES?
YEAH, I WONDER.

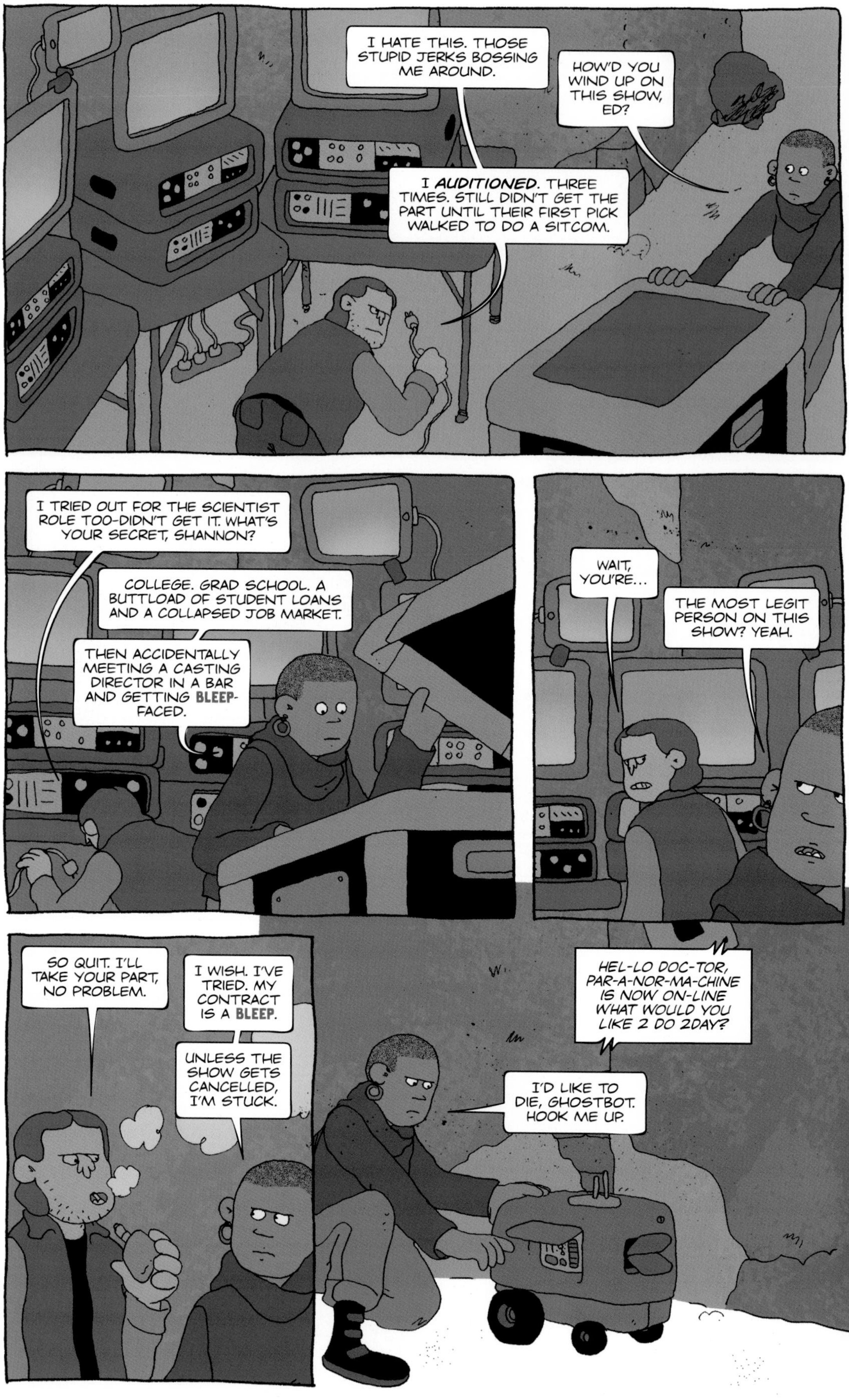
I HATE THIS. THOSE STUPID JERKS BOSSING ME AROUND.
HOW'D YOU WIND UP ON THIS SHOW, ED?
I *AUDITIONED*. THREE TIMES. STILL DIDN'T GET THE PART UNTIL THEIR FIRST PICK WALKED TO DO A SITCOM.
I TRIED OUT FOR THE SCIENTIST ROLE TOO–DIDN'T GET IT. WHAT'S YOUR SECRET, SHANNON?
COLLEGE. GRAD SCHOOL. A BUTTLOAD OF STUDENT LOANS AND A COLLAPSED JOB MARKET.
THEN ACCIDENTALLY MEETING A CASTING DIRECTOR IN A BAR AND GETTING BLEEP-FACED.
WAIT, YOU'RE...
THE MOST LEGIT PERSON ON THIS SHOW? YEAH.
SO QUIT. I'LL TAKE YOUR PART, NO PROBLEM.
I WISH. I'VE TRIED. MY CONTRACT IS A BLEEP.
UNLESS THE SHOW GETS CANCELLED, I'M STUCK.
HEL-LO DOC-TOR, PAR-A-NOR-MA-CHINE IS NOW ON-LINE WHAT WOULD YOU LIKE 2 DO 2DAY?
I'D LIKE TO DIE, GHOSTBOT. HOOK ME UP.

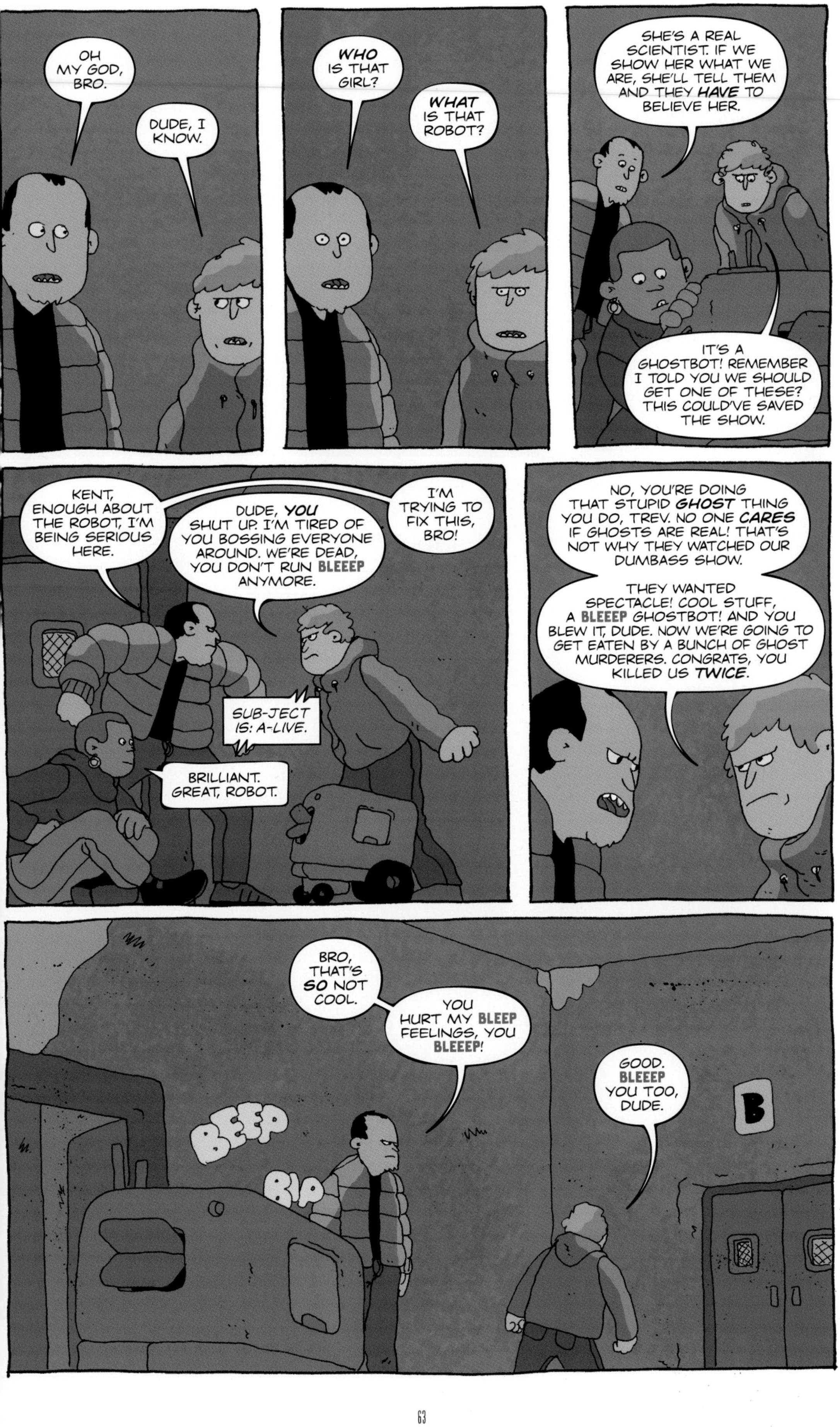
OH MY GOD, BRO.
DUDE, I KNOW.
WHO IS THAT GIRL?
WHAT IS THAT ROBOT?
SHE'S A REAL SCIENTIST. IF WE SHOW HER WHAT WE ARE, SHE'LL TELL THEM AND THEY HAVE TO BELIEVE HER.
IT'S A GHOSTBOT! REMEMBER I TOLD YOU WE SHOULD GET ONE OF THESE? THIS COULD'VE SAVED THE SHOW.
KENT, ENOUGH ABOUT THE ROBOT, I'M BEING SERIOUS HERE.
I'M TRYING TO FIX THIS, BRO!
DUDE, YOU SHUT UP. I'M TIRED OF YOU BOSSING EVERYONE AROUND. WE'RE DEAD, YOU DON'T RUN BLEEEP ANYMORE.
SUB-JECT IS: A-LIVE.
BRILLIANT. GREAT, ROBOT.
NO, YOU'RE DOING THAT STUPID GHOST THING YOU DO, TREV. NO ONE CARES IF GHOSTS ARE REAL! THAT'S NOT WHY THEY WATCHED OUR DUMBASS SHOW.
THEY WANTED SPECTACLE! COOL STUFF, A BLEEEP GHOSTBOT! AND YOU BLEW IT, DUDE. NOW WE'RE GOING TO GET EATEN BY A BUNCH OF GHOST MURDERERS. CONGRATS, YOU KILLED US TWICE.
BRO, THAT'S SO NOT COOL.
YOU HURT MY BLEEP FEELINGS, YOU BLEEEP!
BEEP
BIP
GOOD. BLEEEP YOU TOO, DUDE.
B

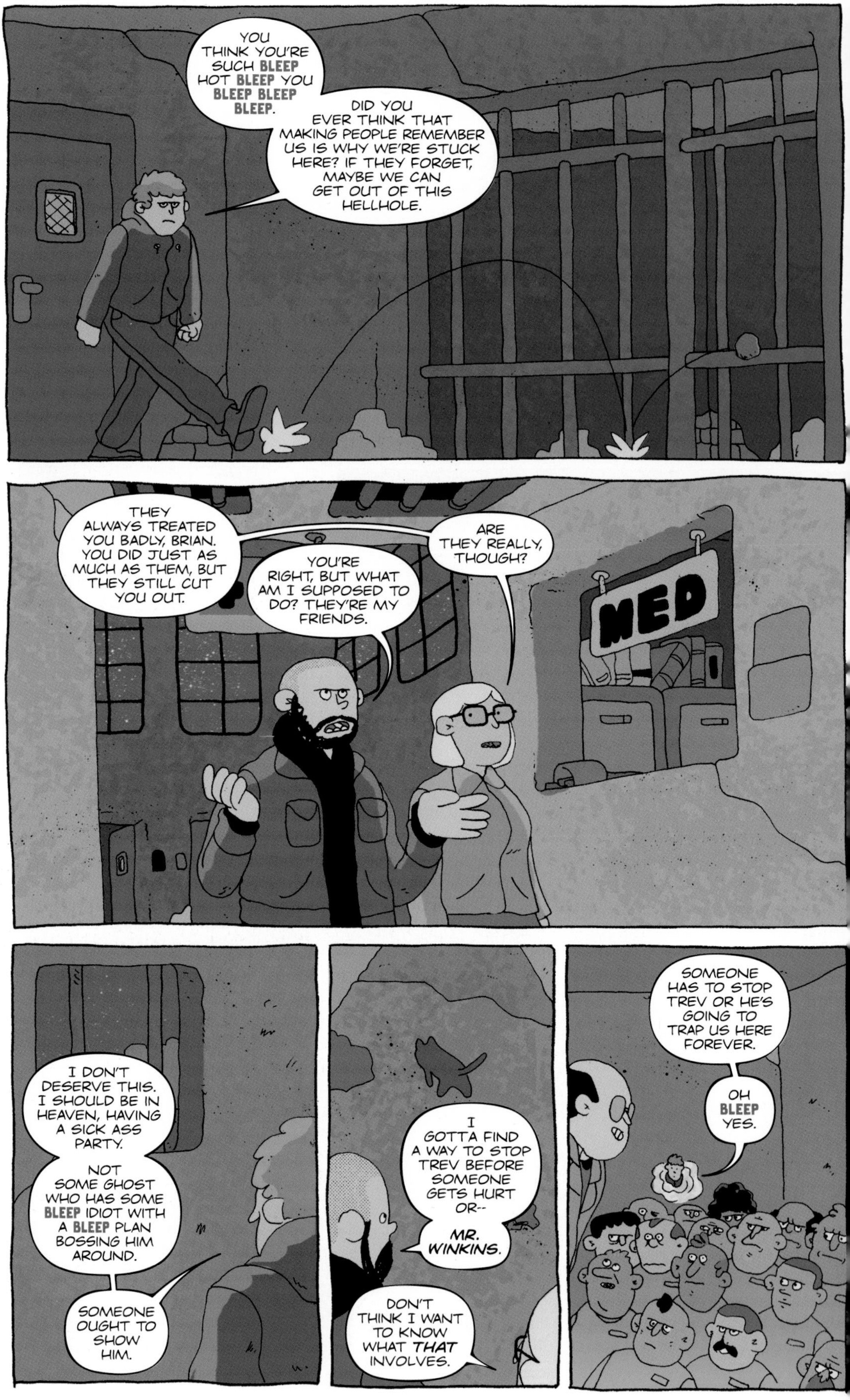
YOU THINK YOU'RE SUCH BLEEP HOT BLEEP YOU BLEEP BLEEP BLEEP.
DID YOU EVER THINK THAT MAKING PEOPLE REMEMBER US IS WHY WE'RE STUCK HERE? IF THEY FORGET, MAYBE WE CAN GET OUT OF THIS HELLHOLE.
THEY ALWAYS TREATED YOU BADLY, BRIAN. YOU DID JUST AS MUCH AS THEM, BUT THEY STILL CUT YOU OUT.
YOU'RE RIGHT, BUT WHAT AM I SUPPOSED TO DO? THEY'RE MY FRIENDS.
ARE THEY REALLY, THOUGH?
MED
I DON'T DESERVE THIS. I SHOULD BE IN HEAVEN, HAVING A SICK ASS PARTY.
NOT SOME GHOST WHO HAS SOME BLEEP IDIOT WITH A BLEEP PLAN BOSSING HIM AROUND.
SOMEONE OUGHT TO SHOW HIM.
I GOTTA FIND A WAY TO STOP TREV BEFORE SOMEONE GETS HURT OR--
MR. WINKINS.
DON'T THINK I WANT TO KNOW WHAT THAT INVOLVES.
SOMEONE HAS TO STOP TREV OR HE'S GOING TO TRAP US HERE FOREVER.
OH BLEEP YES.

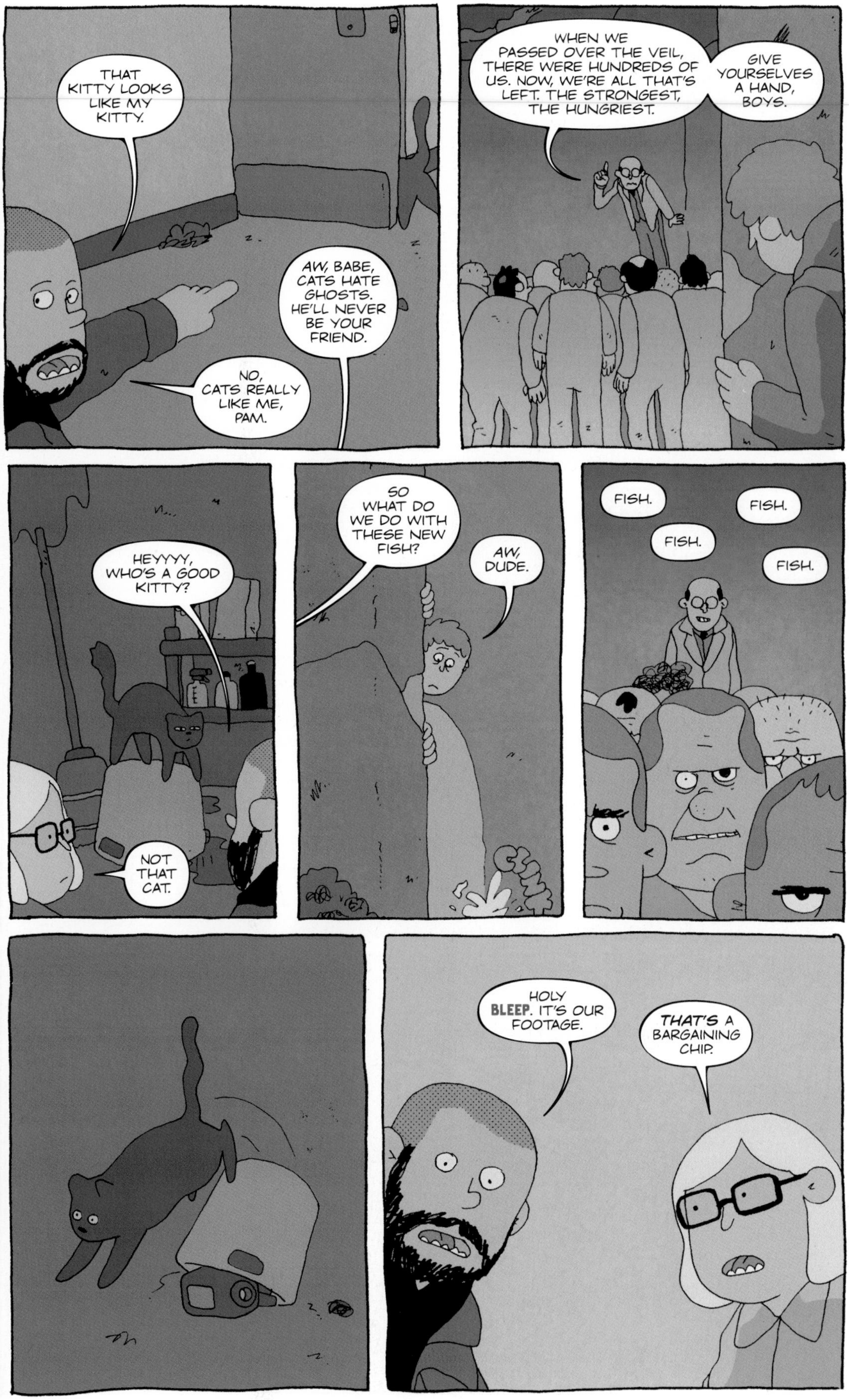
THAT KITTY LOOKS LIKE MY KITTY.
AW, BABE, CATS HATE GHOSTS. HE'LL NEVER BE YOUR FRIEND.
NO, CATS REALLY LIKE ME, PAM.
WHEN WE PASSED OVER THE VEIL, THERE WERE HUNDREDS OF US. NOW, WE'RE ALL THAT'S LEFT. THE STRONGEST, THE HUNGRIEST.
GIVE YOURSELVES A HAND, BOYS.
HEYYYY, WHO'S A GOOD KITTY?
NOT THAT CAT.
SO WHAT DO WE DO WITH THESE NEW FISH?
AW, DUDE.
FISH.
FISH.
FISH.
FISH.
HOLY **BLEEP**. IT'S OUR FOOTAGE.
THAT'S A BARGAINING CHIP.

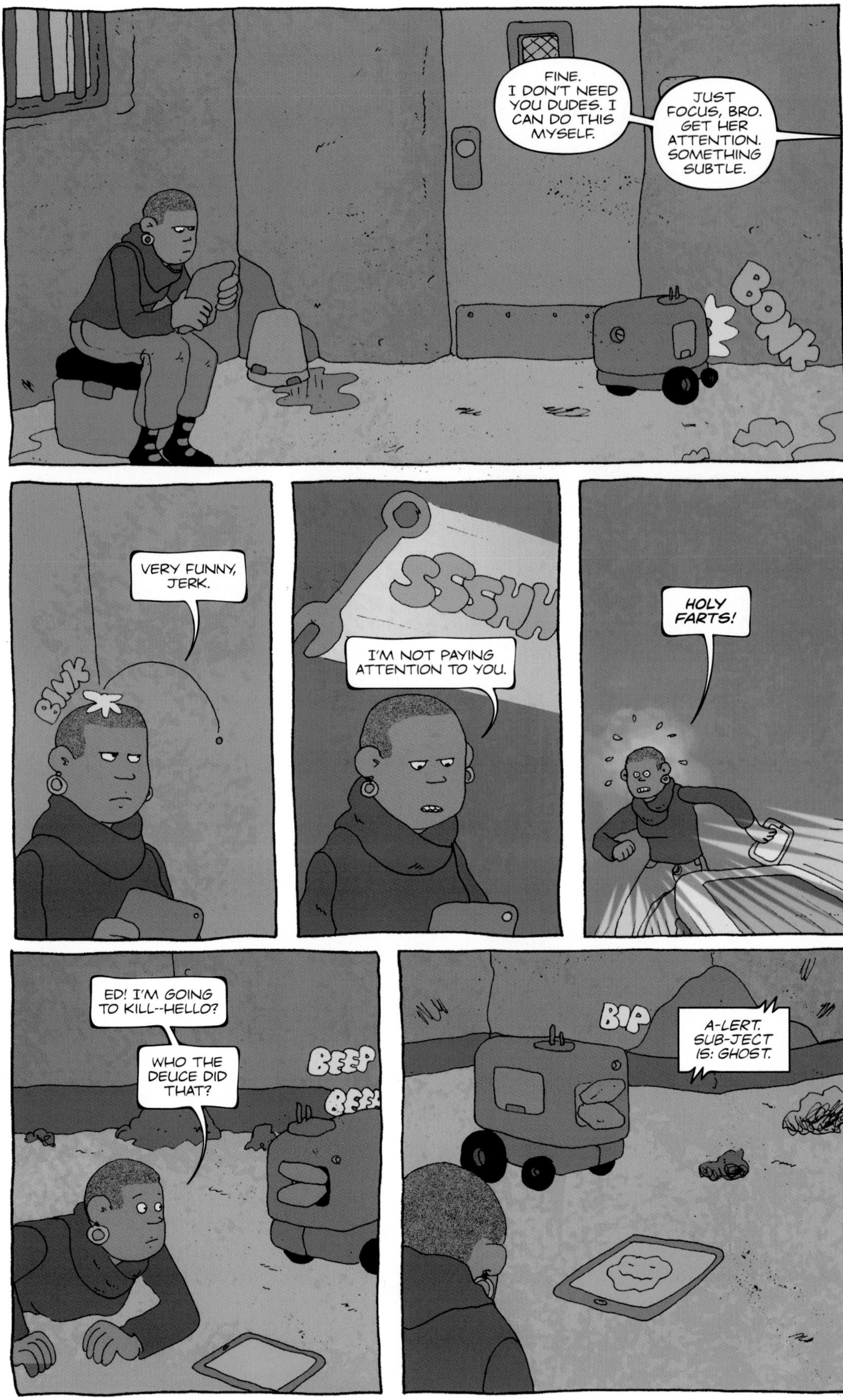
FINE. I DON'T NEED YOU DUDES. I CAN DO THIS MYSELF.
JUST FOCUS, BRO. GET HER ATTENTION. SOMETHING SUBTLE.
BONK
BINK
VERY FUNNY, JERK.
SSSHH
I'M NOT PAYING ATTENTION TO YOU.
HOLY FARTS!
ED! I'M GOING TO KILL--HELLO?
WHO THE DEUCE DID THAT?
BEEP
BIP
A-LERT. SUB-JECT IS: GHOST.

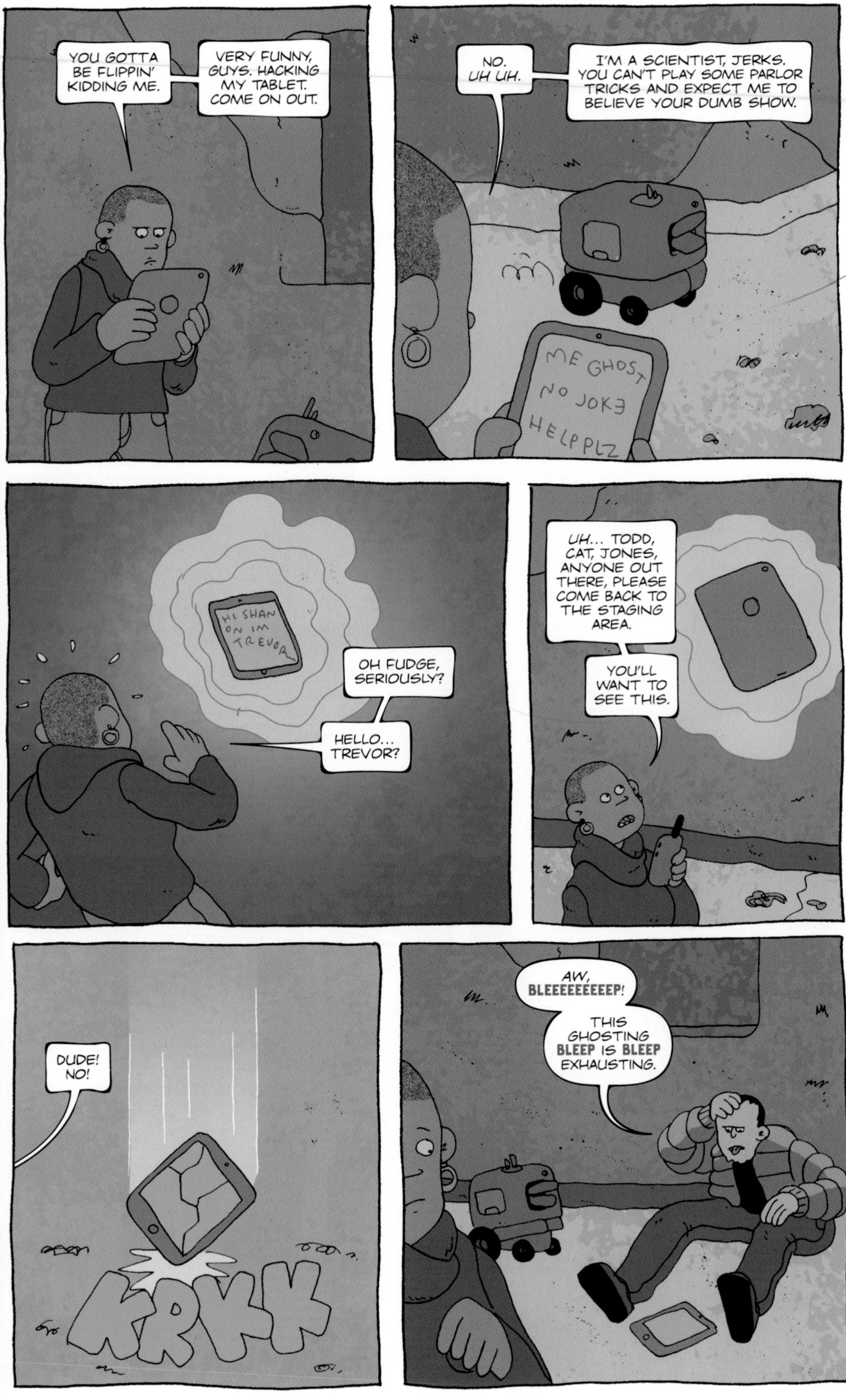
YOU GOTTA BE FLIPPIN' KIDDING ME.
VERY FUNNY, GUYS. HACKING MY TABLET. COME ON OUT.
NO. UH UH.
I'M A SCIENTIST, JERKS. YOU CAN'T PLAY SOME PARLOR TRICKS AND EXPECT ME TO BELIEVE YOUR DUMB SHOW.
ME GHOST NO JOKE HELP PLZ
HI SHAN ON IM TREVOR
OH FUDGE, SERIOUSLY?
HELLO... TREVOR?
UH... TODD, CAT, JONES, ANYONE OUT THERE, PLEASE COME BACK TO THE STAGING AREA.
YOU'LL WANT TO SEE THIS.
DUDE! NO!
KRKK
AW, BLEEEEEEEEEP!
THIS GHOSTING BLEEP IS BLEEP EXHAUSTING.

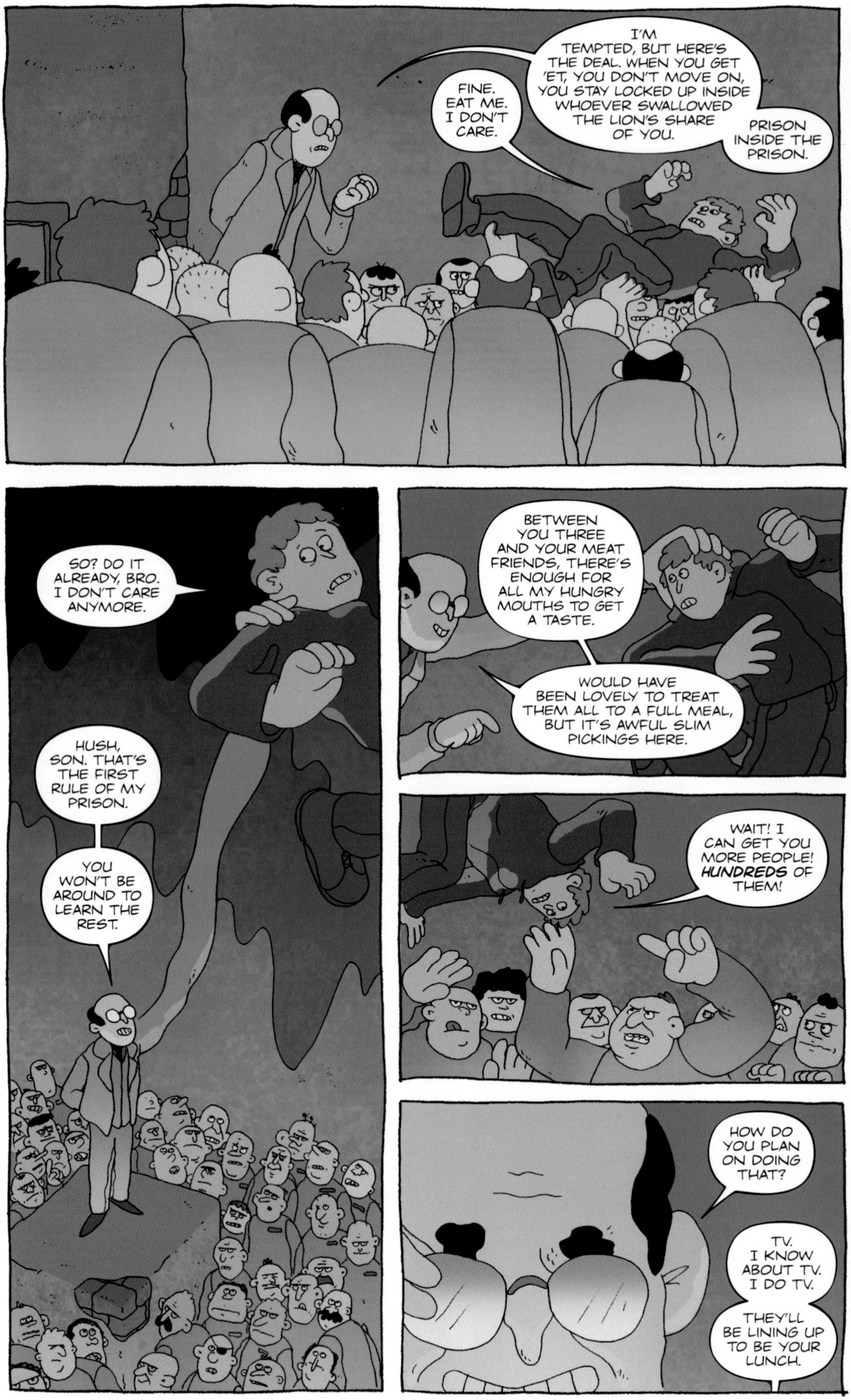

FINE. EAT ME. I DON'T CARE.
I'M TEMPTED, BUT HERE'S THE DEAL. WHEN YOU GET 'ET, YOU DON'T MOVE ON, YOU STAY LOCKED UP INSIDE WHOEVER SWALLOWED THE LION'S SHARE OF YOU.
PRISON INSIDE THE PRISON.
SO? DO IT ALREADY, BRO. I DON'T CARE ANYMORE.
HUSH, SON. THAT'S THE FIRST RULE OF MY PRISON.
YOU WON'T BE AROUND TO LEARN THE REST.
BETWEEN YOU THREE AND YOUR MEAT FRIENDS, THERE'S ENOUGH FOR ALL MY HUNGRY MOUTHS TO GET A TASTE.
WOULD HAVE BEEN LOVELY TO TREAT THEM ALL TO A FULL MEAL, BUT IT'S AWFUL SLIM PICKINGS HERE.
WAIT! I CAN GET YOU MORE PEOPLE! **HUNDREDS** OF THEM!
HOW DO YOU PLAN ON DOING THAT?
TV. I KNOW ABOUT TV. I DO TV.
THEY'LL BE LINING UP TO BE YOUR LUNCH.

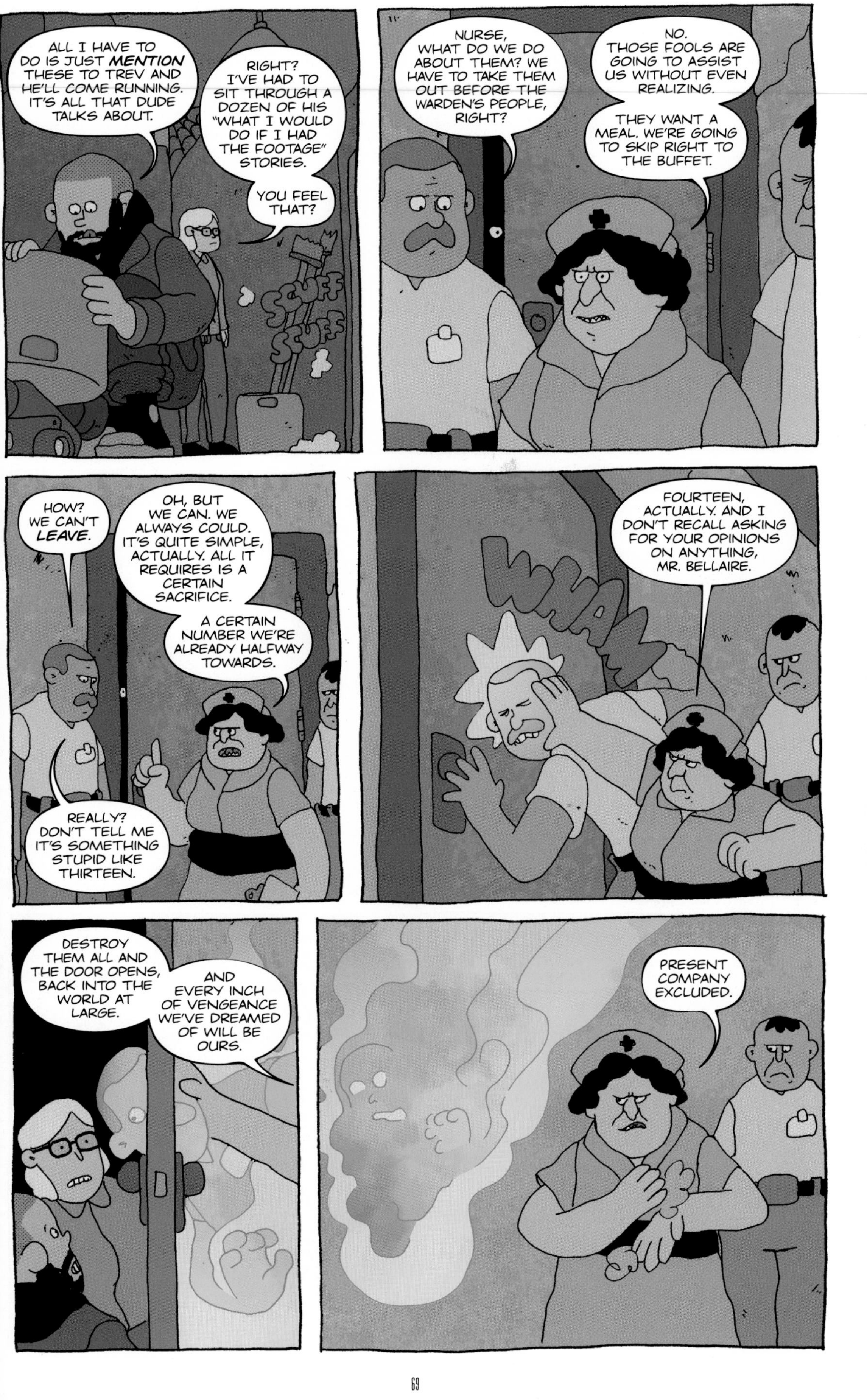
ALL I HAVE TO DO IS JUST **MENTION** THESE TO TREV AND HE'LL COME RUNNING. IT'S ALL THAT DUDE TALKS ABOUT.
RIGHT? I'VE HAD TO SIT THROUGH A DOZEN OF HIS "WHAT I WOULD DO IF I HAD THE FOOTAGE" STORIES.
YOU FEEL THAT?
SCUFF
SCUFF
NURSE, WHAT DO WE DO ABOUT THEM? WE HAVE TO TAKE THEM OUT BEFORE THE WARDEN'S PEOPLE, RIGHT?
NO. THOSE FOOLS ARE GOING TO ASSIST US WITHOUT EVEN REALIZING.
THEY WANT A MEAL. WE'RE GOING TO SKIP RIGHT TO THE BUFFET.
HOW? WE CAN'T ***LEAVE***.
OH, BUT WE CAN. WE ALWAYS COULD. IT'S QUITE SIMPLE, ACTUALLY. ALL IT REQUIRES IS A CERTAIN SACRIFICE.
A CERTAIN NUMBER WE'RE ALREADY HALFWAY TOWARDS.
REALLY? DON'T TELL ME IT'S SOMETHING STUPID LIKE THIRTEEN.
WHAM
FOURTEEN, ACTUALLY. AND I DON'T RECALL ASKING FOR YOUR OPINIONS ON ANYTHING, MR. BELLAIRE.
DESTROY THEM ALL AND THE DOOR OPENS, BACK INTO THE WORLD AT LARGE.
AND EVERY INCH OF VENGEANCE WE'VE DREAMED OF WILL BE OURS.
PRESENT COMPANY EXCLUDED.

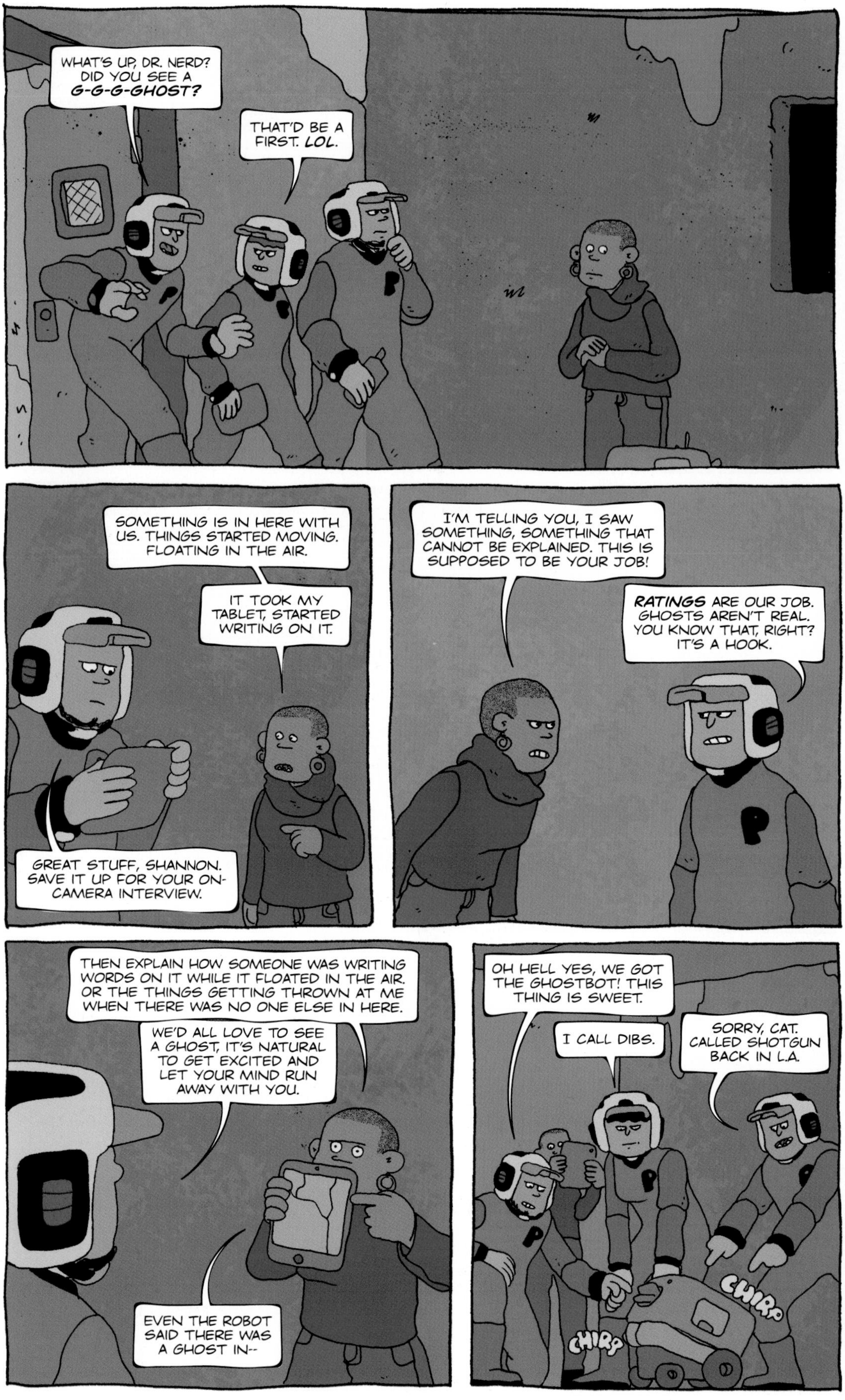
WHAT'S UP, DR. NERD? DID YOU SEE A *G-G-G-GHOST?*
THAT'D BE A FIRST. *LOL.*
SOMETHING IS IN HERE WITH US. THINGS STARTED MOVING. FLOATING IN THE AIR.
IT TOOK MY TABLET, STARTED WRITING ON IT.
GREAT STUFF, SHANNON. SAVE IT UP FOR YOUR ON-CAMERA INTERVIEW.
I'M TELLING YOU, I SAW SOMETHING, SOMETHING THAT CANNOT BE EXPLAINED. THIS IS SUPPOSED TO BE YOUR JOB!
RATINGS ARE OUR JOB. GHOSTS AREN'T REAL. YOU KNOW THAT, RIGHT? IT'S A HOOK.
THEN EXPLAIN HOW SOMEONE WAS WRITING WORDS ON IT WHILE IT FLOATED IN THE AIR. OR THE THINGS GETTING THROWN AT ME WHEN THERE WAS NO ONE ELSE IN HERE.
WE'D ALL LOVE TO SEE A GHOST, IT'S NATURAL TO GET EXCITED AND LET YOUR MIND RUN AWAY WITH YOU.
EVEN THE ROBOT SAID THERE WAS A GHOST IN--
OH HELL YES, WE GOT THE GHOSTBOT! THIS THING IS SWEET.
I CALL DIBS.
SORRY, CAT. CALLED SHOTGUN BACK IN L.A.
CHIRP
CHIRP

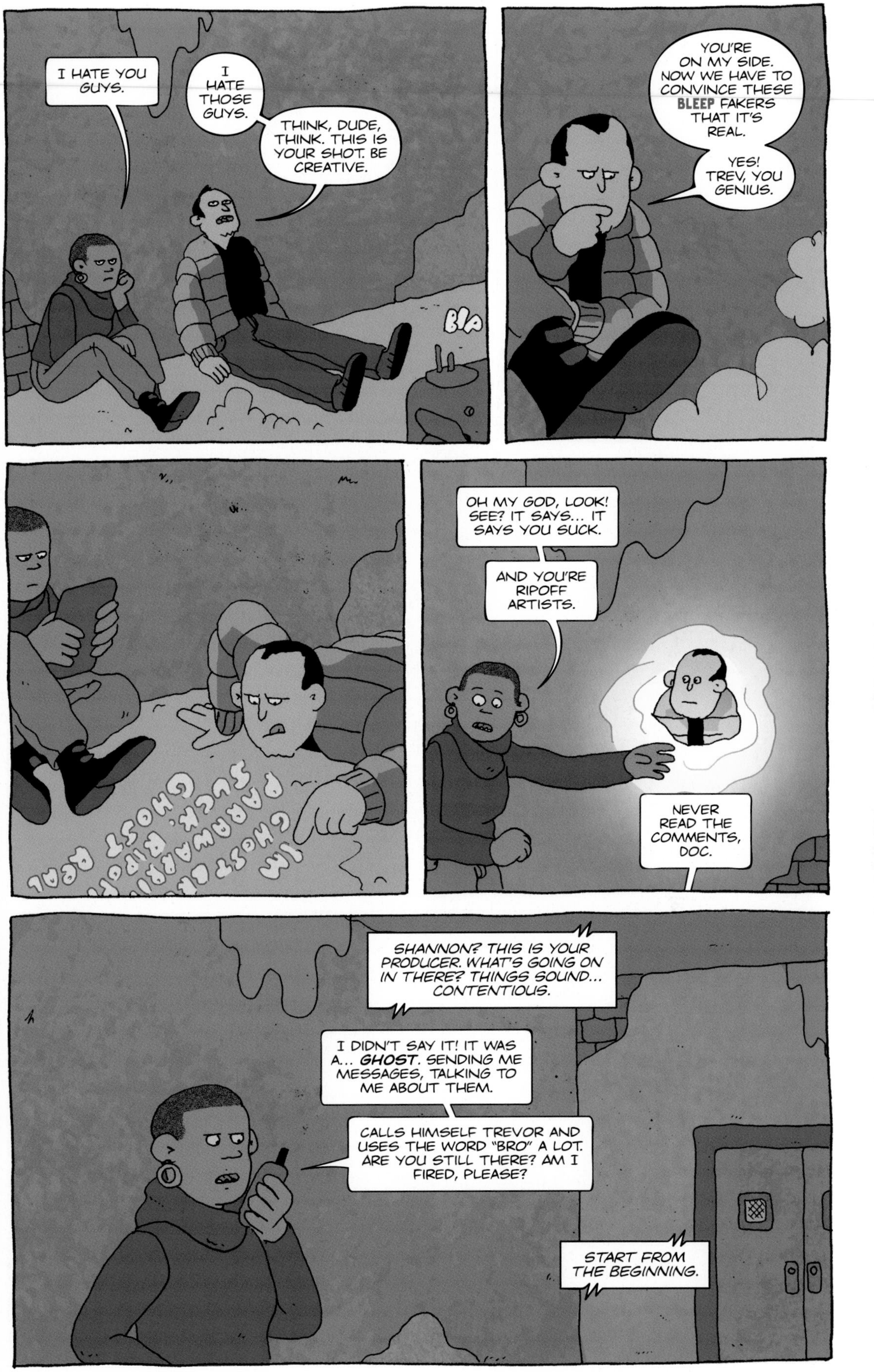

I HATE YOU GUYS.
I HATE THOSE GUYS.
THINK, DUDE, THINK. THIS IS YOUR SHOT. BE CREATIVE.
BIP
YOU'RE ON MY SIDE. NOW WE HAVE TO CONVINCE THESE BLEEP FAKERS THAT IT'S REAL.
YES! TREV, YOU GENIUS.
OH MY GOD, LOOK! SEE? IT SAYS... IT SAYS YOU SUCK.
AND YOU'RE RIPOFF ARTISTS.
NEVER READ THE COMMENTS, DOC.
SHANNON? THIS IS YOUR PRODUCER. WHAT'S GOING ON IN THERE? THINGS SOUND... CONTENTIOUS.
I DIDN'T SAY IT! IT WAS A... GHOST. SENDING ME MESSAGES, TALKING TO ME ABOUT THEM.
CALLS HIMSELF TREVOR AND USES THE WORD "BRO" A LOT. ARE YOU STILL THERE? AM I FIRED, PLEASE?
START FROM THE BEGINNING.

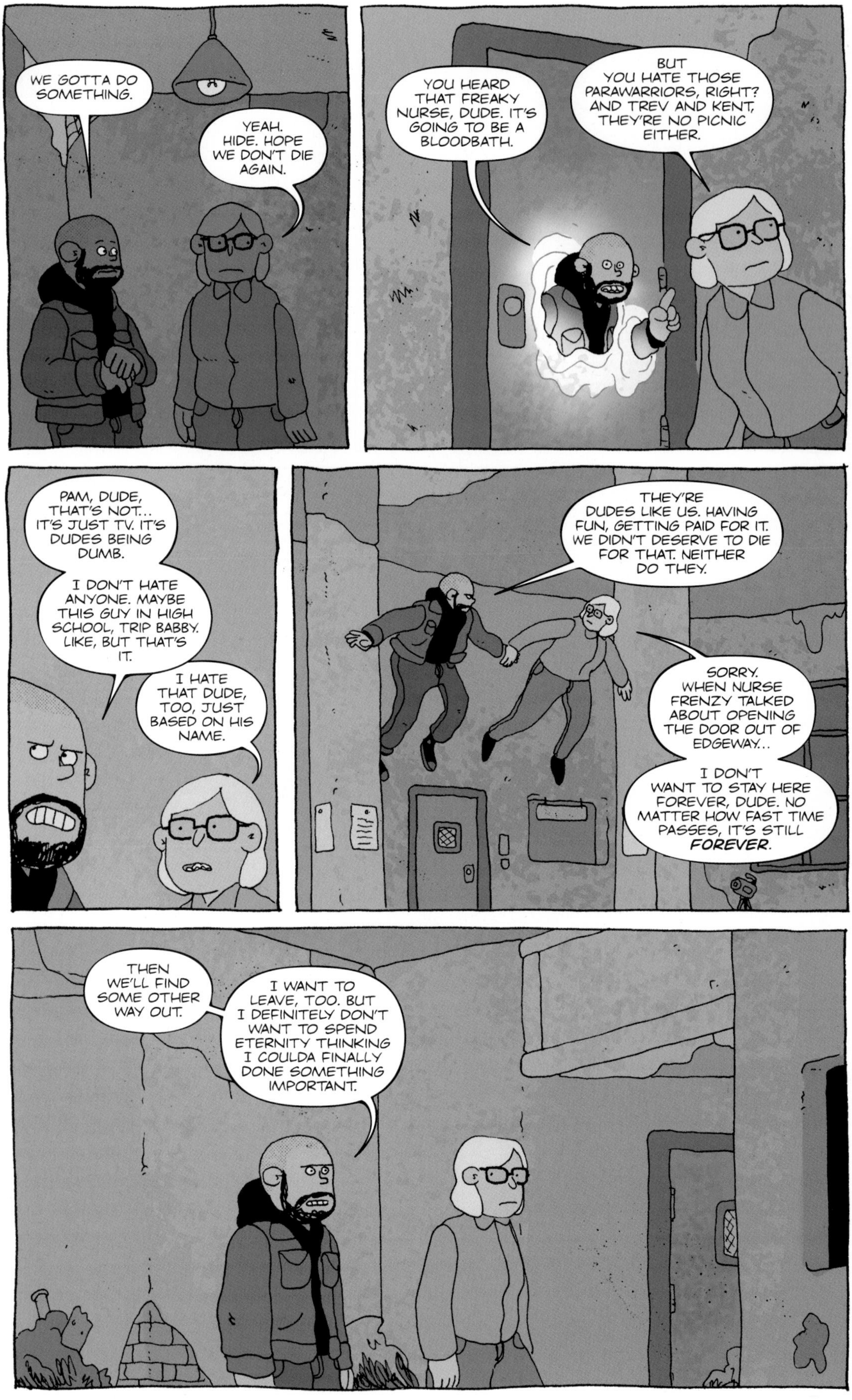
WE GOTTA DO SOMETHING.
YEAH. HIDE. HOPE WE DON'T DIE AGAIN.
YOU HEARD THAT FREAKY NURSE, DUDE. IT'S GOING TO BE A BLOODBATH.
BUT YOU HATE THOSE PARAWARRIORS, RIGHT? AND TREV AND KENT, THEY'RE NO PICNIC EITHER.
PAM, DUDE, THAT'S NOT... IT'S JUST TV. IT'S DUDES BEING DUMB.
I DON'T HATE ANYONE. MAYBE THIS GUY IN HIGH SCHOOL, TRIP BABBY. LIKE, BUT THAT'S IT.
I HATE THAT DUDE, TOO, JUST BASED ON HIS NAME.
THEY'RE DUDES LIKE US. HAVING FUN, GETTING PAID FOR IT. WE DIDN'T DESERVE TO DIE FOR THAT. NEITHER DO THEY.
SORRY. WHEN NURSE FRENZY TALKED ABOUT OPENING THE DOOR OUT OF EDGEWAY...
I DON'T WANT TO STAY HERE FOREVER, DUDE. NO MATTER HOW FAST TIME PASSES, IT'S STILL ***FOREVER***.
THEN WE'LL FIND SOME OTHER WAY OUT.
I WANT TO LEAVE, TOO. BUT I DEFINITELY DON'T WANT TO SPEND ETERNITY THINKING I COULDA FINALLY DONE SOMETHING IMPORTANT.

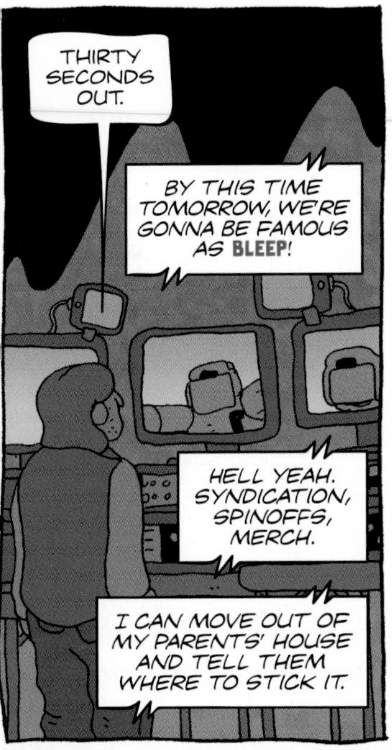
THIRTY SECONDS OUT.
BY THIS TIME TOMORROW, WE'RE GONNA BE FAMOUS AS BLEEP!
HELL YEAH. SYNDICATION, SPINOFFS, MERCH.
I CAN MOVE OUT OF MY PARENTS' HOUSE AND TELL THEM WHERE TO STICK IT.

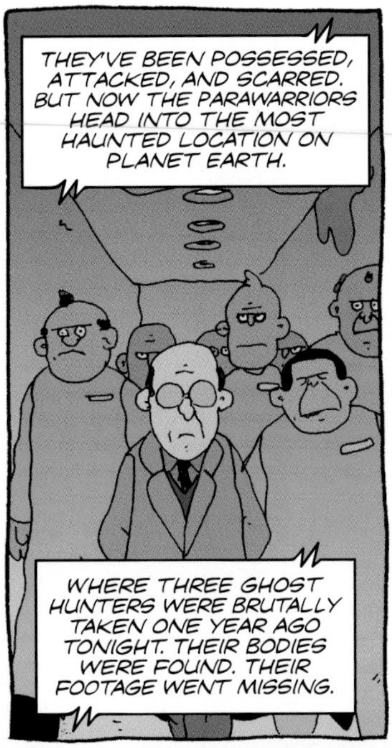
THEY'VE BEEN POSSESSED, ATTACKED, AND SCARRED. BUT NOW THE PARAWARRIORS HEAD INTO THE MOST HAUNTED LOCATION ON PLANET EARTH.
WHERE THREE GHOST HUNTERS WERE BRUTALLY TAKEN ONE YEAR AGO TONIGHT. THEIR BODIES WERE FOUND. THEIR FOOTAGE WENT MISSING.

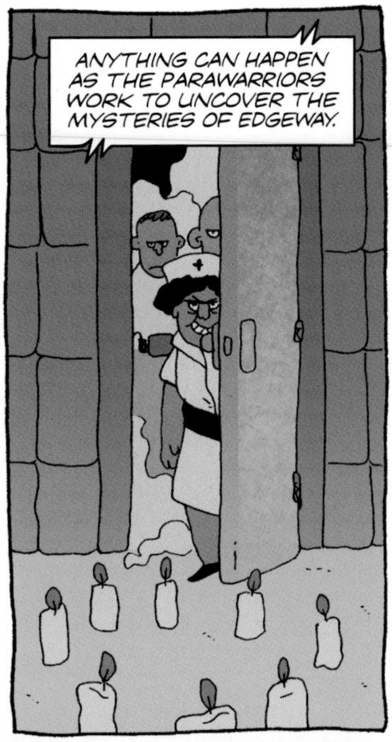
ANYTHING CAN HAPPEN AS THE PARAWARRIORS WORK TO UNCOVER THE MYSTERIES OF EDGEWAY.

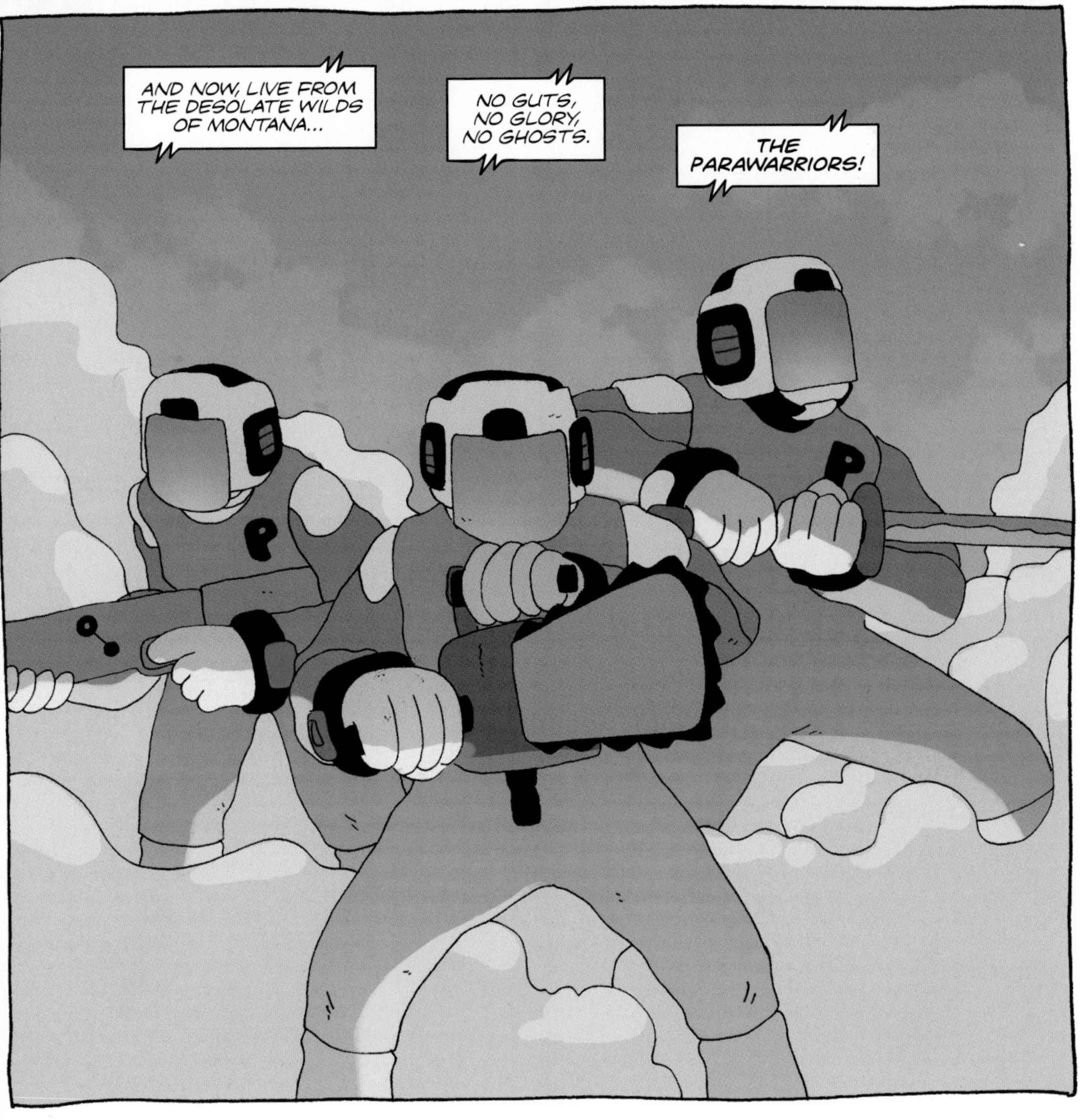
AND NOW, LIVE FROM THE DESOLATE WILDS OF MONTANA...
NO GUTS, NO GLORY, NO GHOSTS.
THE PARAWARRIORS!

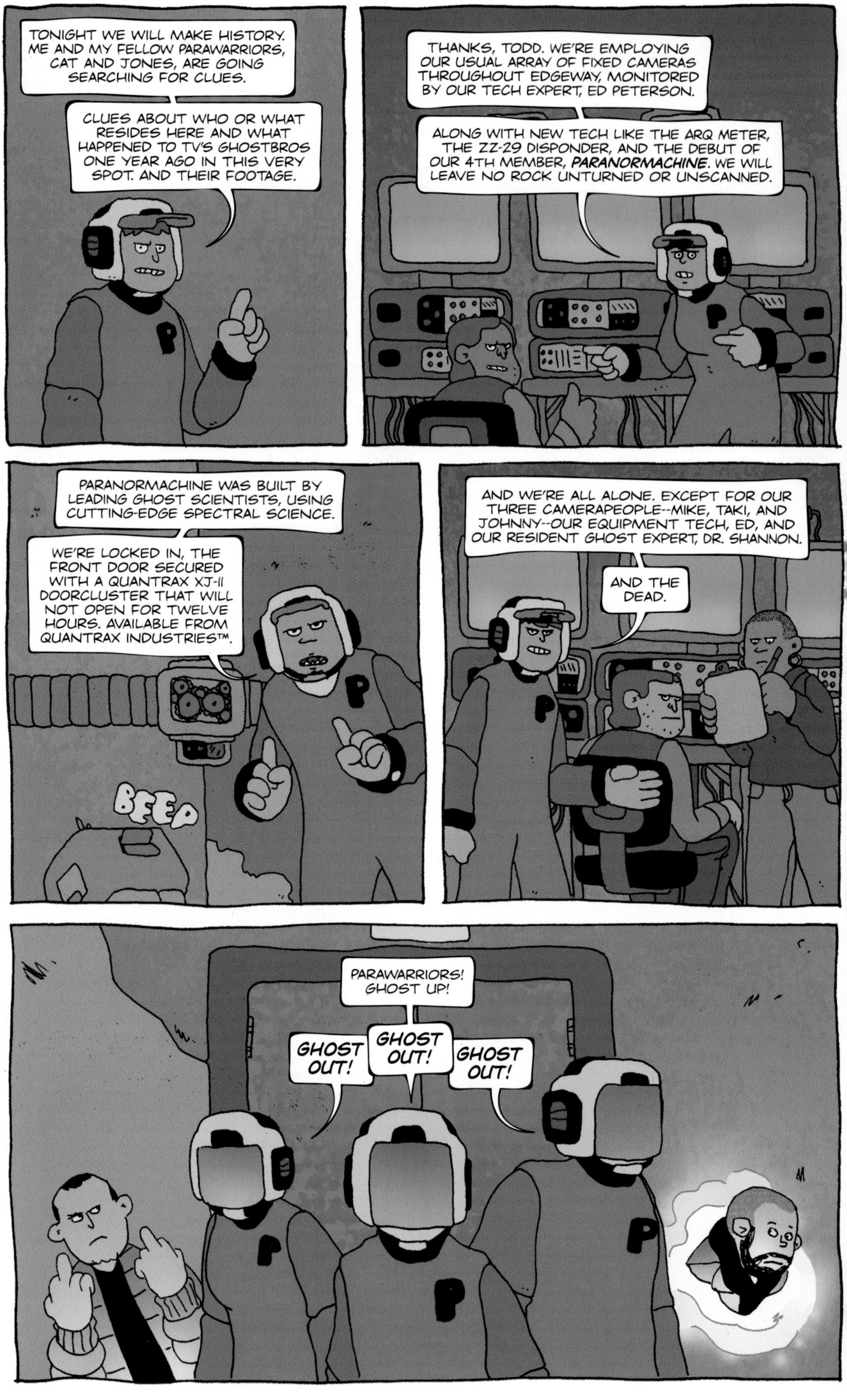
TONIGHT WE WILL MAKE HISTORY. ME AND MY FELLOW PARAWARRIORS, CAT AND JONES, ARE GOING SEARCHING FOR CLUES.
CLUES ABOUT WHO OR WHAT RESIDES HERE AND WHAT HAPPENED TO TV'S GHOSTBROS ONE YEAR AGO IN THIS VERY SPOT. AND THEIR FOOTAGE.
THANKS, TODD. WE'RE EMPLOYING OUR USUAL ARRAY OF FIXED CAMERAS THROUGHOUT EDGEWAY, MONITORED BY OUR TECH EXPERT, ED PETERSON.
ALONG WITH NEW TECH LIKE THE ARQ METER, THE ZZ-29 DISPONDER, AND THE DEBUT OF OUR 4TH MEMBER, ***PARANORMACHINE***. WE WILL LEAVE NO ROCK UNTURNED OR UNSCANNED.
PARANORMACHINE WAS BUILT BY LEADING GHOST SCIENTISTS, USING CUTTING-EDGE SPECTRAL SCIENCE.
WE'RE LOCKED IN, THE FRONT DOOR SECURED WITH A QUANTRAX XJ-11 DOORCLUSTER THAT WILL NOT OPEN FOR TWELVE HOURS. AVAILABLE FROM QUANTRAX INDUSTRIES™.
BEEP
AND WE'RE ALL ALONE. EXCEPT FOR OUR THREE CAMERAPEOPLE--MIKE, TAKI, AND JOHNNY--OUR EQUIPMENT TECH, ED, AND OUR RESIDENT GHOST EXPERT, DR. SHANNON.
AND THE DEAD.
PARAWARRIORS! GHOST UP!
GHOST OUT!
GHOST OUT!
GHOST OUT!

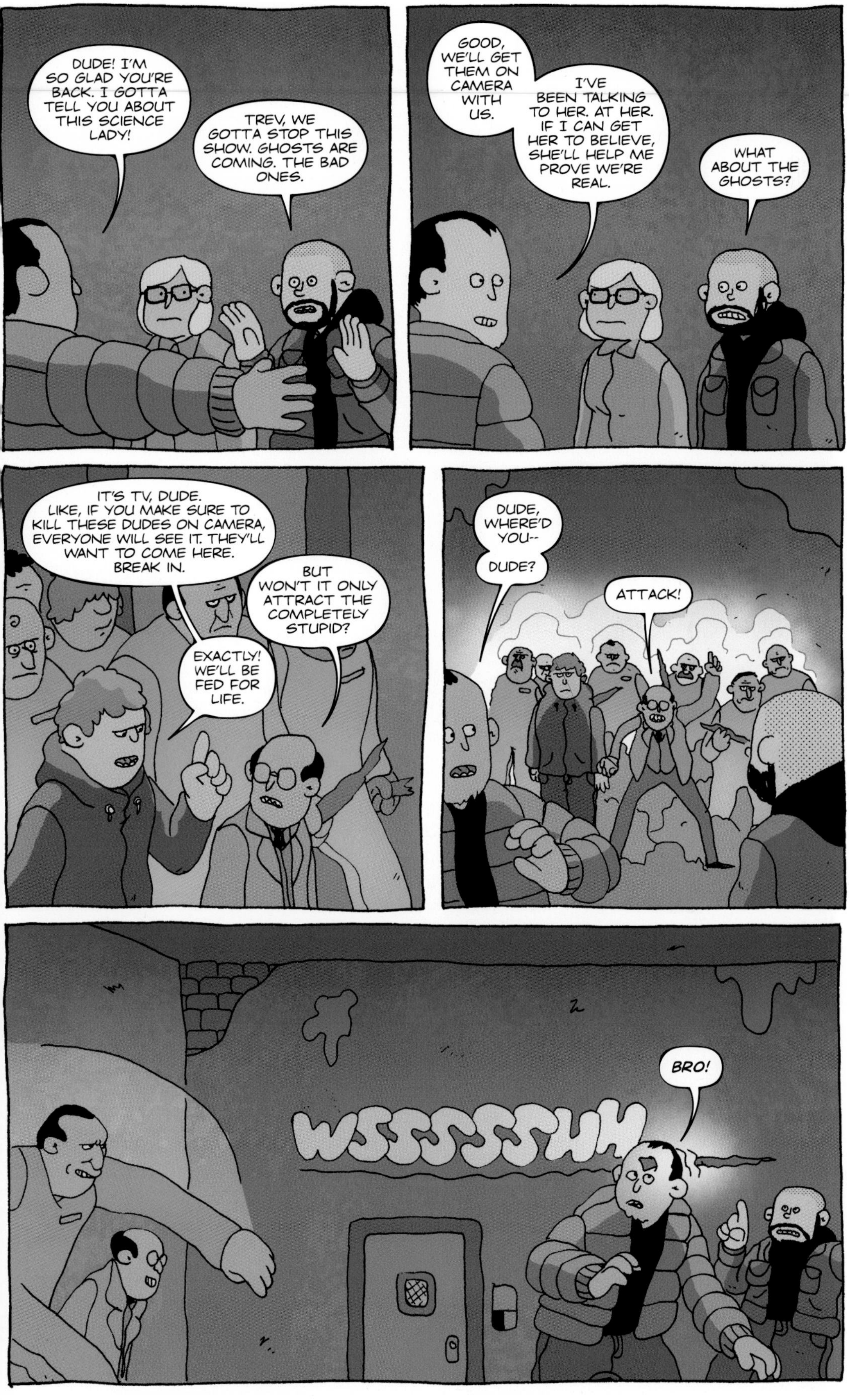

DUDE! I'M SO GLAD YOU'RE BACK. I GOTTA TELL YOU ABOUT THIS SCIENCE LADY!
TREV, WE GOTTA STOP THIS SHOW. GHOSTS ARE COMING. THE BAD ONES.
GOOD, WE'LL GET THEM ON CAMERA WITH US.
I'VE BEEN TALKING TO HER. AT HER. IF I CAN GET HER TO BELIEVE, SHE'LL HELP ME PROVE WE'RE REAL.
WHAT ABOUT THE GHOSTS?
IT'S TV, DUDE. LIKE, IF YOU MAKE SURE TO KILL THESE DUDES ON CAMERA, EVERYONE WILL SEE IT. THEY'LL WANT TO COME HERE. BREAK IN.
BUT WON'T IT ONLY ATTRACT THE COMPLETELY STUPID?
EXACTLY! WE'LL BE FED FOR LIFE.
DUDE, WHERE'D YOU--
DUDE?
ATTACK!
BRO!
WSSSSSSHH

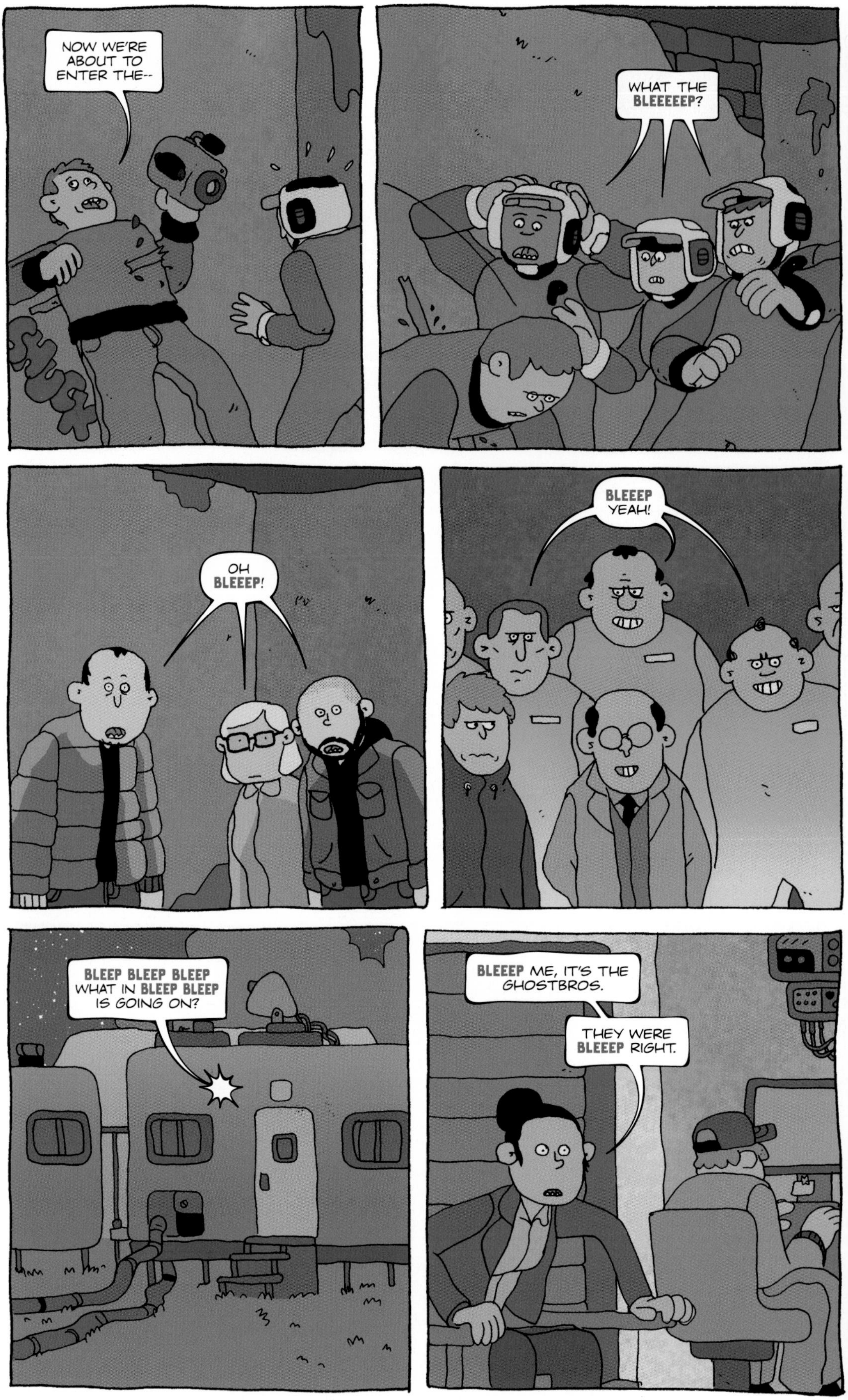
NOW WE'RE ABOUT TO ENTER THE--
WHAT THE BLEEEEEP?
OH BLEEEP!
BLEEEP YEAH!
BLEEP BLEEP BLEEP WHAT IN BLEEP BLEEP IS GOING ON?
BLEEEP ME, IT'S THE GHOSTBROS.
THEY WERE BLEEEP RIGHT.

CHAPTER
FOUR

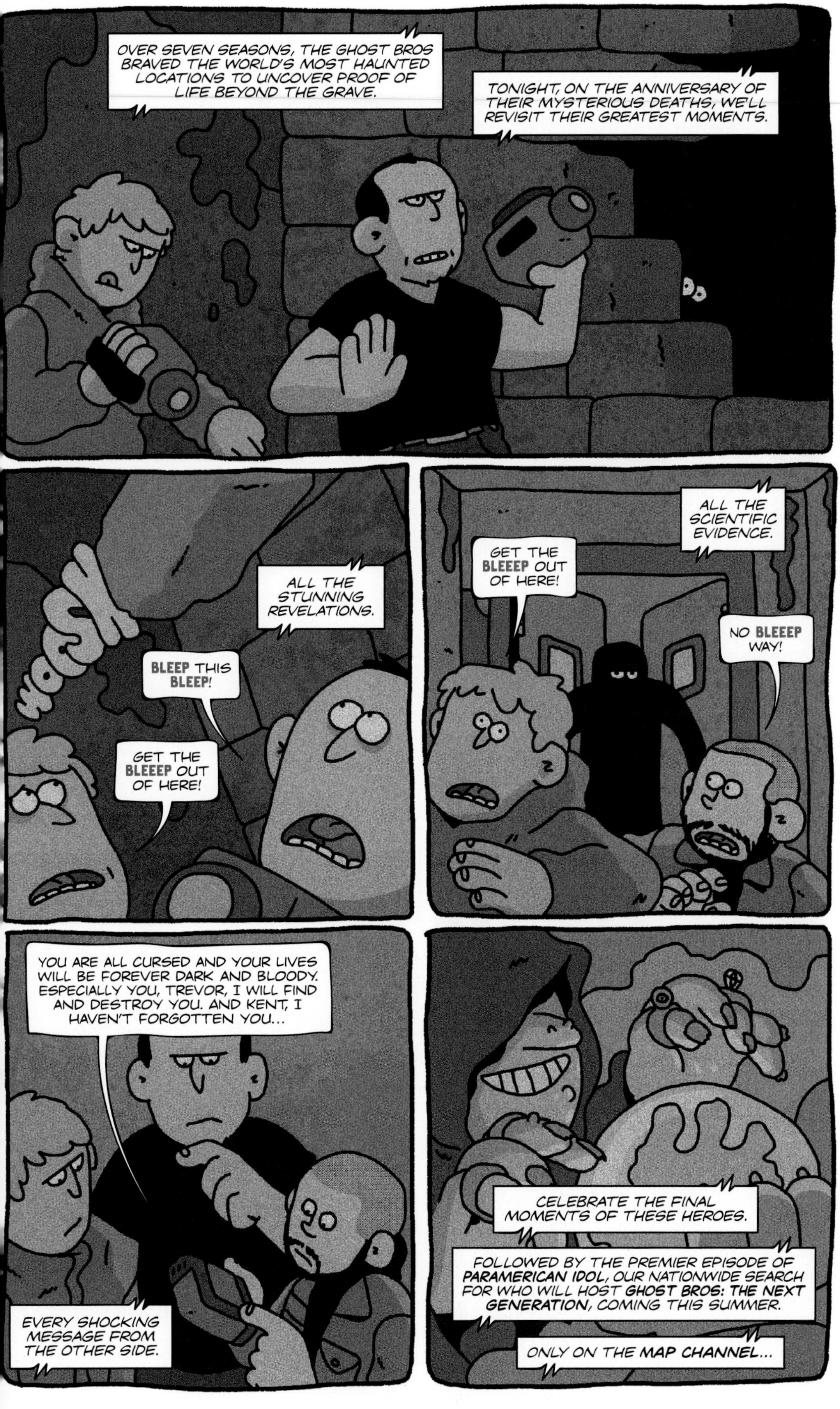
OVER SEVEN SEASONS, THE GHOST BROS BRAVED THE WORLD'S MOST HAUNTED LOCATIONS TO UNCOVER PROOF OF LIFE BEYOND THE GRAVE.
TONIGHT, ON THE ANNIVERSARY OF THEIR MYSTERIOUS DEATHS, WE'LL REVISIT THEIR GREATEST MOMENTS.
WOOSH
ALL THE STUNNING REVELATIONS.
BLEEP THIS BLEEP!
GET THE BLEEEP OUT OF HERE!
ALL THE SCIENTIFIC EVIDENCE.
GET THE BLEEEP OUT OF HERE!
NO BLEEEP WAY!
YOU ARE ALL CURSED AND YOUR LIVES WILL BE FOREVER DARK AND BLOODY. ESPECIALLY YOU, TREVOR, I WILL FIND AND DESTROY YOU. AND KENT, I HAVEN'T FORGOTTEN YOU...
EVERY SHOCKING MESSAGE FROM THE OTHER SIDE.
CELEBRATE THE FINAL MOMENTS OF THESE HEROES.
FOLLOWED BY THE PREMIER EPISODE OF PARAMERICAN IDOL, OUR NATIONWIDE SEARCH FOR WHO WILL HOST GHOST BROS: THE NEXT GENERATION, COMING THIS SUMMER.
ONLY ON THE MAP CHANNEL...

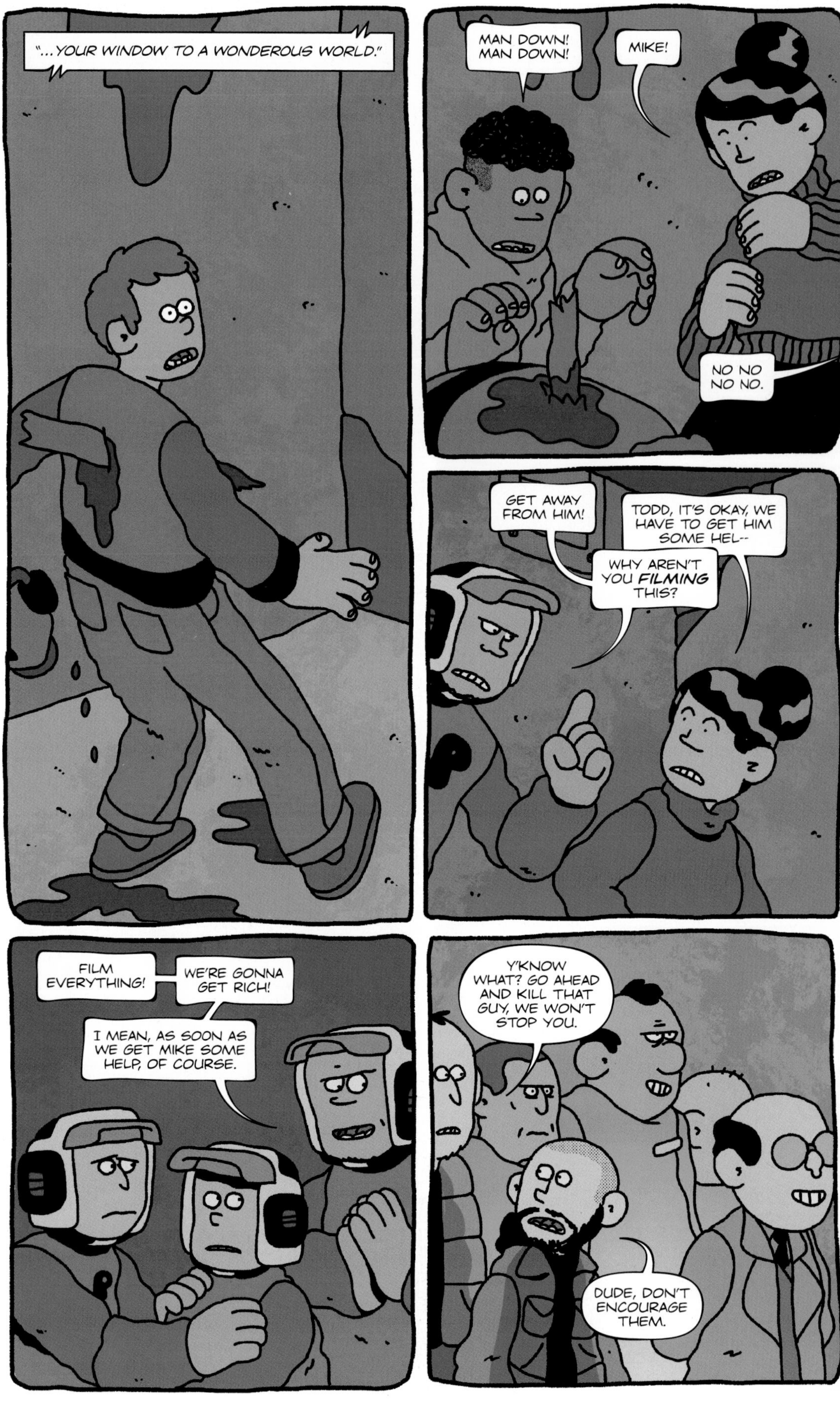
"...YOUR WINDOW TO A WONDEROUS WORLD."
MAN DOWN! MAN DOWN!
MIKE!
NO NO NO NO.
GET AWAY FROM HIM!
TODD, IT'S OKAY, WE HAVE TO GET HIM SOME HEL--
WHY AREN'T YOU **FILMING** THIS?
FILM EVERYTHING!
WE'RE GONNA GET RICH!
I MEAN, AS SOON AS WE GET MIKE SOME HELP, OF COURSE.
Y'KNOW WHAT? GO AHEAD AND KILL THAT GUY, WE WON'T STOP YOU.
DUDE, DON'T ENCOURAGE THEM.

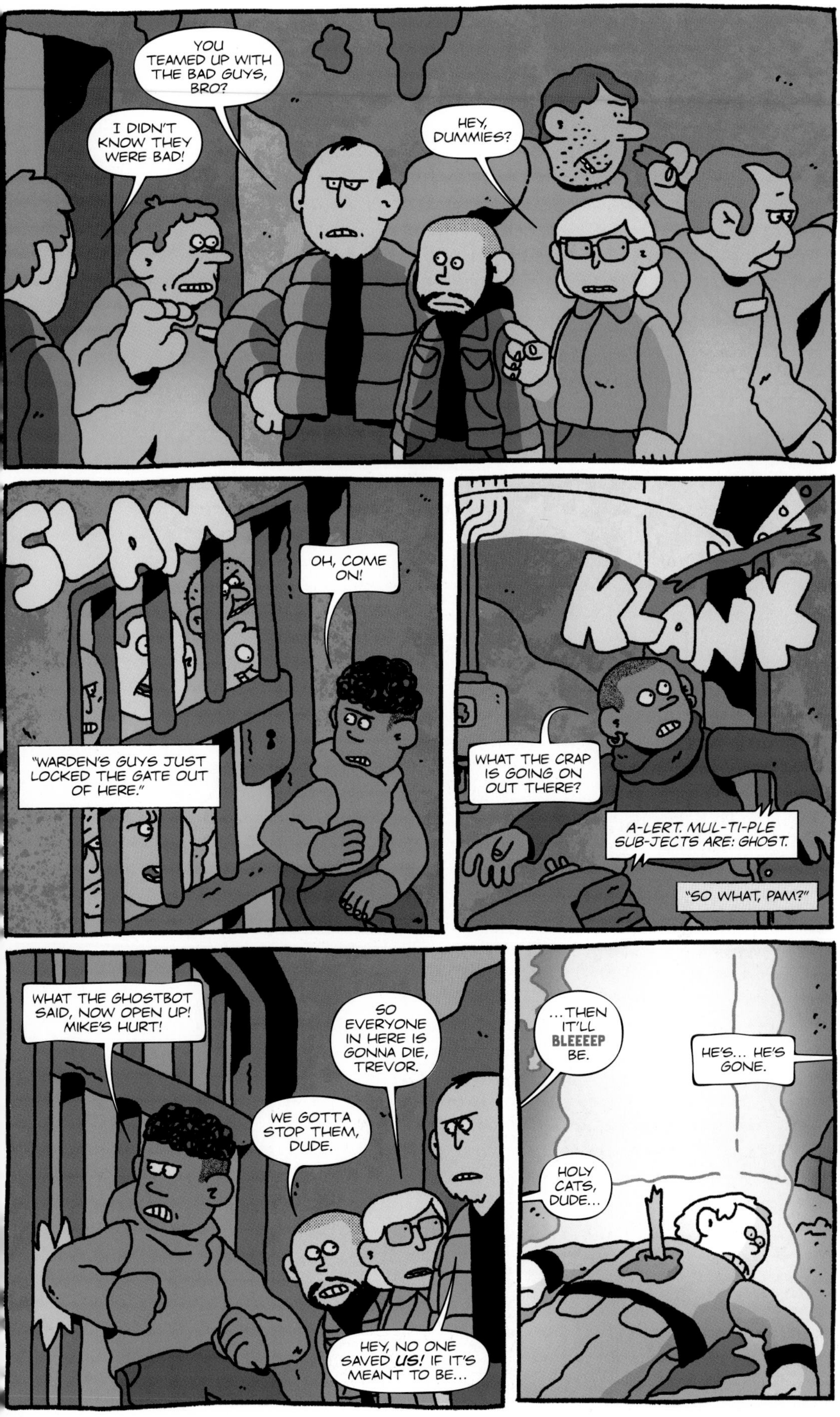
YOU TEAMED UP WITH THE BAD GUYS, BRO?
I DIDN'T KNOW THEY WERE BAD!
HEY, DUMMIES?
SLAM
OH, COME ON!
"WARDEN'S GUYS JUST LOCKED THE GATE OUT OF HERE."
KLANK
WHAT THE CRAP IS GOING ON OUT THERE?
A-LERT. MUL-TI-PLE SUB-JECTS ARE: GHOST.
"SO WHAT, PAM?"
WHAT THE GHOSTBOT SAID, NOW OPEN UP! MIKE'S HURT!
SO EVERYONE IN HERE IS GONNA DIE, TREVOR.
WE GOTTA STOP THEM, DUDE.
HEY, NO ONE SAVED *US!* IF IT'S MEANT TO BE...
...THEN IT'LL **BLEEEEP** BE.
HE'S... HE'S GONE.
HOLY CATS, DUDE...

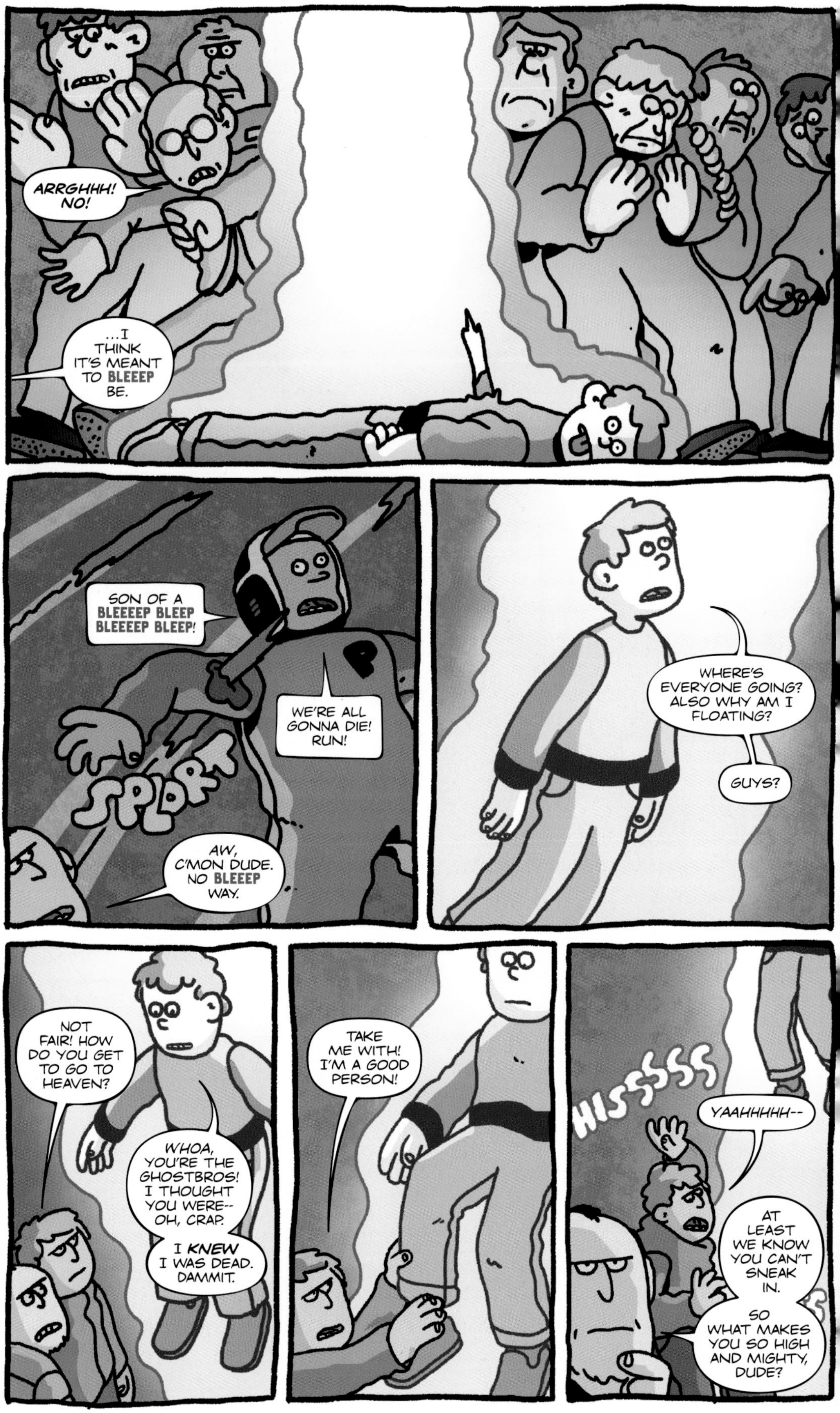
ARRGHHH! NO!
...I THINK IT'S MEANT TO BLEEEP BE.
SON OF A BLEEEEP BLEEP BLEEEEP BLEEP!
WE'RE ALL GONNA DIE! RUN!
SPLORT
AW, C'MON DUDE. NO BLEEEP WAY.
WHERE'S EVERYONE GOING? ALSO WHY AM I FLOATING?
GUYS?
NOT FAIR! HOW DO YOU GET TO GO TO HEAVEN?
WHOA, YOU'RE THE GHOSTBROS! I THOUGHT YOU WERE-- OH, CRAP.
I KNEW I WAS DEAD. DAMMIT.
TAKE ME WITH! I'M A GOOD PERSON!
HISSSSS
YAAHHHHH--
AT LEAST WE KNOW YOU CAN'T SNEAK IN.
SO WHAT MAKES YOU SO HIGH AND MIGHTY, DUDE?

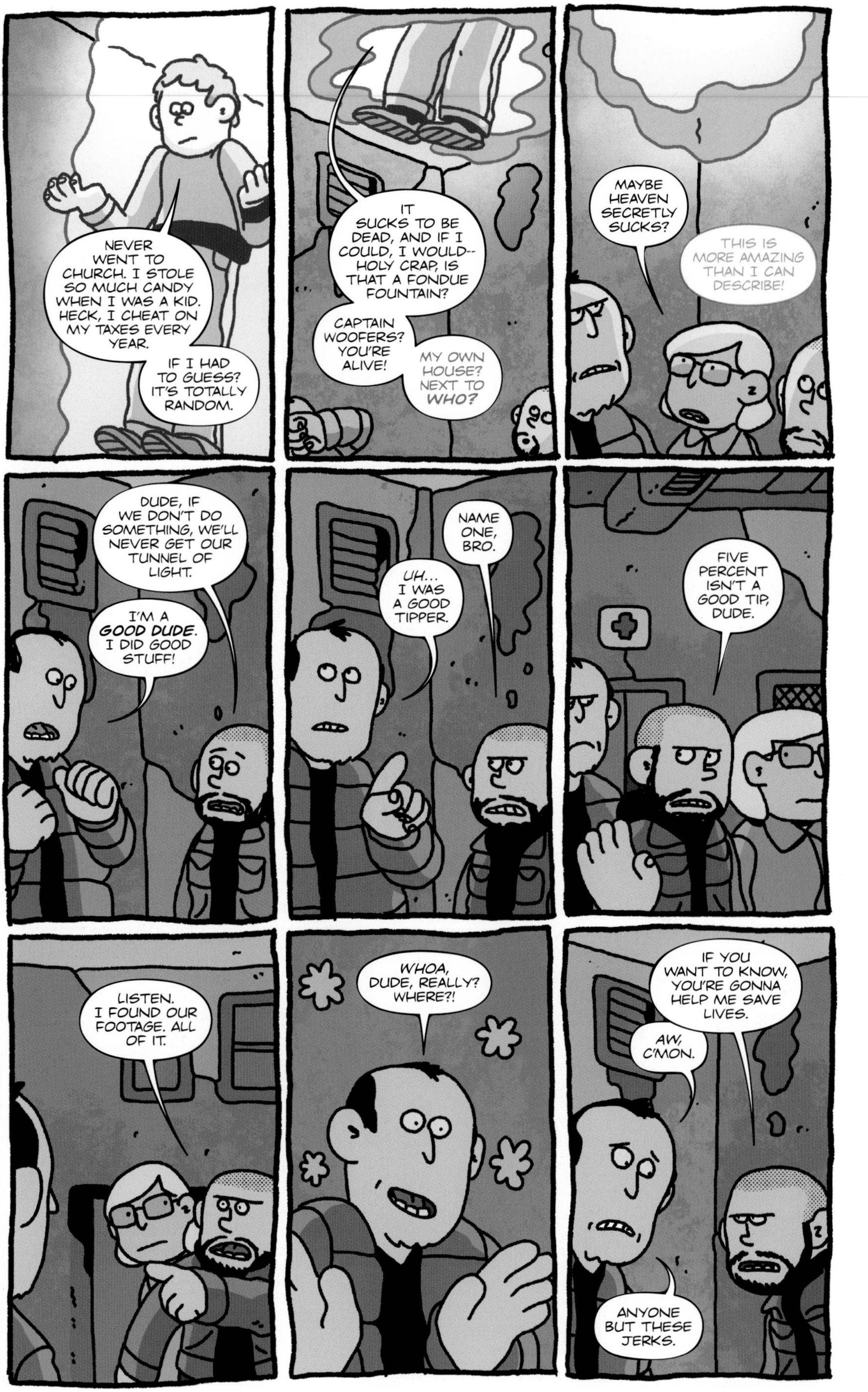

NEVER WENT TO CHURCH. I STOLE SO MUCH CANDY WHEN I WAS A KID. HECK, I CHEAT ON MY TAXES EVERY YEAR.
IF I HAD TO GUESS? IT'S TOTALLY RANDOM.
IT SUCKS TO BE DEAD, AND IF I COULD, I WOULD-- HOLY CRAP, IS THAT A FONDUE FOUNTAIN?
CAPTAIN WOOFERS? YOU'RE ALIVE!
MY OWN HOUSE? NEXT TO *WHO?*
MAYBE HEAVEN SECRETLY SUCKS?
THIS IS MORE AMAZING THAN I CAN DESCRIBE!
DUDE, IF WE DON'T DO SOMETHING, WE'LL NEVER GET OUR TUNNEL OF LIGHT.
I'M A **GOOD DUDE**. I DID GOOD STUFF!
NAME ONE, BRO.
UH... I WAS A GOOD TIPPER.
FIVE PERCENT ISN'T A GOOD TIP, DUDE.
LISTEN. I FOUND OUR FOOTAGE. ALL OF IT.
WHOA, DUDE, REALLY? WHERE?!
IF YOU WANT TO KNOW, YOU'RE GONNA HELP ME SAVE LIVES.
AW, C'MON.
ANYONE BUT THESE JERKS.

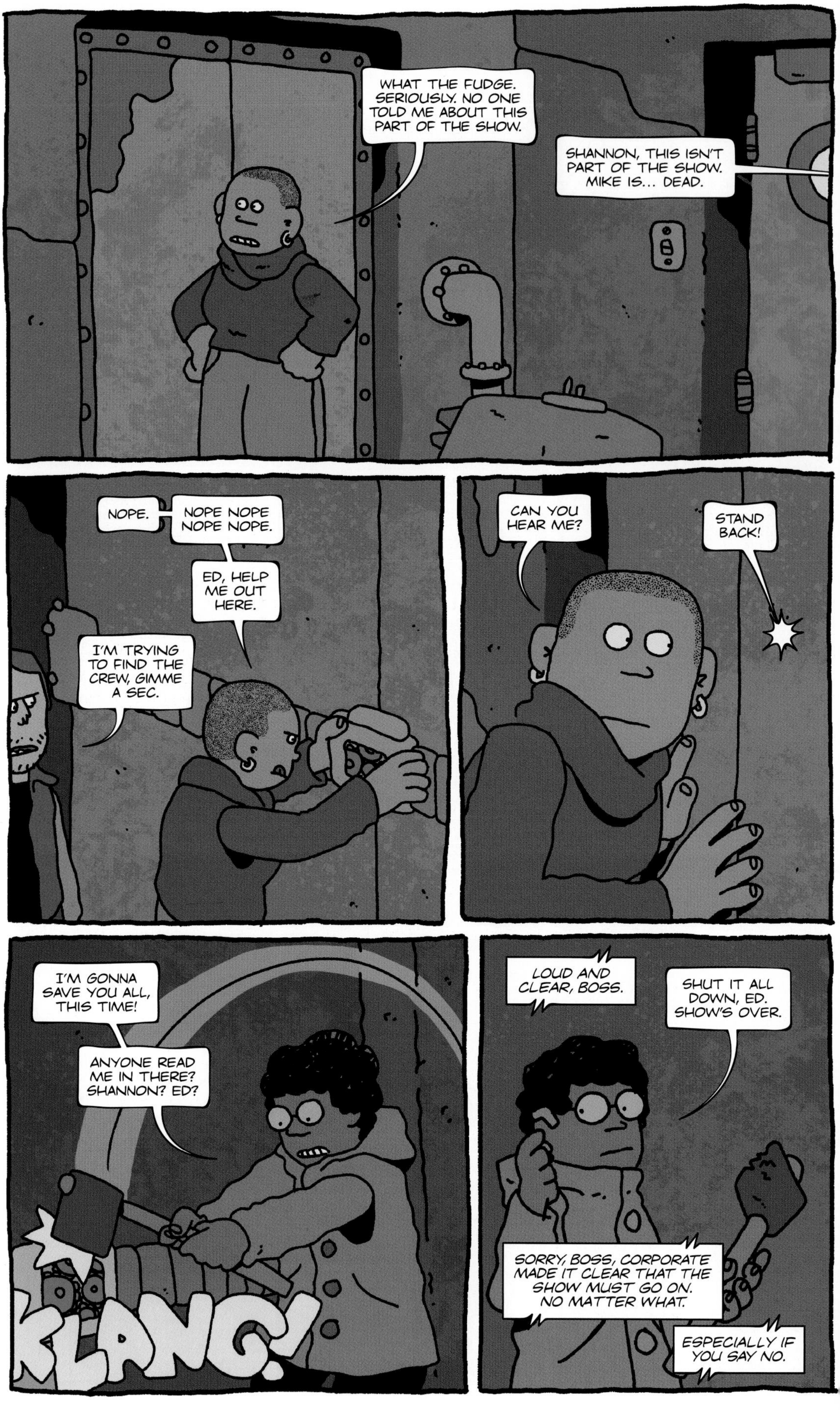

WHAT THE FUDGE. SERIOUSLY. NO ONE TOLD ME ABOUT THIS PART OF THE SHOW.
SHANNON, THIS ISN'T PART OF THE SHOW. MIKE IS... DEAD.
NOPE.
NOPE NOPE NOPE NOPE.
ED, HELP ME OUT HERE.
I'M TRYING TO FIND THE CREW, GIMME A SEC.
CAN YOU HEAR ME?
STAND BACK!
I'M GONNA SAVE YOU ALL, THIS TIME!
ANYONE READ ME IN THERE? SHANNON? ED?
KLANG!
LOUD AND CLEAR, BOSS.
SHUT IT ALL DOWN, ED. SHOW'S OVER.
SORRY, BOSS, CORPORATE MADE IT CLEAR THAT THE SHOW MUST GO ON. NO MATTER WHAT.
ESPECIALLY IF YOU SAY NO.

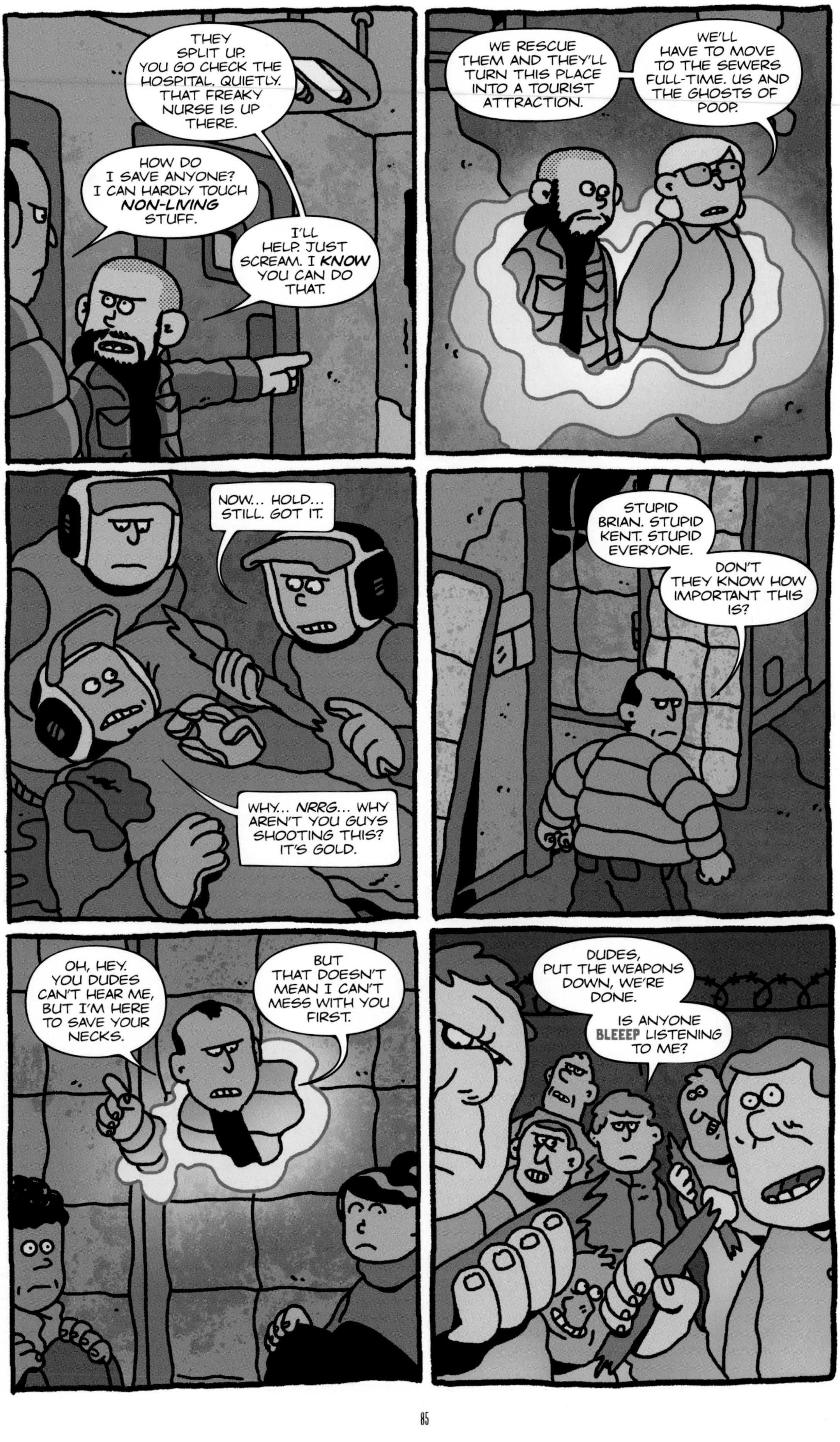
THEY SPLIT UP. YOU GO CHECK THE HOSPITAL. QUIETLY. THAT FREAKY NURSE IS UP THERE.
HOW DO I SAVE ANYONE? I CAN HARDLY TOUCH **NON-LIVING** STUFF.
I'LL HELP. JUST SCREAM. I **KNOW** YOU CAN DO THAT.
WE RESCUE THEM AND THEY'LL TURN THIS PLACE INTO A TOURIST ATTRACTION.
WE'LL HAVE TO MOVE TO THE SEWERS FULL-TIME. US AND THE GHOSTS OF POOP.
NOW... HOLD... STILL. GOT IT.
WHY... *NRRG*... WHY AREN'T YOU GUYS SHOOTING THIS? IT'S GOLD.
STUPID BRIAN. STUPID KENT. STUPID EVERYONE.
DON'T THEY KNOW HOW IMPORTANT THIS IS?
OH, HEY. YOU DUDES CAN'T HEAR ME, BUT I'M HERE TO SAVE YOUR NECKS.
BUT THAT DOESN'T MEAN I CAN'T MESS WITH YOU FIRST.
DUDES, PUT THE WEAPONS DOWN, WE'RE DONE.
IS ANYONE BLEEEP LISTENING TO ME?

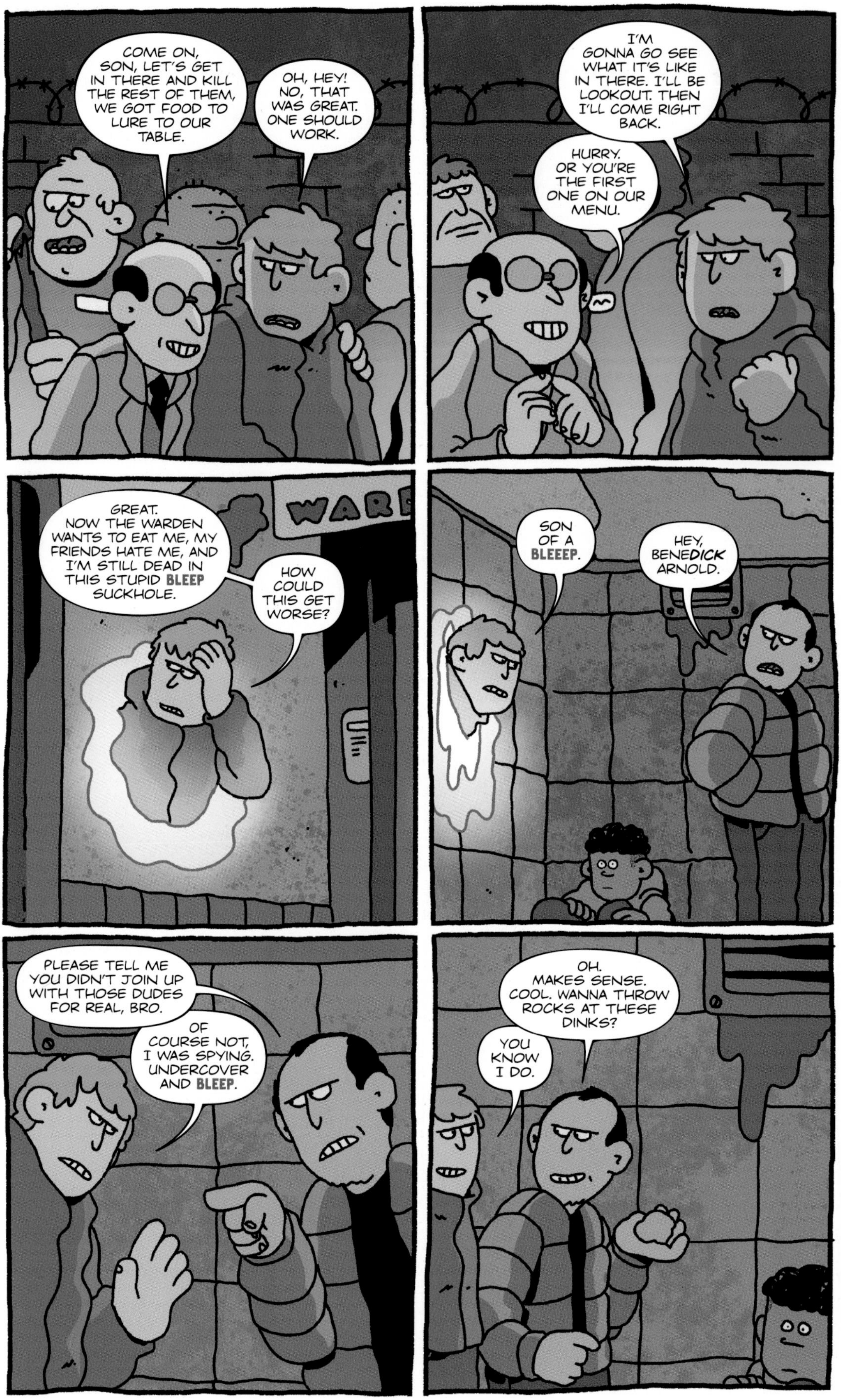
COME ON, SON, LET'S GET IN THERE AND KILL THE REST OF THEM, WE GOT FOOD TO LURE TO OUR TABLE.
OH, HEY! NO, THAT WAS GREAT. ONE SHOULD WORK.
I'M GONNA GO SEE WHAT IT'S LIKE IN THERE. I'LL BE LOOKOUT. THEN I'LL COME RIGHT BACK.
HURRY. OR YOU'RE THE FIRST ONE ON OUR MENU.
WARD
GREAT. NOW THE WARDEN WANTS TO EAT ME, MY FRIENDS HATE ME, AND I'M STILL DEAD IN THIS STUPID BLEEP SUCKHOLE.
HOW COULD THIS GET WORSE?
SON OF A BLEEEP.
HEY, BENEDICK ARNOLD.
PLEASE TELL ME YOU DIDN'T JOIN UP WITH THOSE DUDES FOR REAL, BRO.
OF COURSE NOT, I WAS SPYING. UNDERCOVER AND BLEEP.
OH. MAKES SENSE. COOL. WANNA THROW ROCKS AT THESE DINKS?
YOU KNOW I DO.

DO YOU THINK TREV GOT THE POINT?

NO OFFENSE, BRIAN, BUT HE'S NOT THE BRIGHTEST BULB.

DUDE, HE'S SMARTER THAN ME.

BRIAN. THAT'S WHAT THOSE GUYS **TOLD** YOU OVER AND OVER, BUT **YOU'RE** THE ONE WHO FOUND THE TAPES.

YOU MASTERED THE GHOST SKILLS FIRST. AND BEST.

YEAH, BUT...

NO BUTS! KENT IS A GIANT SELLOUT. TREV IS A SELFISH BABY.

THEY'RE STILL MY FRIENDS, PAM.

I KNOW. I HAD SOME **BLEEP** FRIENDS, TOO.

YOU'RE RIGHT, BUT I'M STUCK WITH THEM FOREVER. MIGHT AS WELL MAKE THE BEST OF IT.

MAYBE NOT.

C'MON. WANNA BEAT UP SOME DEAD GUYS?

YOU'RE SO COOL.

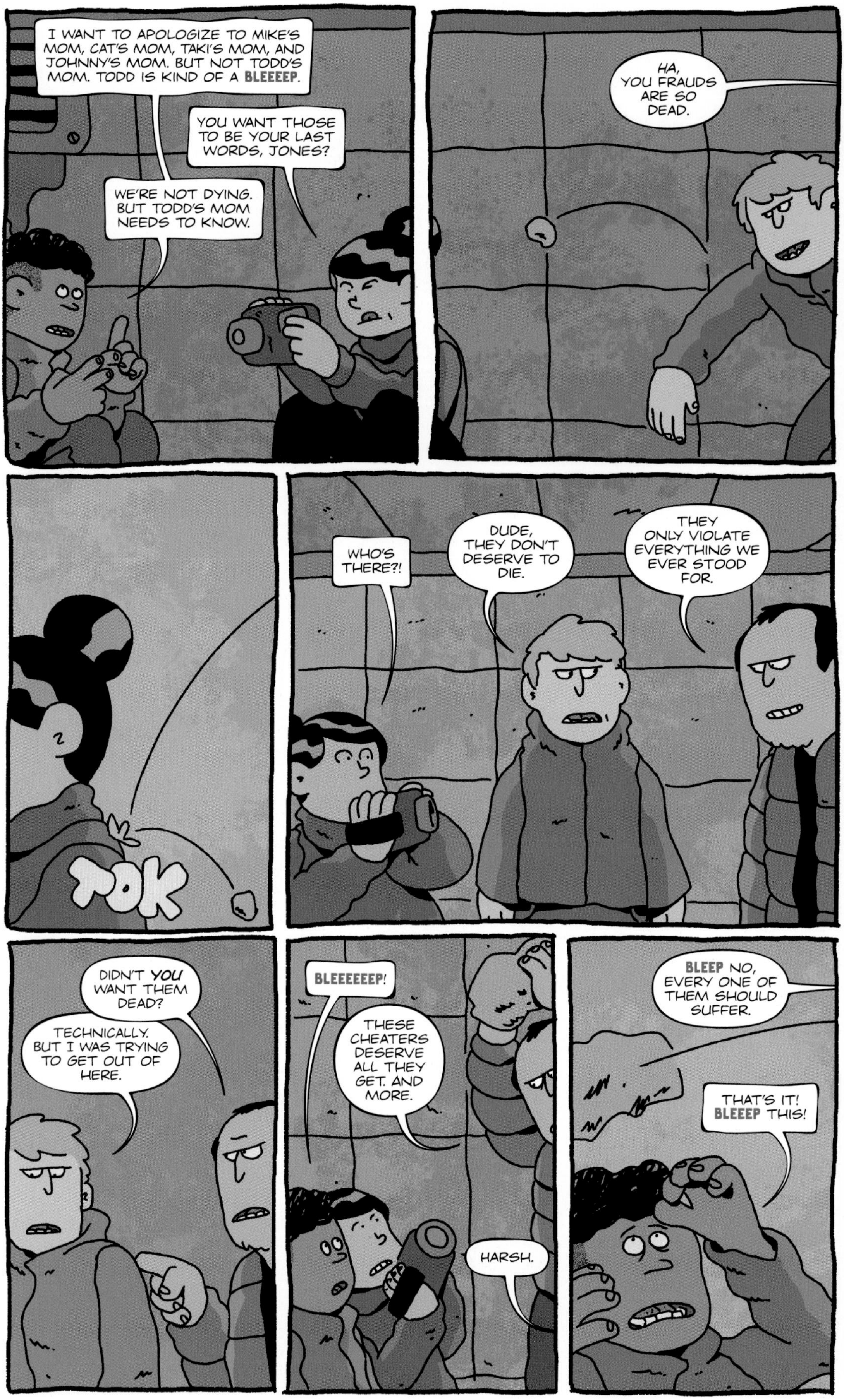
I WANT TO APOLOGIZE TO MIKE'S MOM, CAT'S MOM, TAKI'S MOM, AND JOHNNY'S MOM. BUT NOT TODD'S MOM. TODD IS KIND OF A BLEEEEP.
YOU WANT THOSE TO BE YOUR LAST WORDS, JONES?
WE'RE NOT DYING. BUT TODD'S MOM NEEDS TO KNOW.
HA, YOU FRAUDS ARE SO DEAD.
TOK
WHO'S THERE?!
DUDE, THEY DON'T DESERVE TO DIE.
THEY ONLY VIOLATE EVERYTHING WE EVER STOOD FOR.
DIDN'T YOU WANT THEM DEAD?
TECHNICALLY. BUT I WAS TRYING TO GET OUT OF HERE.
BLEEEEEEP!
THESE CHEATERS DESERVE ALL THEY GET. AND MORE.
HARSH.
BLEEP NO, EVERY ONE OF THEM SHOULD SUFFER.
THAT'S IT! BLEEEP THIS!

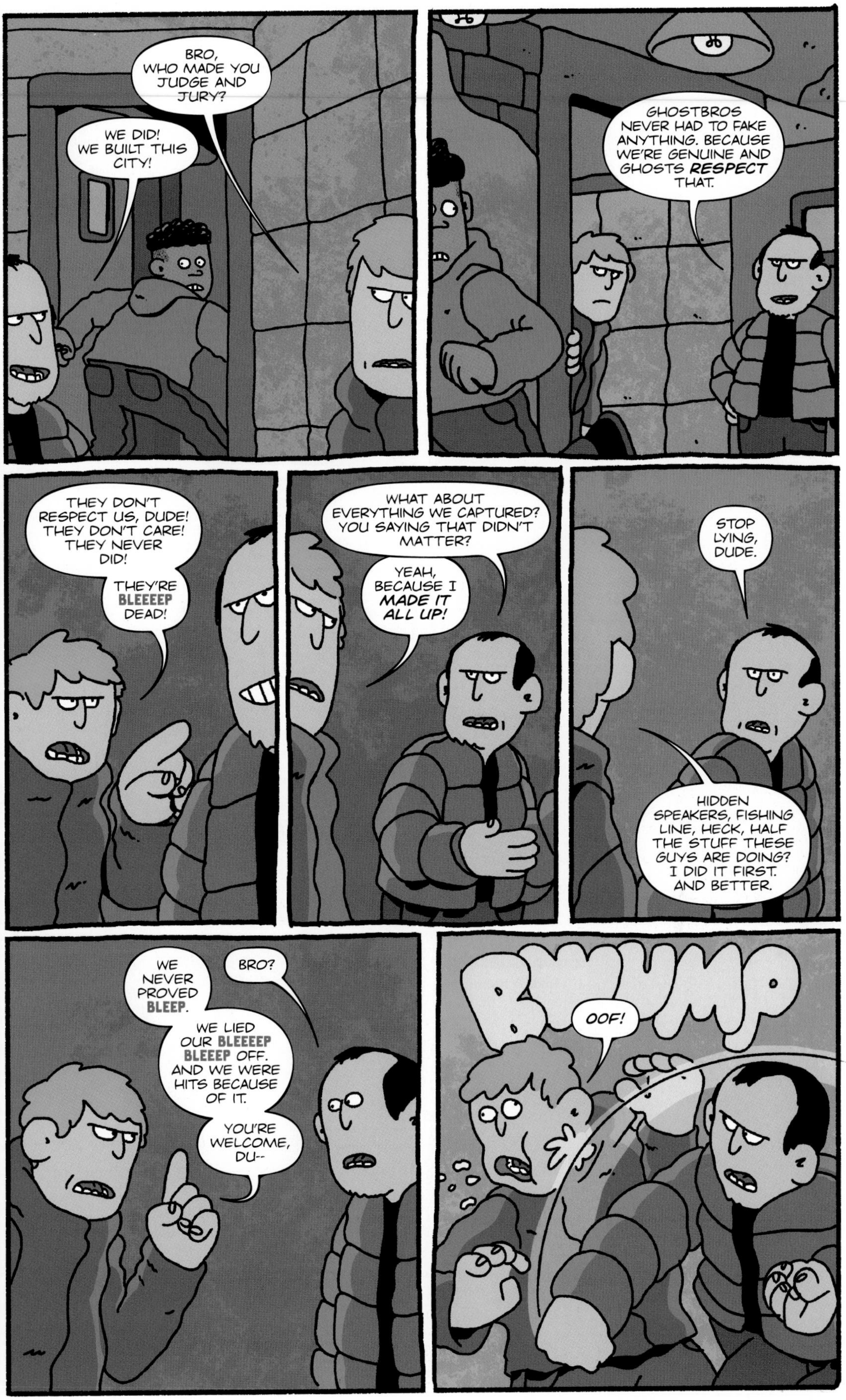

BRO, WHO MADE YOU JUDGE AND JURY?
WE DID! WE BUILT THIS CITY!
GHOSTBROS NEVER HAD TO FAKE ANYTHING. BECAUSE WE'RE GENUINE AND GHOSTS RESPECT THAT.
THEY DON'T RESPECT US, DUDE! THEY DON'T CARE! THEY NEVER DID!
THEY'RE BLEEEEP DEAD!
WHAT ABOUT EVERYTHING WE CAPTURED? YOU SAYING THAT DIDN'T MATTER?
YEAH, BECAUSE I MADE IT ALL UP!
STOP LYING, DUDE.
HIDDEN SPEAKERS, FISHING LINE, HECK, HALF THE STUFF THESE GUYS ARE DOING? I DID IT FIRST. AND BETTER.
WE NEVER PROVED BLEEP.
BRO?
WE LIED OUR BLEEEEP BLEEEP OFF. AND WE WERE HITS BECAUSE OF IT.
YOU'RE WELCOME, DU--
BWUMP
OOF!

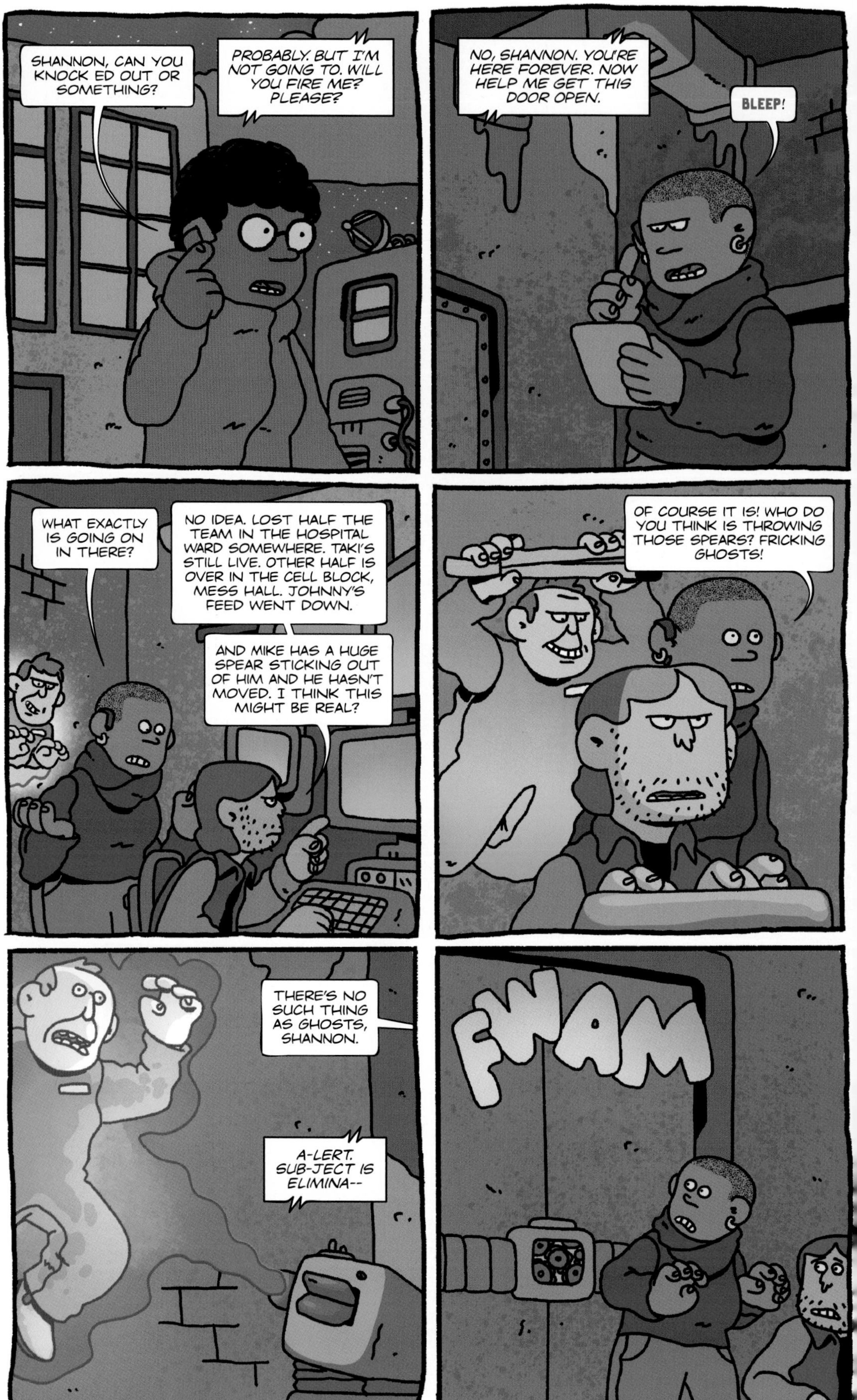

SHANNON, CAN YOU KNOCK ED OUT OR SOMETHING?
PROBABLY. BUT I'M NOT GOING TO. WILL YOU FIRE ME? PLEASE?
NO, SHANNON. YOU'RE HERE FOREVER. NOW HELP ME GET THIS DOOR OPEN.
BLEEP!
WHAT EXACTLY IS GOING ON IN THERE?
NO IDEA. LOST HALF THE TEAM IN THE HOSPITAL WARD SOMEWHERE. TAKI'S STILL LIVE. OTHER HALF IS OVER IN THE CELL BLOCK, MESS HALL. JOHNNY'S FEED WENT DOWN.
AND MIKE HAS A HUGE SPEAR STICKING OUT OF HIM AND HE HASN'T MOVED. I THINK THIS MIGHT BE REAL?
OF COURSE IT IS! WHO DO YOU THINK IS THROWING THOSE SPEARS? FRICKING GHOSTS!
THERE'S NO SUCH THING AS GHOSTS, SHANNON.
A-LERT. SUB-JECT IS ELIMINA--
FWAM

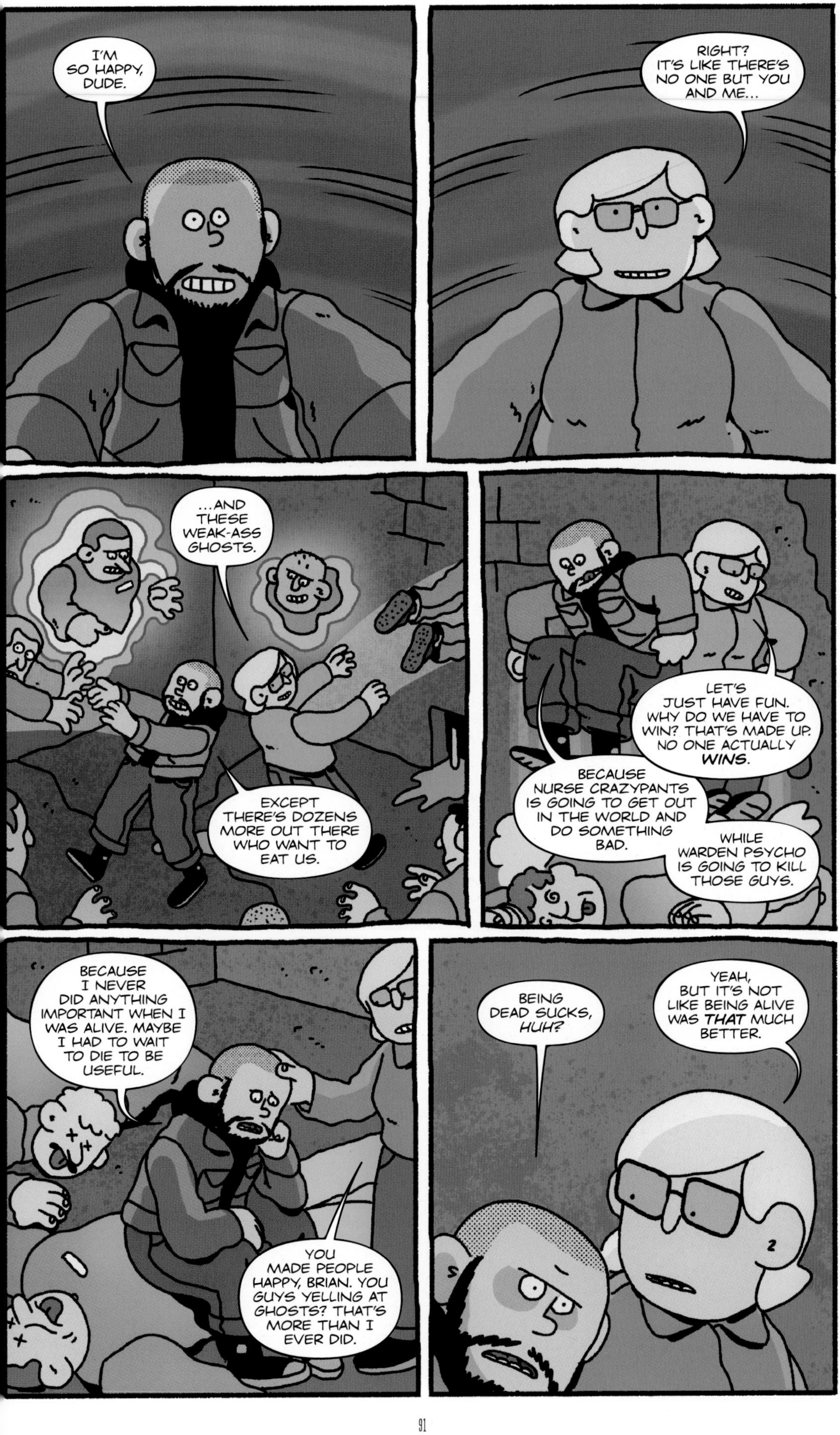

I'M SO HAPPY, DUDE.
RIGHT? IT'S LIKE THERE'S NO ONE BUT YOU AND ME...
...AND THESE WEAK-ASS GHOSTS.
EXCEPT THERE'S DOZENS MORE OUT THERE WHO WANT TO EAT US.
LET'S JUST HAVE FUN. WHY DO WE HAVE TO WIN? THAT'S MADE UP. NO ONE ACTUALLY **WINS**.
BECAUSE NURSE CRAZYPANTS IS GOING TO GET OUT IN THE WORLD AND DO SOMETHING BAD.
WHILE WARDEN PSYCHO IS GOING TO KILL THOSE GUYS.
BECAUSE I NEVER DID ANYTHING IMPORTANT WHEN I WAS ALIVE. MAYBE I HAD TO WAIT TO DIE TO BE USEFUL.
YOU MADE PEOPLE HAPPY, BRIAN. YOU GUYS YELLING AT GHOSTS? THAT'S MORE THAN I EVER DID.
BEING DEAD SUCKS, *HUH?*
YEAH, BUT IT'S NOT LIKE BEING ALIVE WAS ***THAT*** MUCH BETTER.

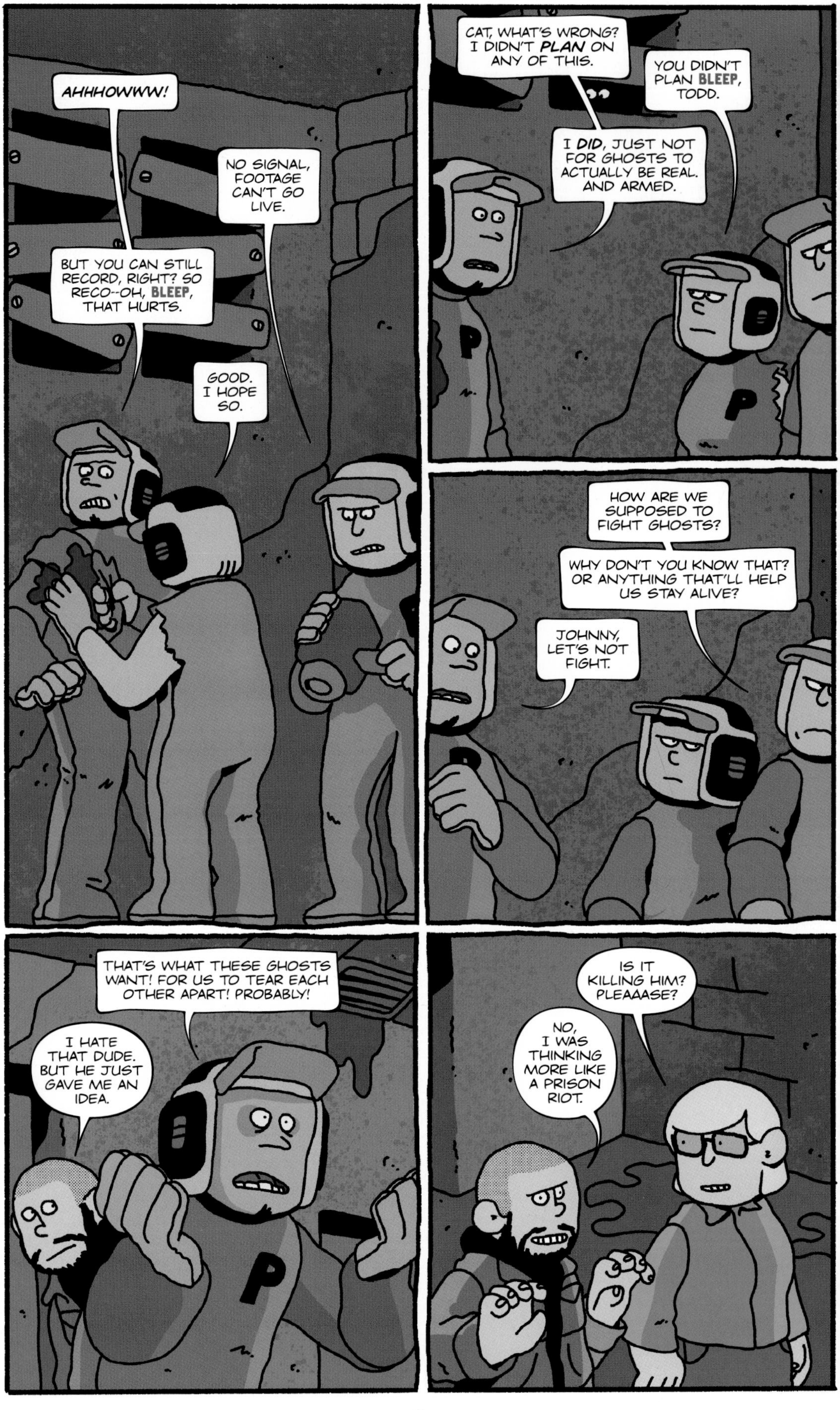
AHHHOWWW!
NO SIGNAL, FOOTAGE CAN'T GO LIVE.
BUT YOU CAN STILL RECORD, RIGHT? SO RECO--OH, BLEEP, THAT HURTS.
GOOD. I HOPE SO.
CAT, WHAT'S WRONG? I DIDN'T PLAN ON ANY OF THIS.
YOU DIDN'T PLAN BLEEP, TODD.
I DID, JUST NOT FOR GHOSTS TO ACTUALLY BE REAL. AND ARMED.
HOW ARE WE SUPPOSED TO FIGHT GHOSTS?
WHY DON'T YOU KNOW THAT? OR ANYTHING THAT'LL HELP US STAY ALIVE?
JOHNNY, LET'S NOT FIGHT.
THAT'S WHAT THESE GHOSTS WANT! FOR US TO TEAR EACH OTHER APART! PROBABLY!
I HATE THAT DUDE. BUT HE JUST GAVE ME AN IDEA.
IS IT KILLING HIM? PLEAAASE?
NO, I WAS THINKING MORE LIKE A PRISON RIOT.

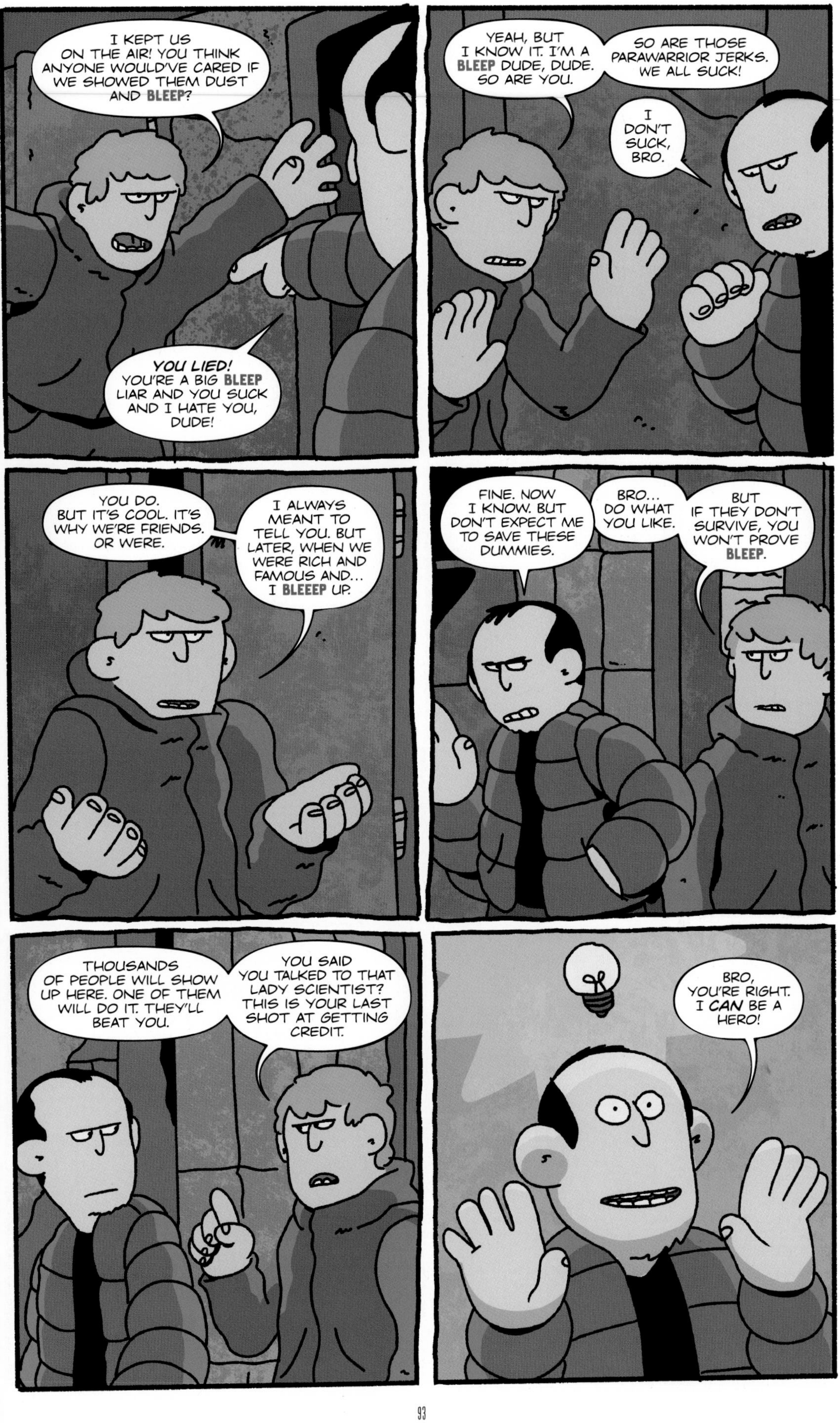

I KEPT US ON THE AIR! YOU THINK ANYONE WOULD'VE CARED IF WE SHOWED THEM DUST AND BLEEP?
YOU LIED! YOU'RE A BIG BLEEP LIAR AND YOU SUCK AND I HATE YOU, DUDE!
YEAH, BUT I KNOW IT. I'M A BLEEP DUDE, DUDE. SO ARE YOU.
SO ARE THOSE PARAWARRIOR JERKS. WE ALL SUCK!
I DON'T SUCK, BRO.
YOU DO. BUT IT'S COOL. IT'S WHY WE'RE FRIENDS. OR WERE.
I ALWAYS MEANT TO TELL YOU. BUT LATER, WHEN WE WERE RICH AND FAMOUS AND... I BLEEEP UP.
FINE. NOW I KNOW. BUT DON'T EXPECT ME TO SAVE THESE DUMMIES.
BRO... DO WHAT YOU LIKE.
BUT IF THEY DON'T SURVIVE, YOU WON'T PROVE BLEEP.
THOUSANDS OF PEOPLE WILL SHOW UP HERE. ONE OF THEM WILL DO IT. THEY'LL BEAT YOU.
YOU SAID YOU TALKED TO THAT LADY SCIENTIST? THIS IS YOUR LAST SHOT AT GETTING CREDIT.
BRO, YOU'RE RIGHT. I CAN BE A HERO!

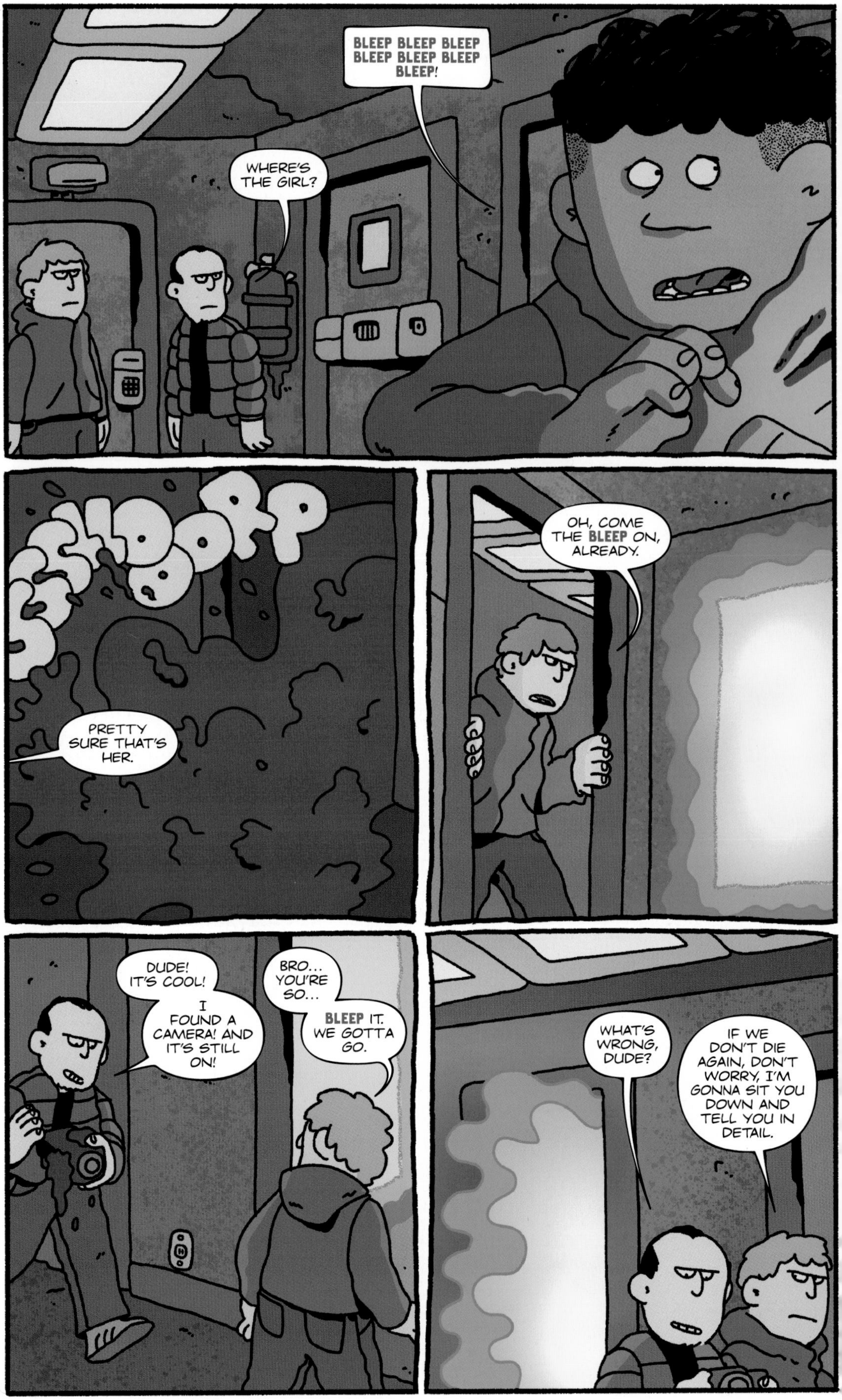
WHERE'S THE GIRL?
BLEEP BLEEP BLEEP BLEEP BLEEP BLEEP BLEEP!
SSHLOORP
PRETTY SURE THAT'S HER.
OH, COME THE BLEEP ON, ALREADY.
DUDE! IT'S COOL!
I FOUND A CAMERA! AND IT'S STILL ON!
BRO... YOU'RE SO...
BLEEP IT. WE GOTTA GO.
WHAT'S WRONG, DUDE?
IF WE DON'T DIE AGAIN, DON'T WORRY, I'M GONNA SIT YOU DOWN AND TELL YOU IN DETAIL.

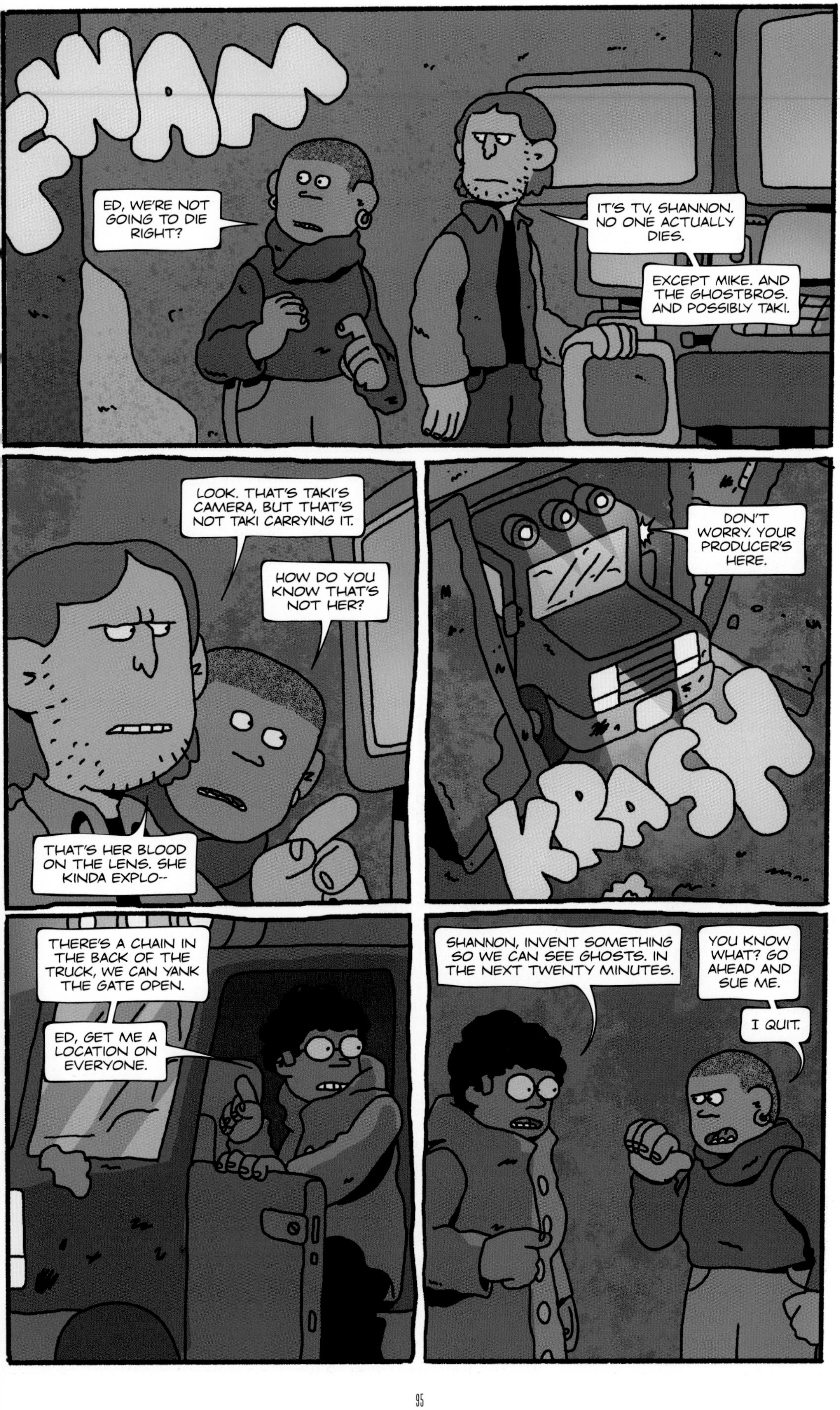
WHAM
ED, WE'RE NOT GOING TO DIE RIGHT?
IT'S TV, SHANNON. NO ONE ACTUALLY DIES.
EXCEPT MIKE. AND THE GHOSTBROS. AND POSSIBLY TAKI.
LOOK. THAT'S TAKI'S CAMERA, BUT THAT'S NOT TAKI CARRYING IT.
HOW DO YOU KNOW THAT'S NOT HER?
THAT'S HER BLOOD ON THE LENS. SHE KINDA EXPLO--
DON'T WORRY. YOUR PRODUCER'S HERE.
KRASH
THERE'S A CHAIN IN THE BACK OF THE TRUCK, WE CAN YANK THE GATE OPEN.
ED, GET ME A LOCATION ON EVERYONE.
SHANNON, INVENT SOMETHING SO WE CAN SEE GHOSTS. IN THE NEXT TWENTY MINUTES.
YOU KNOW WHAT? GO AHEAD AND SUE ME.
I QUIT.

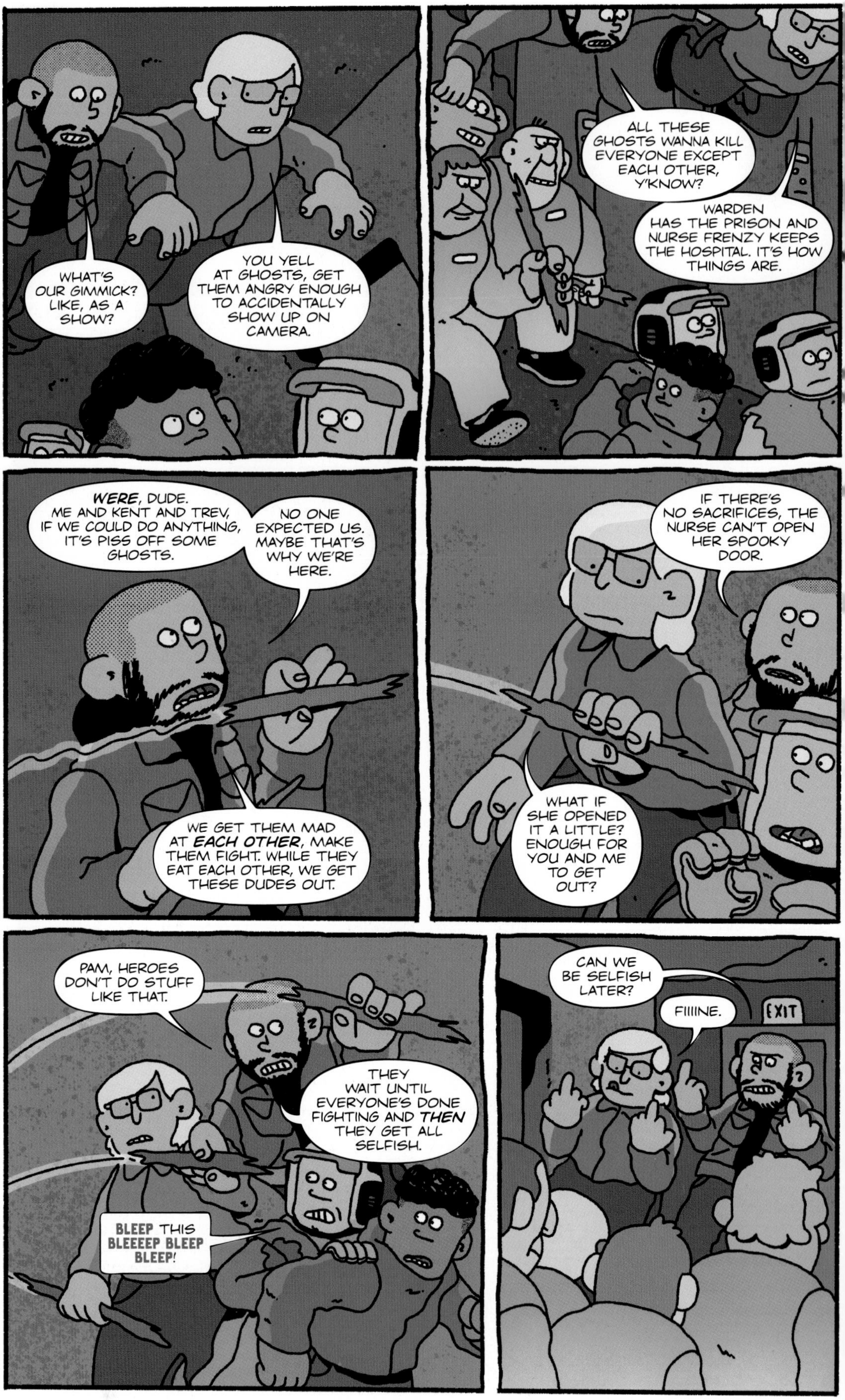
WHAT'S OUR GIMMICK? LIKE, AS A SHOW?
YOU YELL AT GHOSTS, GET THEM ANGRY ENOUGH TO ACCIDENTALLY SHOW UP ON CAMERA.
ALL THESE GHOSTS WANNA KILL EVERYONE EXCEPT EACH OTHER, Y'KNOW?
WARDEN HAS THE PRISON AND NURSE FRENZY KEEPS THE HOSPITAL. IT'S HOW THINGS ARE.
WERE, DUDE. ME AND KENT AND TREV, IF WE COULD DO ANYTHING, IT'S PISS OFF SOME GHOSTS.
NO ONE EXPECTED US. MAYBE THAT'S WHY WE'RE HERE.
WE GET THEM MAD AT *EACH OTHER*, MAKE THEM FIGHT. WHILE THEY EAT EACH OTHER, WE GET THESE DUDES OUT.
IF THERE'S NO SACRIFICES, THE NURSE CAN'T OPEN HER SPOOKY DOOR.
WHAT IF SHE OPENED IT A LITTLE? ENOUGH FOR YOU AND ME TO GET OUT?
PAM, HEROES DON'T DO STUFF LIKE THAT.
THEY WAIT UNTIL EVERYONE'S DONE FIGHTING AND *THEN* THEY GET ALL SELFISH.
BLEEP THIS **BLEEEEP BLEEP BLEEP**!
CAN WE BE SELFISH LATER?
FIIIINE.
EXIT

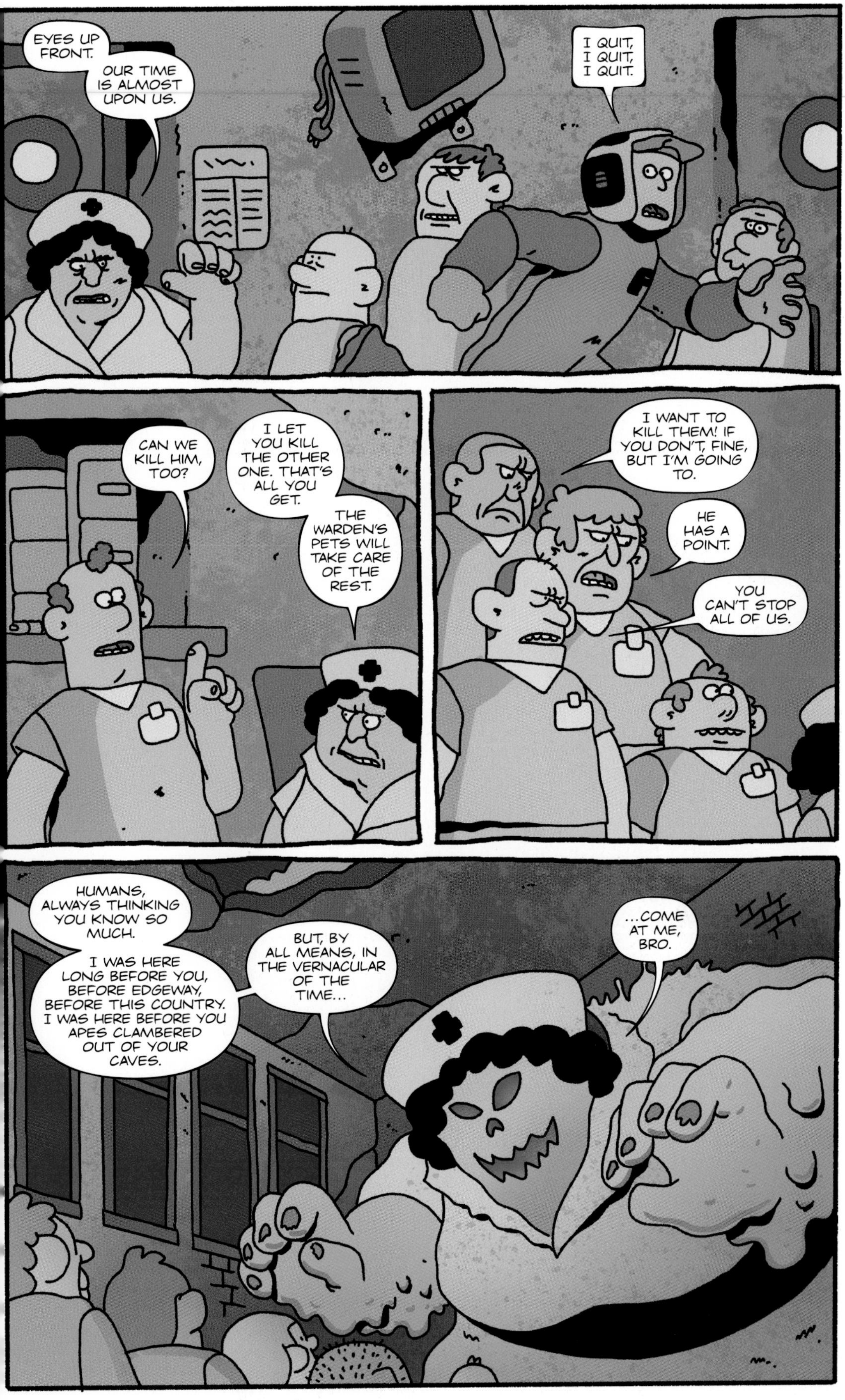
EYES UP FRONT.
OUR TIME IS ALMOST UPON US.
I QUIT, I QUIT, I QUIT.
CAN WE KILL HIM, TOO?
I LET YOU KILL THE OTHER ONE. THAT'S ALL YOU GET.
THE WARDEN'S PETS WILL TAKE CARE OF THE REST.
I WANT TO KILL THEM! IF YOU DON'T, FINE, BUT I'M GOING TO.
HE HAS A POINT.
YOU CAN'T STOP ALL OF US.
HUMANS, ALWAYS THINKING YOU KNOW SO MUCH.
I WAS HERE LONG BEFORE YOU, BEFORE EDGEWAY, BEFORE THIS COUNTRY. I WAS HERE BEFORE YOU APES CLAMBERED OUT OF YOUR CAVES.
BUT, BY ALL MEANS, IN THE VERNACULAR OF THE TIME...
...COME AT ME, BRO.

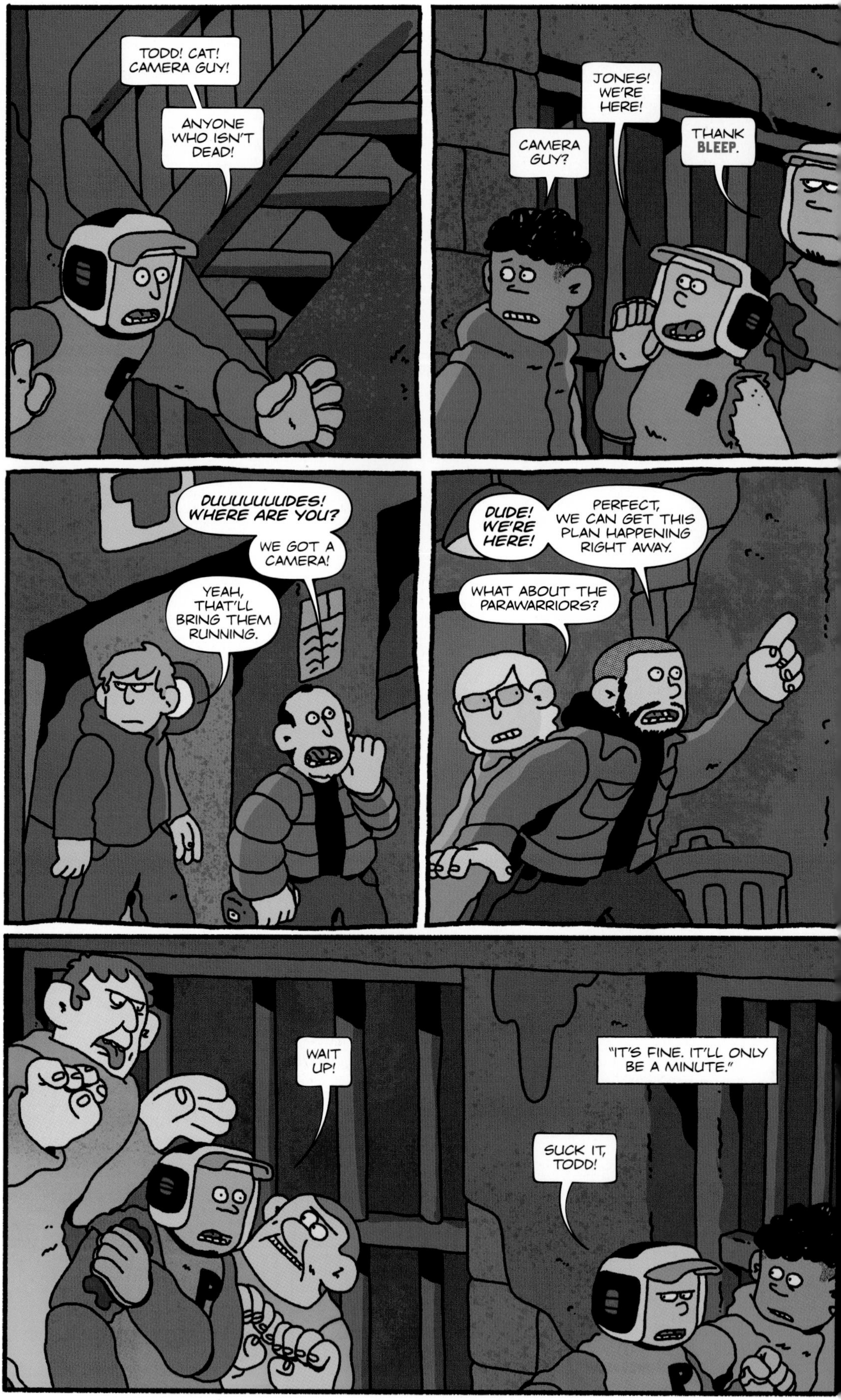
TODD! CAT! CAMERA GUY!
ANYONE WHO ISN'T DEAD!
CAMERA GUY?
JONES! WE'RE HERE!
THANK **BLEEP**.
DUUUUUUUDES! WHERE ARE YOU?
WE GOT A CAMERA!
YEAH, THAT'LL BRING THEM RUNNING.
DUDE! WE'RE HERE!
PERFECT, WE CAN GET THIS PLAN HAPPENING RIGHT AWAY.
WHAT ABOUT THE PARAWARRIORS?
WAIT UP!
"IT'S FINE. IT'LL ONLY BE A MINUTE."
SUCK IT, TODD!

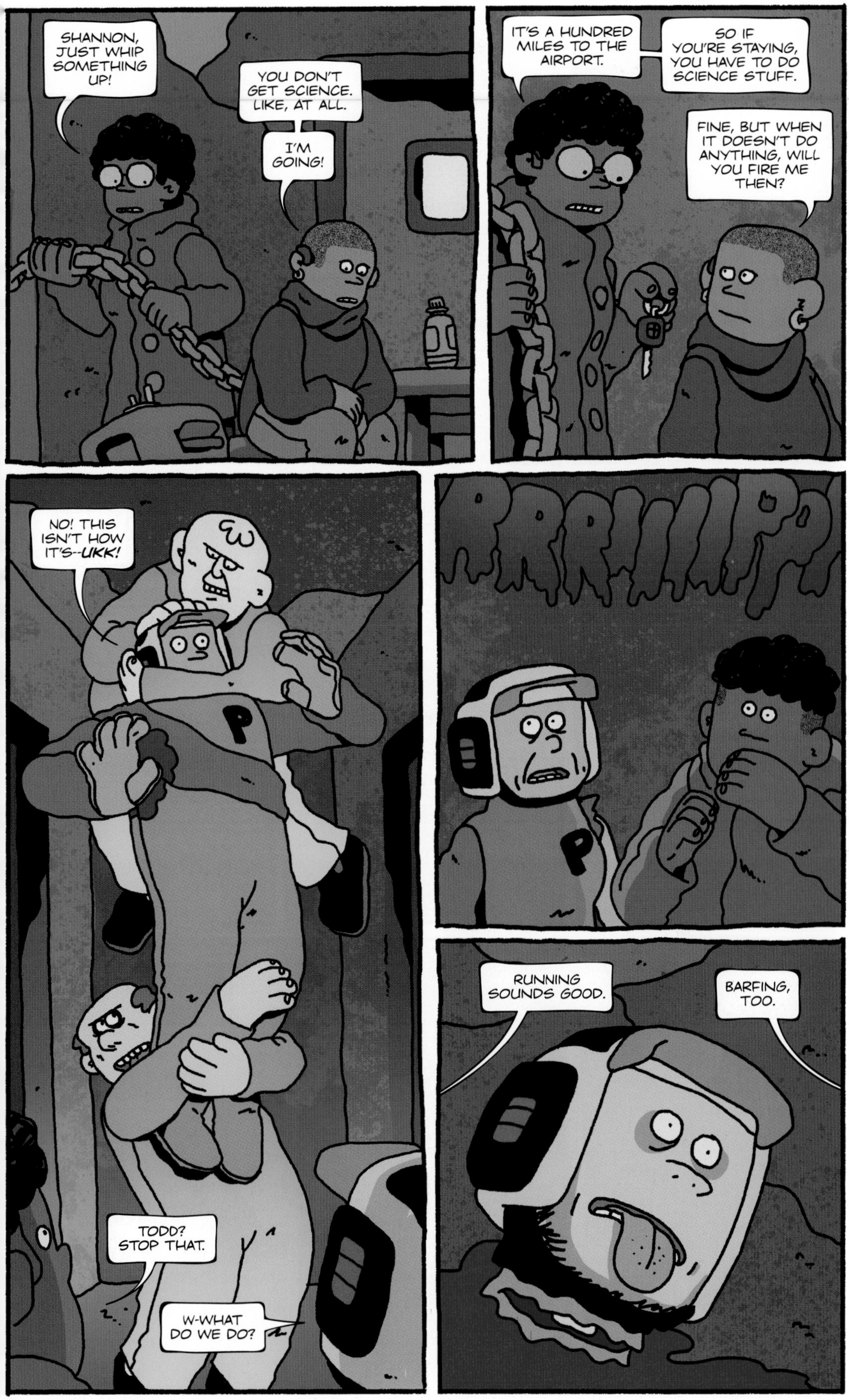
SHANNON, JUST WHIP SOMETHING UP!
YOU DON'T GET SCIENCE. LIKE, AT ALL.
I'M GOING!
IT'S A HUNDRED MILES TO THE AIRPORT.
SO IF YOU'RE STAYING, YOU HAVE TO DO SCIENCE STUFF.
FINE, BUT WHEN IT DOESN'T DO ANYTHING, WILL YOU FIRE ME THEN?
NO! THIS ISN'T HOW IT'S--*UKK!*
TODD? STOP THAT.
W-WHAT DO WE DO?
PRRIIIIPP
RUNNING SOUNDS GOOD.
BARFING, TOO.

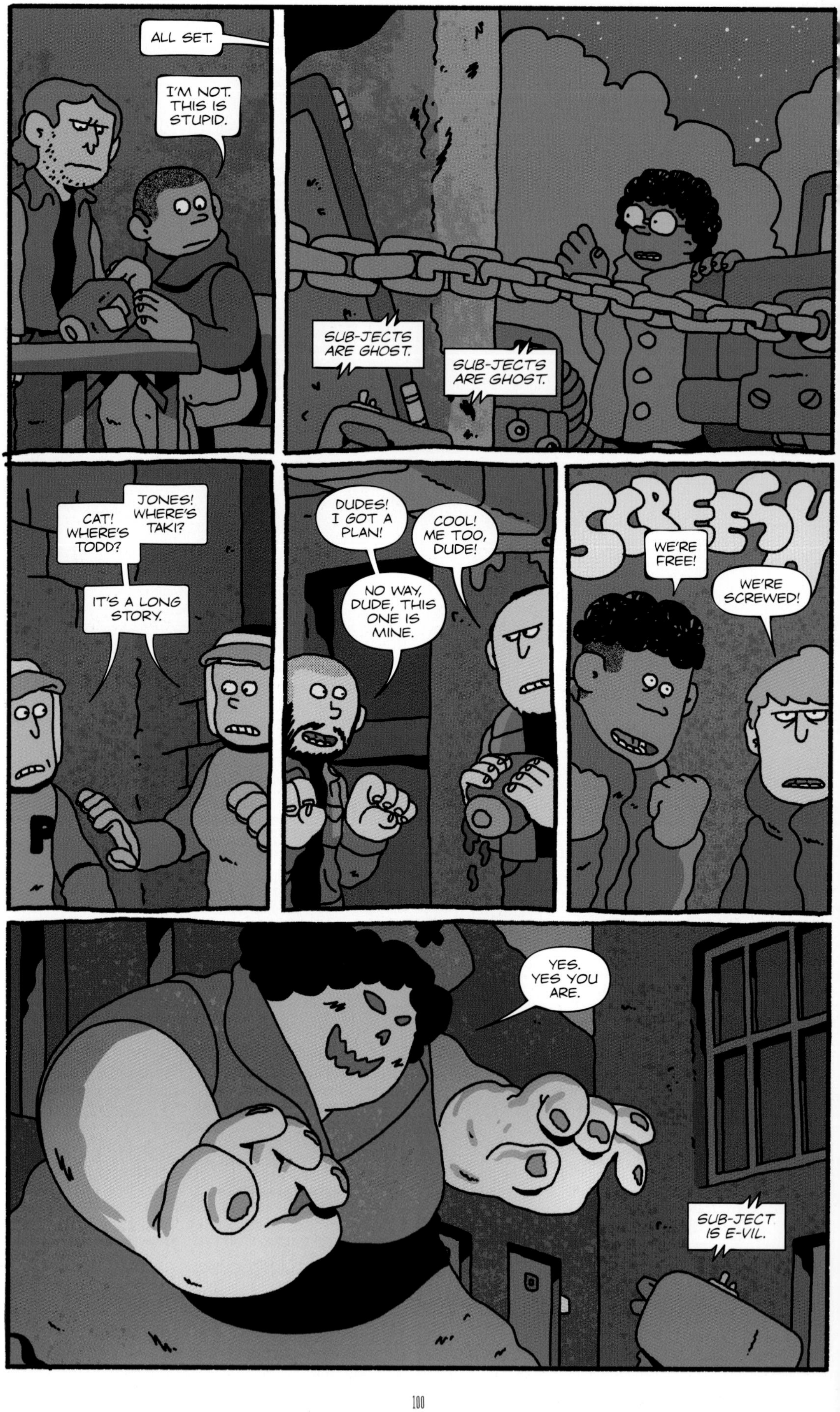
ALL SET.
I'M NOT. THIS IS STUPID.
SUB-JECTS ARE GHOST.
SUB-JECTS ARE GHOST.
CAT! WHERE'S TODD?
JONES! WHERE'S TAKI?
IT'S A LONG STORY.
DUDES! I GOT A PLAN!
COOL! ME TOO, DUDE!
NO WAY, DUDE, THIS ONE IS MINE.
SCREESH
WE'RE FREE!
WE'RE SCREWED!
YES. YES YOU ARE.
SUB-JECT IS E-VIL.

CHAPTER FIVE

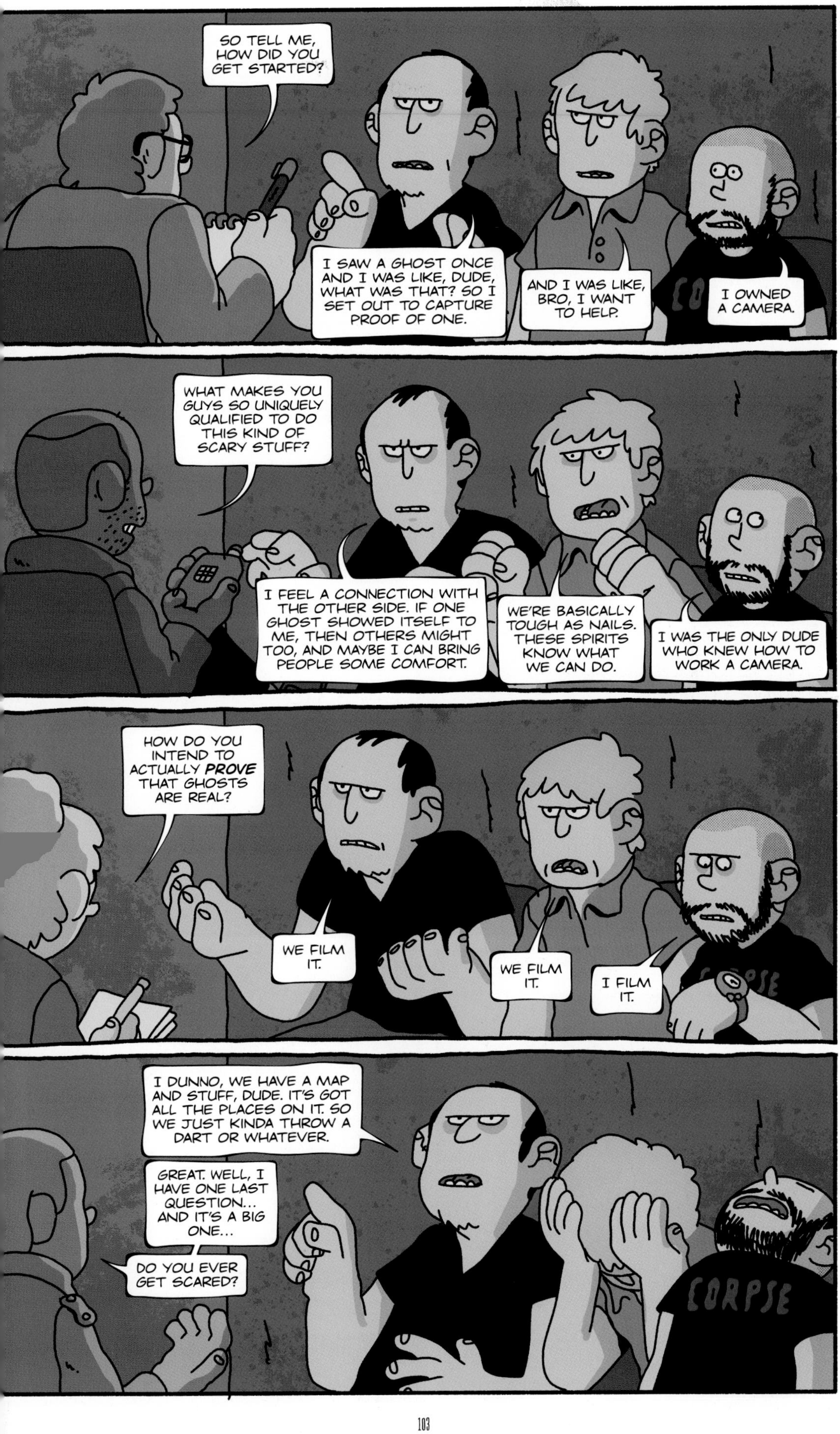
SO TELL ME, HOW DID YOU GET STARTED?
I SAW A GHOST ONCE AND I WAS LIKE, DUDE, WHAT WAS THAT? SO I SET OUT TO CAPTURE PROOF OF ONE.
AND I WAS LIKE, BRO, I WANT TO HELP.
I OWNED A CAMERA.
WHAT MAKES YOU GUYS SO UNIQUELY QUALIFIED TO DO THIS KIND OF SCARY STUFF?
I FEEL A CONNECTION WITH THE OTHER SIDE. IF ONE GHOST SHOWED ITSELF TO ME, THEN OTHERS MIGHT TOO, AND MAYBE I CAN BRING PEOPLE SOME COMFORT.
WE'RE BASICALLY TOUGH AS NAILS. THESE SPIRITS KNOW WHAT WE CAN DO.
I WAS THE ONLY DUDE WHO KNEW HOW TO WORK A CAMERA.
HOW DO YOU INTEND TO ACTUALLY **PROVE** THAT GHOSTS ARE REAL?
WE FILM IT.
WE FILM IT.
I FILM IT.
CORPSE
I DUNNO, WE HAVE A MAP AND STUFF, DUDE. IT'S GOT ALL THE PLACES ON IT. SO WE JUST KINDA THROW A DART OR WHATEVER.
GREAT. WELL, I HAVE ONE LAST QUESTION... AND IT'S A BIG ONE...
DO YOU EVER GET SCARED?
CORPSE

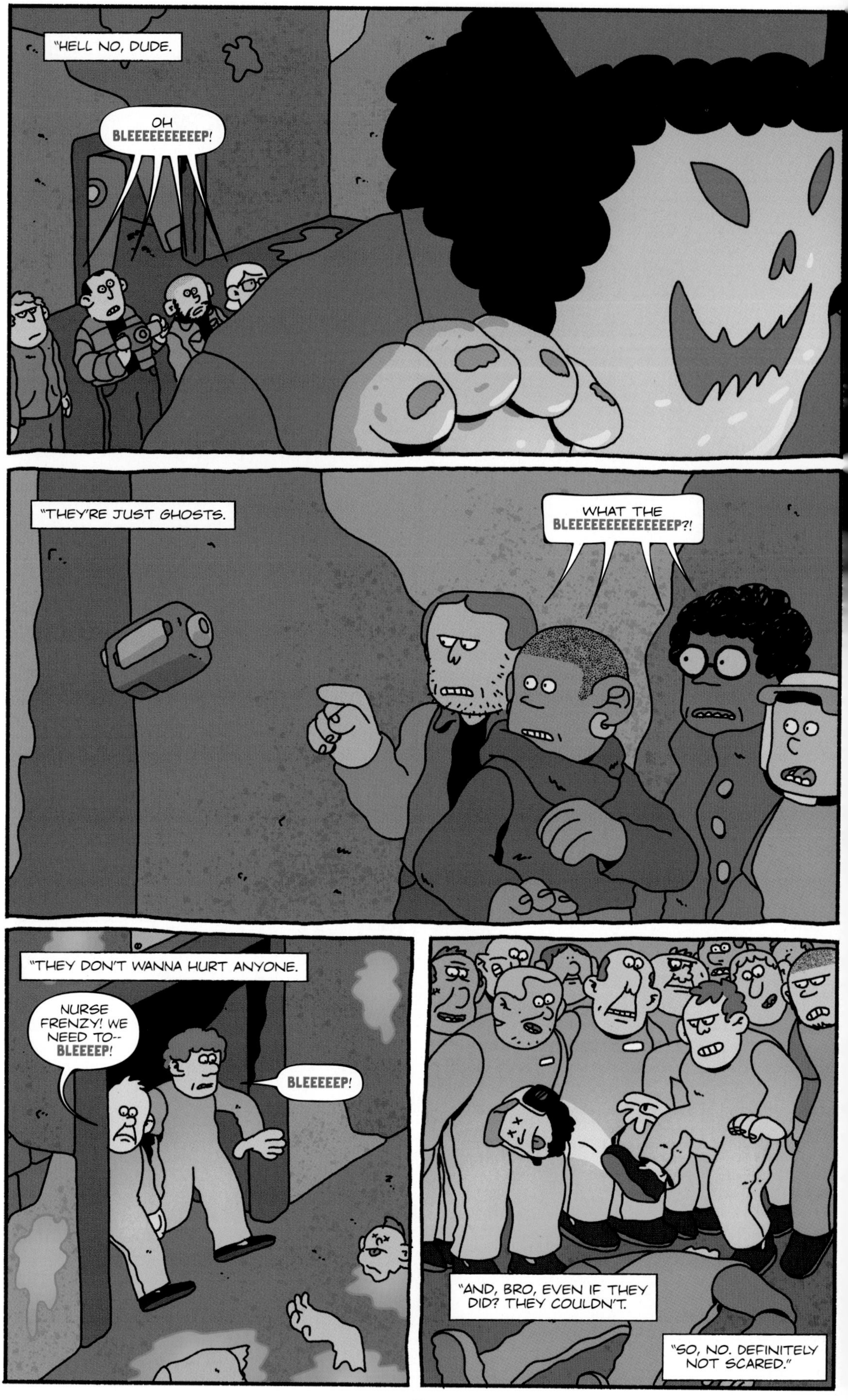

"HELL NO, DUDE.
OH BLEEEEEEEEEEP!
"THEY'RE JUST GHOSTS.
WHAT THE BLEEEEEEEEEEEEEEEP?!
"THEY DON'T WANNA HURT ANYONE.
NURSE FRENZY! WE NEED TO-- BLEEEEP!
BLEEEEEP!
"AND, BRO, EVEN IF THEY DID? THEY COULDN'T.
"SO, NO. DEFINITELY NOT SCARED."

DUDE, I CAN'T DIE AGAIN. I JUST FIGURED OUT HOW TO LIFT STUFF.

I HAVE BEEN WAITING **MILLENNIA** TO ESCAPE FROM THIS PLACE, TO MAKE MY WAY OUT INTO THE WORLD AND UNLEASH TRUE HELL.

SO QUIT CRYING AND DIE LIKE A MAN.

LET'S JUST GO BACK TO LIVING IN THE BASEMENT.

CHEESE IT!

WE KINDA HAVE TO SAVE THOSE DUMMIES FIRST.

PLEASE TELL ME SOMEONE GOT FOOTAGE OF THAT.

JANELLE, NO OFFENSE, BUT **BLEEP** YOU.

AND **BLEEP** THIS WHOLE THING. WE'RE DONE. TODD IS **DEAD**. MIKE? TAKI? DEAD!

I HAD FRIENDS WHO DIED HERE, TOO, AND I WANT TO FIND OUT WHY. I WANT TO PROVE WHAT THEY COULDN'T.

I JUST WANNA GET FIRED.

YOU HAVE NO IDEA WHAT YOU'RE DOING.

YOU TWO ARE FREE TO LEAVE ANYTIME YOU LIKE. WE CAN PUT ANYONE BEHIND THOSE MASKS.

GREAT. TALK TO MY LAWYER, YOU **BLEEP**.

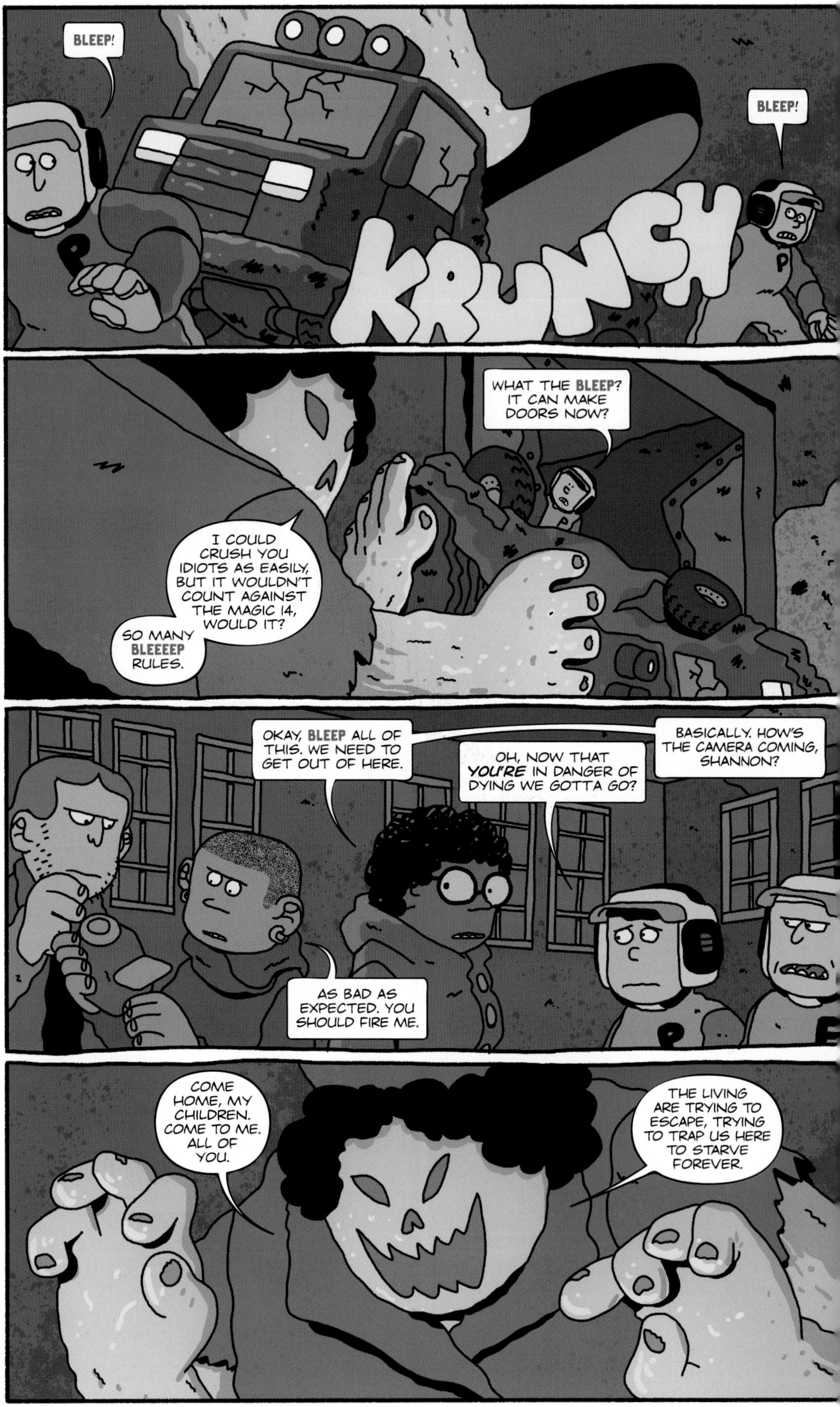
BLEEP!
BLEEP!
KRUNCH
WHAT THE BLEEP? IT CAN MAKE DOORS NOW?
I COULD CRUSH YOU IDIOTS AS EASILY, BUT IT WOULDN'T COUNT AGAINST THE MAGIC 14, WOULD IT?
SO MANY BLEEEEP RULES.
OKAY, BLEEP ALL OF THIS. WE NEED TO GET OUT OF HERE.
OH, NOW THAT YOU'RE IN DANGER OF DYING WE GOTTA GO?
BASICALLY. HOW'S THE CAMERA COMING, SHANNON?
AS BAD AS EXPECTED. YOU SHOULD FIRE ME.
COME HOME, MY CHILDREN. COME TO ME. ALL OF YOU.
THE LIVING ARE TRYING TO ESCAPE, TRYING TO TRAP US HERE TO STARVE FOREVER.

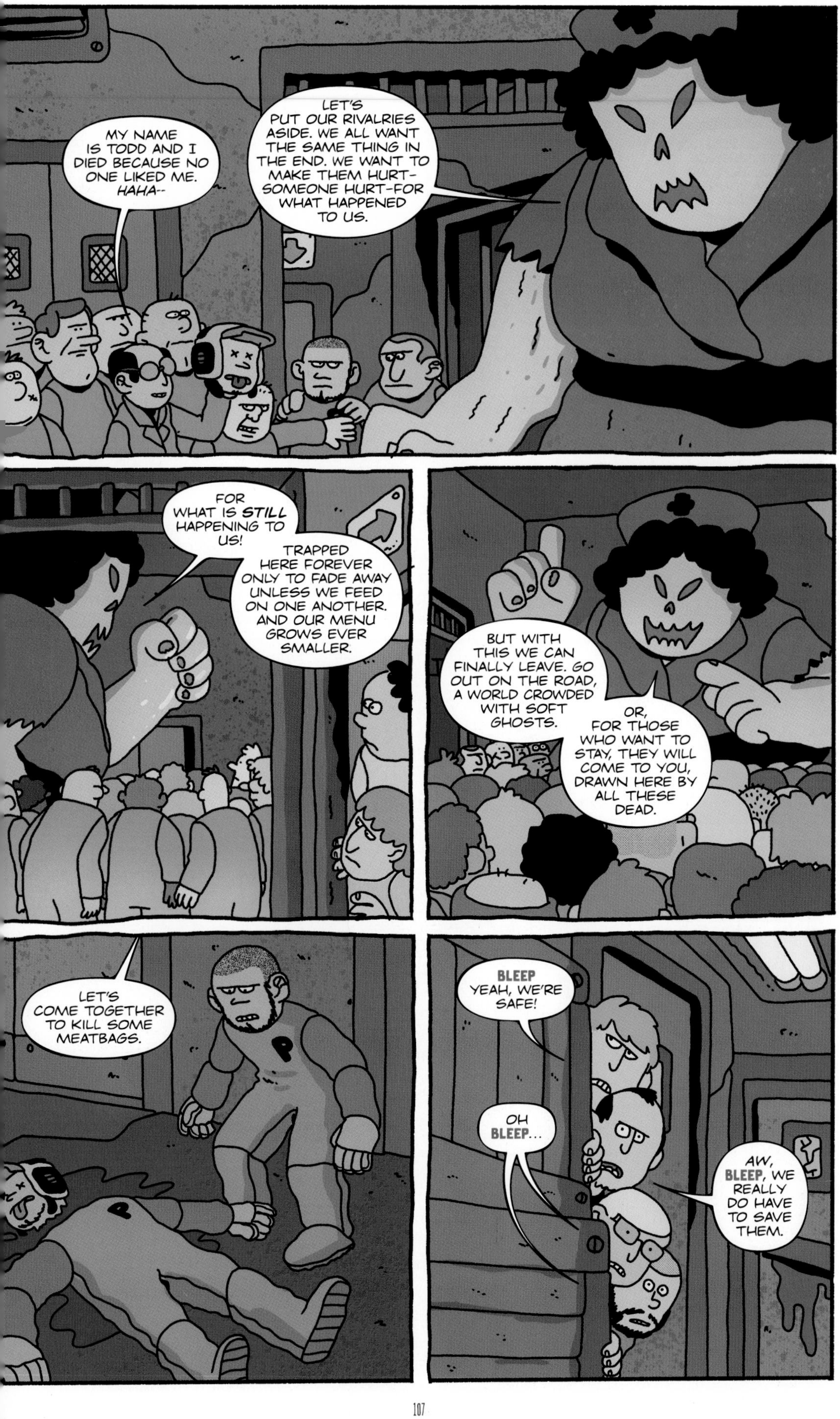

MY NAME IS TODD AND I DIED BECAUSE NO ONE LIKED ME. *HAHA*--
LET'S PUT OUR RIVALRIES ASIDE. WE ALL WANT THE SAME THING IN THE END. WE WANT TO MAKE THEM HURT-SOMEONE HURT-FOR WHAT HAPPENED TO US.
FOR WHAT IS **STILL** HAPPENING TO US!
TRAPPED HERE FOREVER ONLY TO FADE AWAY UNLESS WE FEED ON ONE ANOTHER. AND OUR MENU GROWS EVER SMALLER.
BUT WITH THIS WE CAN FINALLY LEAVE. GO OUT ON THE ROAD, A WORLD CROWDED WITH SOFT GHOSTS.
OR, FOR THOSE WHO WANT TO STAY, THEY WILL COME TO YOU, DRAWN HERE BY ALL THESE DEAD.
LET'S COME TOGETHER TO KILL SOME MEATBAGS.
BLEEP YEAH, WE'RE SAFE!
OH BLEEP...
AW, BLEEP, WE REALLY DO HAVE TO SAVE THEM.

I KNEW YOU'D GET THERE, DUDE.

WE'LL RUN INTERFERENCE IF YOU GOT AN IDEA WHAT TO DO.

I ACTUALLY *DO* HAVE AN IDEA OF WHAT TO DO.

IT MIGHT BE DUMB, THOUGH.

NO BLEEP.

"HEY, WITH MY IDEA, WE COULD LIKE, COMBINE THEM INTO ONE."

"I JUST WANT TO SAVE THESE DUDES, DUDE."

"DON'T YOU WANNA BLEEP HER OFF AT THE SAME TIME, THOUGH?"

"BLEEP YEAH, BRO. LET'S DO IT!"

"OKAY, BUT YOU GOTTA FOLLOW MY ORDERS, KENT."

"*THEN* YOU GOTTA FOLLOW MINE."

"AW, DUDES... FINE."

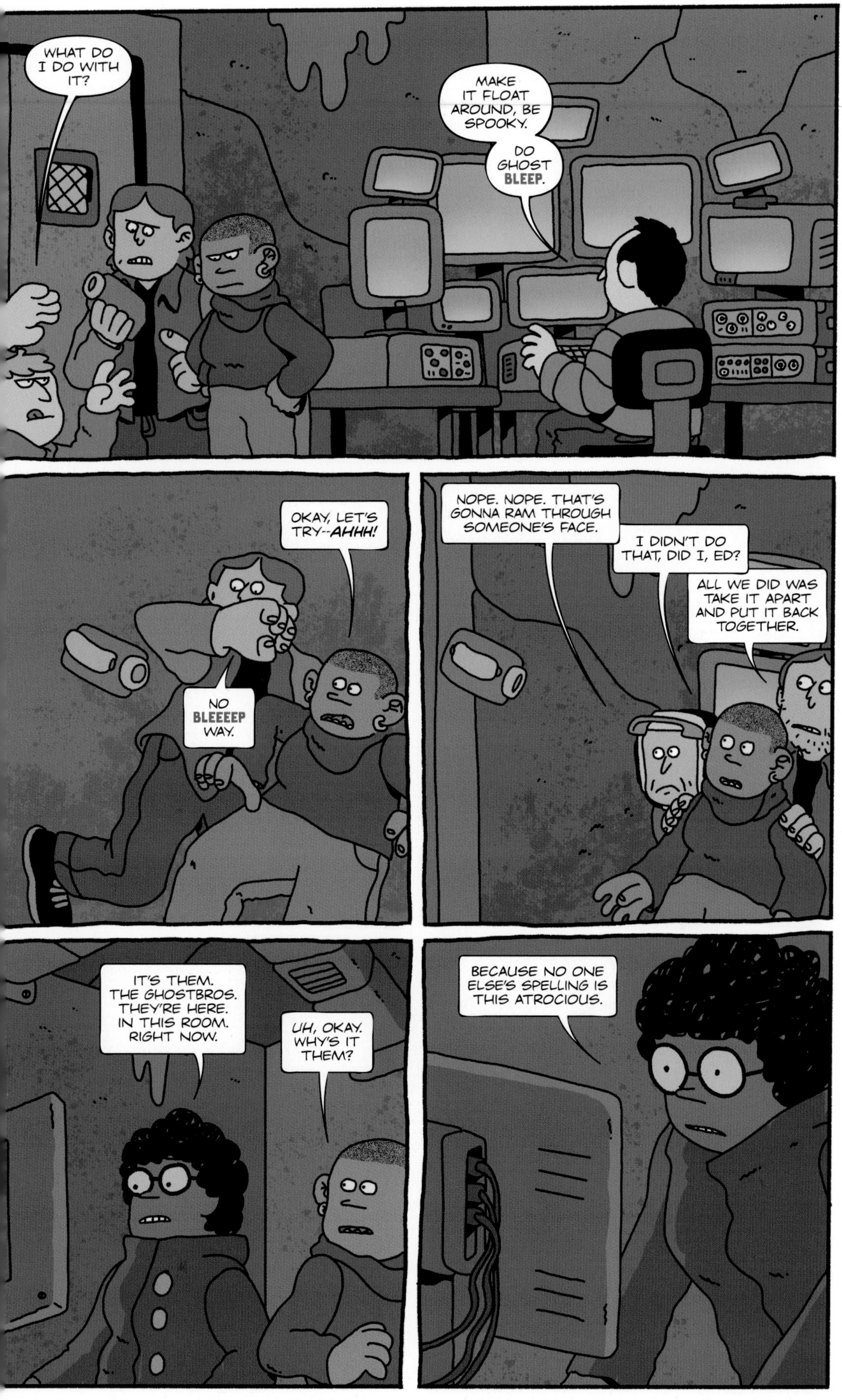
WHAT DO I DO WITH IT?
MAKE IT FLOAT AROUND, BE SPOOKY.
DO GHOST BLEEP.
OKAY, LET'S TRY--AHHH!
NO BLEEEEP WAY.
NOPE. NOPE. THAT'S GONNA RAM THROUGH SOMEONE'S FACE.
I DIDN'T DO THAT, DID I, ED?
ALL WE DID WAS TAKE IT APART AND PUT IT BACK TOGETHER.
IT'S THEM. THE GHOSTBROS. THEY'RE HERE. IN THIS ROOM. RIGHT NOW.
UH, OKAY. WHY'S IT THEM?
BECAUSE NO ONE ELSE'S SPELLING IS THIS ATROCIOUS.

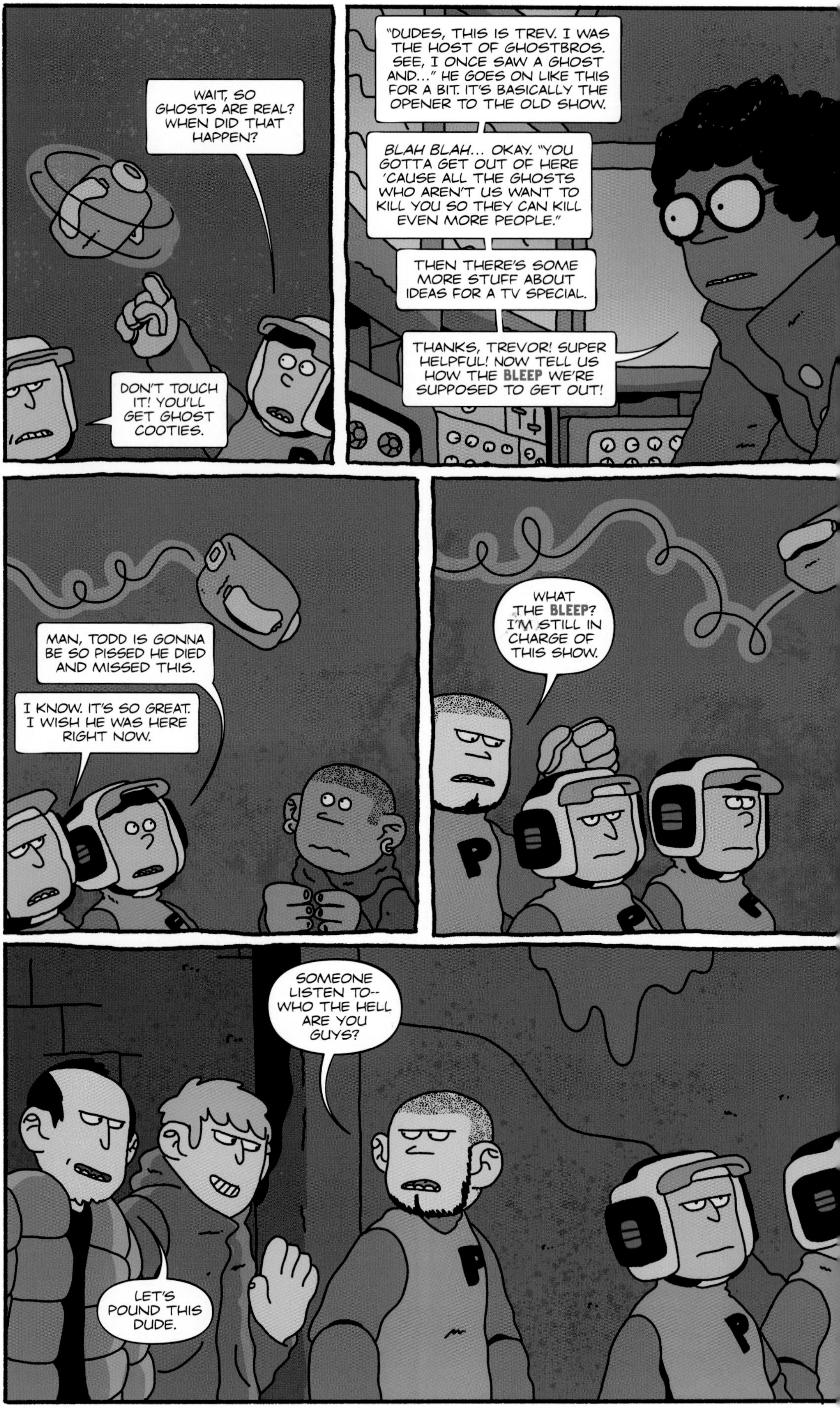

WAIT, SO GHOSTS ARE REAL? WHEN DID THAT HAPPEN?
DON'T TOUCH IT! YOU'LL GET GHOST COOTIES.
"DUDES, THIS IS TREV. I WAS THE HOST OF GHOSTBROS. SEE, I ONCE SAW A GHOST AND..." HE GOES ON LIKE THIS FOR A BIT. IT'S BASICALLY THE OPENER TO THE OLD SHOW.
BLAH BLAH... OKAY. "YOU GOTTA GET OUT OF HERE 'CAUSE ALL THE GHOSTS WHO AREN'T US WANT TO KILL YOU SO THEY CAN KILL EVEN MORE PEOPLE."
THEN THERE'S SOME MORE STUFF ABOUT IDEAS FOR A TV SPECIAL.
THANKS, TREVOR! SUPER HELPFUL! NOW TELL US HOW THE BLEEP WE'RE SUPPOSED TO GET OUT!
MAN, TODD IS GONNA BE SO PISSED HE DIED AND MISSED THIS.
I KNOW. IT'S SO GREAT. I WISH HE WAS HERE RIGHT NOW.
WHAT THE BLEEP? I'M STILL IN CHARGE OF THIS SHOW.
SOMEONE LISTEN TO-- WHO THE HELL ARE YOU GUYS?
LET'S POUND THIS DUDE.

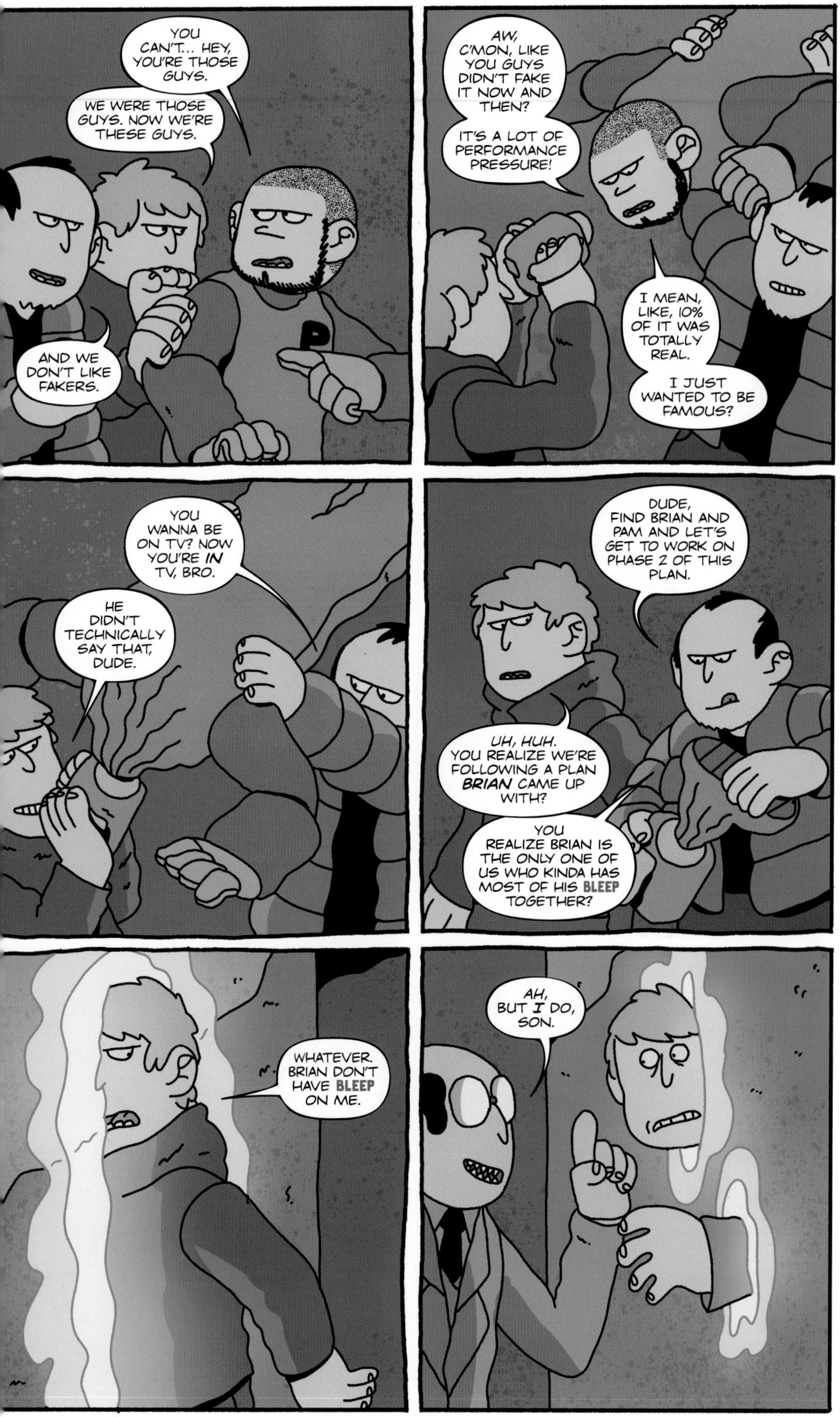

YOU CAN'T... HEY, YOU'RE THOSE GUYS.
WE WERE THOSE GUYS. NOW WE'RE THESE GUYS.
AND WE DON'T LIKE FAKERS.
AW, C'MON, LIKE YOU GUYS DIDN'T FAKE IT NOW AND THEN?
IT'S A LOT OF PERFORMANCE PRESSURE!
I MEAN, LIKE, 10% OF IT WAS TOTALLY REAL.
I JUST WANTED TO BE FAMOUS?
YOU WANNA BE ON TV? NOW YOU'RE IN TV, BRO.
HE DIDN'T TECHNICALLY SAY THAT, DUDE.
DUDE, FIND BRIAN AND PAM AND LET'S GET TO WORK ON PHASE 2 OF THIS PLAN.
UH, HUH. YOU REALIZE WE'RE FOLLOWING A PLAN BRIAN CAME UP WITH?
YOU REALIZE BRIAN IS THE ONLY ONE OF US WHO KINDA HAS MOST OF HIS BLEEP TOGETHER?
WHATEVER. BRIAN DON'T HAVE BLEEP ON ME.
AH, BUT I DO, SON.

WE GOT NOTHING, BRIAN. SHE'S LIKE TWENTY FEET TALL AND SOME KIND OF ANCIENT DEMON OR WHATEVER.

WE DON'T HAVE TO DEFEAT HER OURSELVES. THE GUYS ARE GONNA HELP.

RIGHT. WHAT COULD GO WRONG?

YOU RECENTLY DEAD ARE SO MUCH FUN TO PLAY WITH, I MUST ADMIT.

ALL THOSE STRINGY BITS OF HOPE STILL STUCK TO YOU. THEY TASTE THE BEST.

FWAK

DUDES! HAVE YOU SEEN THE NURSE LATELY? SHE'S **BLEEEP** HUGE. ENOUGH FOR ALL OF YOU TO CHOW DOWN ON FOR WEEKS.

BUT I GET IT, YOU'RE SCARED OF HER. I AM, TOO. THAT'S WHY WE'RE STAYING AS FAR AWAY AS WE CAN GET, RIGHT?

VERY DROLL.

LET'S GO SEE OUR ESTEEMED CO-WORKER AND SEE JUST HOW SCARY SHE IS.

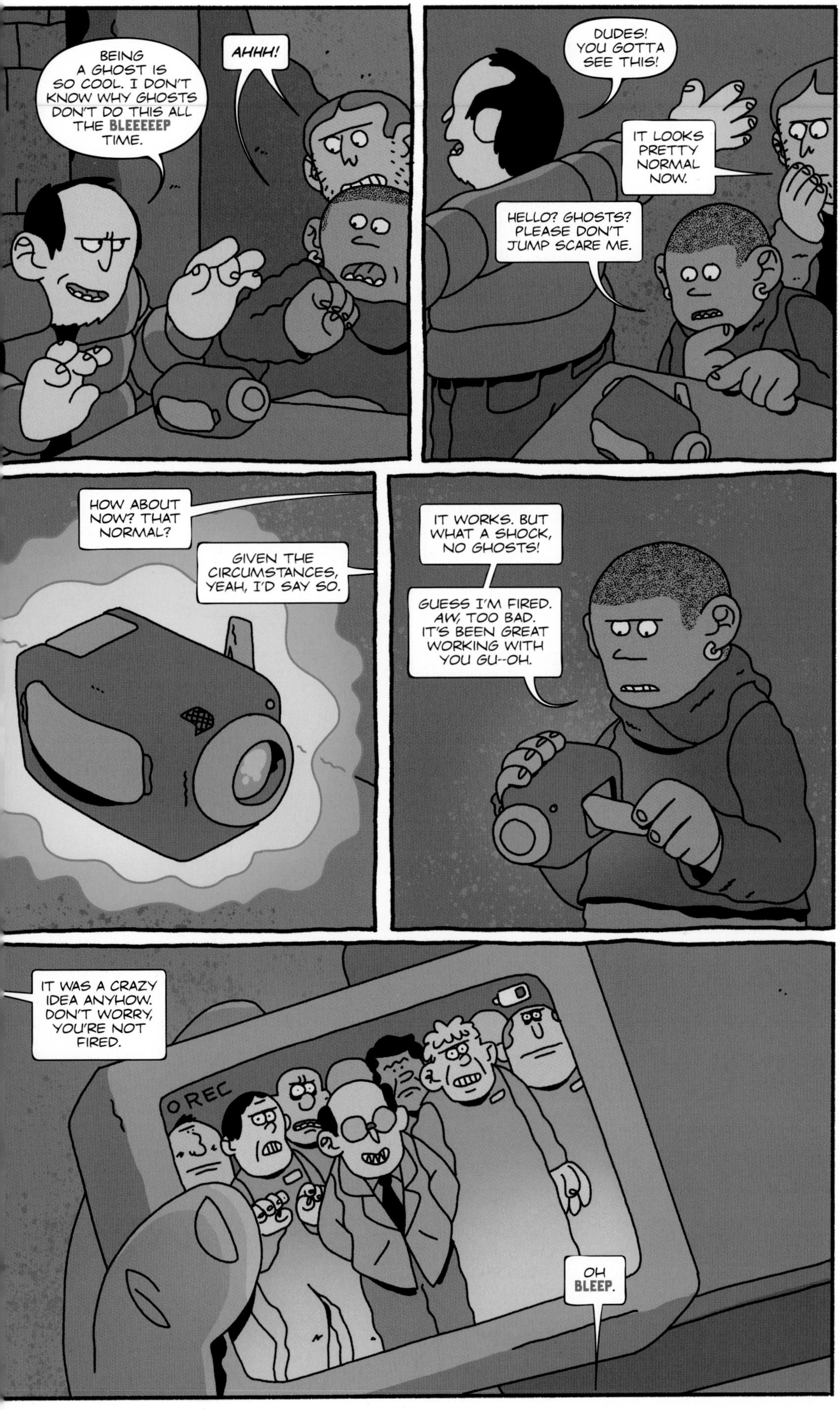
BEING A GHOST IS SO COOL. I DON'T KNOW WHY GHOSTS DON'T DO THIS ALL THE BLEEEEEP TIME.
AHHH!
DUDES! YOU GOTTA SEE THIS!
IT LOOKS PRETTY NORMAL NOW.
HELLO? GHOSTS? PLEASE DON'T JUMP SCARE ME.
HOW ABOUT NOW? THAT NORMAL?
GIVEN THE CIRCUMSTANCES, YEAH, I'D SAY SO.
IT WORKS. BUT WHAT A SHOCK, NO GHOSTS!
GUESS I'M FIRED. AW, TOO BAD. IT'S BEEN GREAT WORKING WITH YOU GU--OH.
IT WAS A CRAZY IDEA ANYHOW. DON'T WORRY, YOU'RE NOT FIRED.
REC
OH BLEEP.

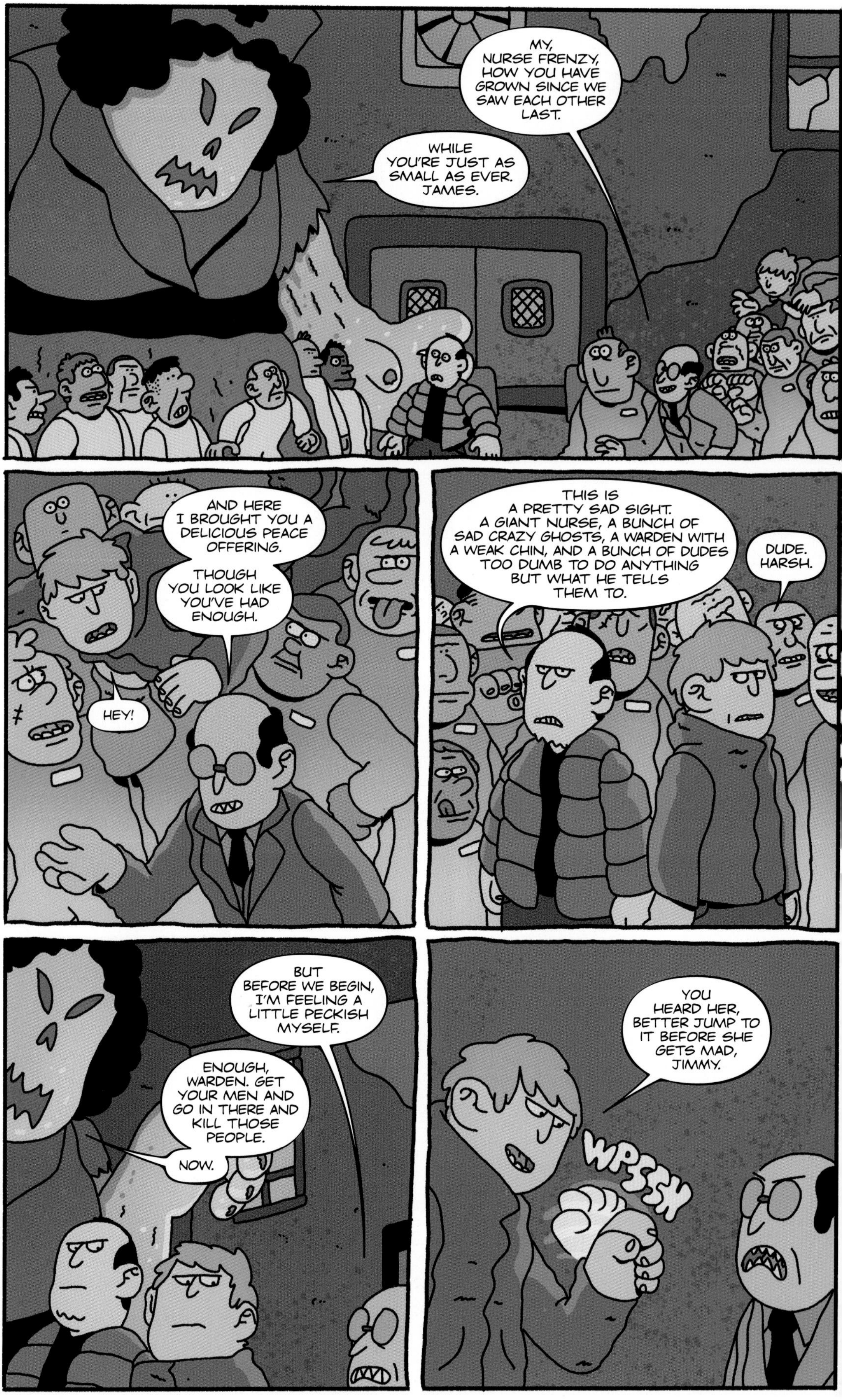
MY, NURSE FRENZY, HOW YOU HAVE GROWN SINCE WE SAW EACH OTHER LAST.
WHILE YOU'RE JUST AS SMALL AS EVER. JAMES.
AND HERE I BROUGHT YOU A DELICIOUS PEACE OFFERING.
THOUGH YOU LOOK LIKE YOU'VE HAD ENOUGH.
HEY!
THIS IS A PRETTY SAD SIGHT. A GIANT NURSE, A BUNCH OF SAD CRAZY GHOSTS, A WARDEN WITH A WEAK CHIN, AND A BUNCH OF DUDES TOO DUMB TO DO ANYTHING BUT WHAT HE TELLS THEM TO.
DUDE. HARSH.
BUT BEFORE WE BEGIN, I'M FEELING A LITTLE PECKISH MYSELF.
ENOUGH, WARDEN. GET YOUR MEN AND GO IN THERE AND KILL THOSE PEOPLE.
NOW.
YOU HEARD HER, BETTER JUMP TO IT BEFORE SHE GETS MAD, JIMMY.
WPSSH

I DON'T CARE HOW HIGH AND MIGHTY YOU MIGHT THINK YOU ARE, I DON'T TAKE THAT TONE FROM ANYONE, LIVING NOR DEAD.

FROM WHAT I CAN SEE, YOU NEED MY MEN MORE THAN WE NEED YOU AND WHAT'S LEFT OF YOUR MENU.

NOW WHAT?

NOW IT'S ALL UP TO BRIAN.

BLEEP ME SIDEWAYS. WE'RE DOOMED.

YOU SURE WE CAN DO THIS?

NO. I DON'T KNOW. I NEVER TRIED.

YOU SCARED?

LITTLE BIT. YOU?

FREAKING OUT. LET'S DO IT BEFORE I CHANGE MY MIND.

I HAVE ALLOWED YOU TO CONTINUE RESIDING HERE FOR LONG ENOUGH. WHATEVER ILLUSIONS YOU HARBOR ABOUT THIS BEING YOUR PRISON? ALLOW ME TO SHATTER THEM.

YOU AND WHAT ARMY, MISSY?

BLEEEEEEEEEEEP!

I AM THE ARMY.

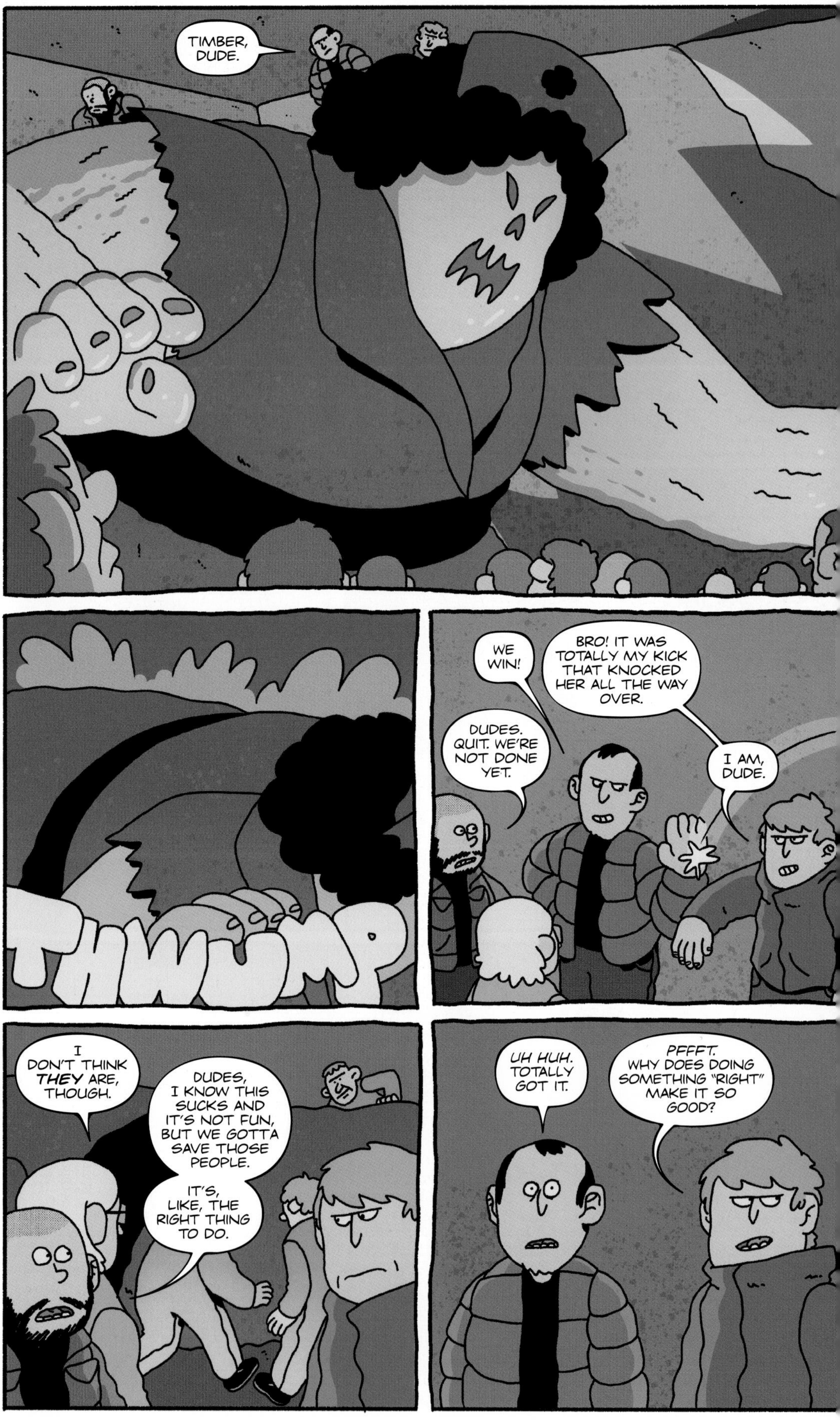

TIMBER, DUDE.
THWUMP
WE WIN!
BRO! IT WAS TOTALLY MY KICK THAT KNOCKED HER ALL THE WAY OVER.
DUDES. QUIT. WE'RE NOT DONE YET.
I AM, DUDE.
I DON'T THINK ***THEY*** ARE, THOUGH.
DUDES, I KNOW THIS SUCKS AND IT'S NOT FUN, BUT WE GOTTA SAVE THOSE PEOPLE.
IT'S, LIKE, THE RIGHT THING TO DO.
UH HUH. TOTALLY GOT IT.
PFFFT. WHY DOES DOING SOMETHING "RIGHT" MAKE IT SO GOOD?

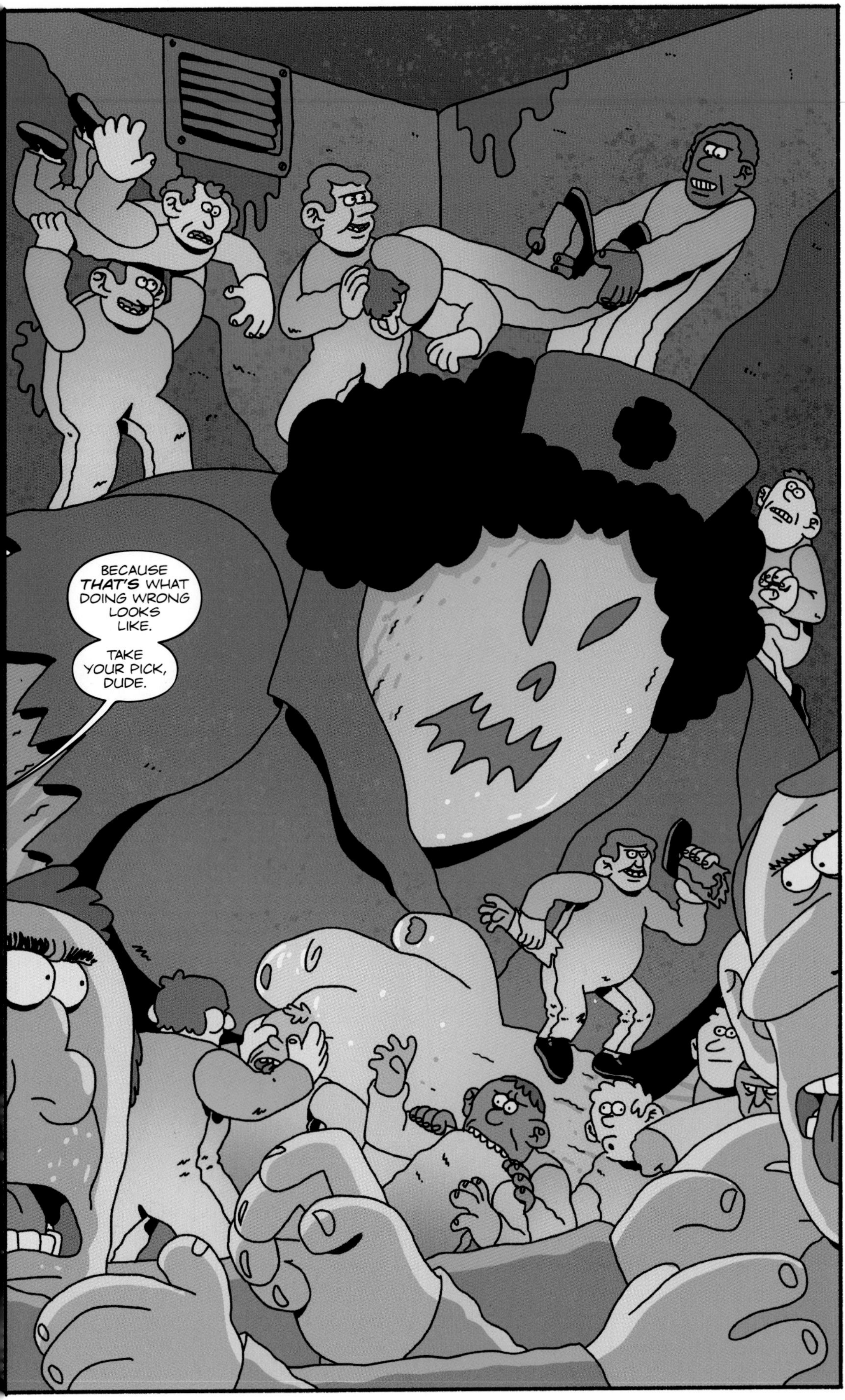
BECAUSE ***THAT'S*** WHAT DOING WRONG LOOKS LIKE.
TAKE YOUR PICK, DUDE.

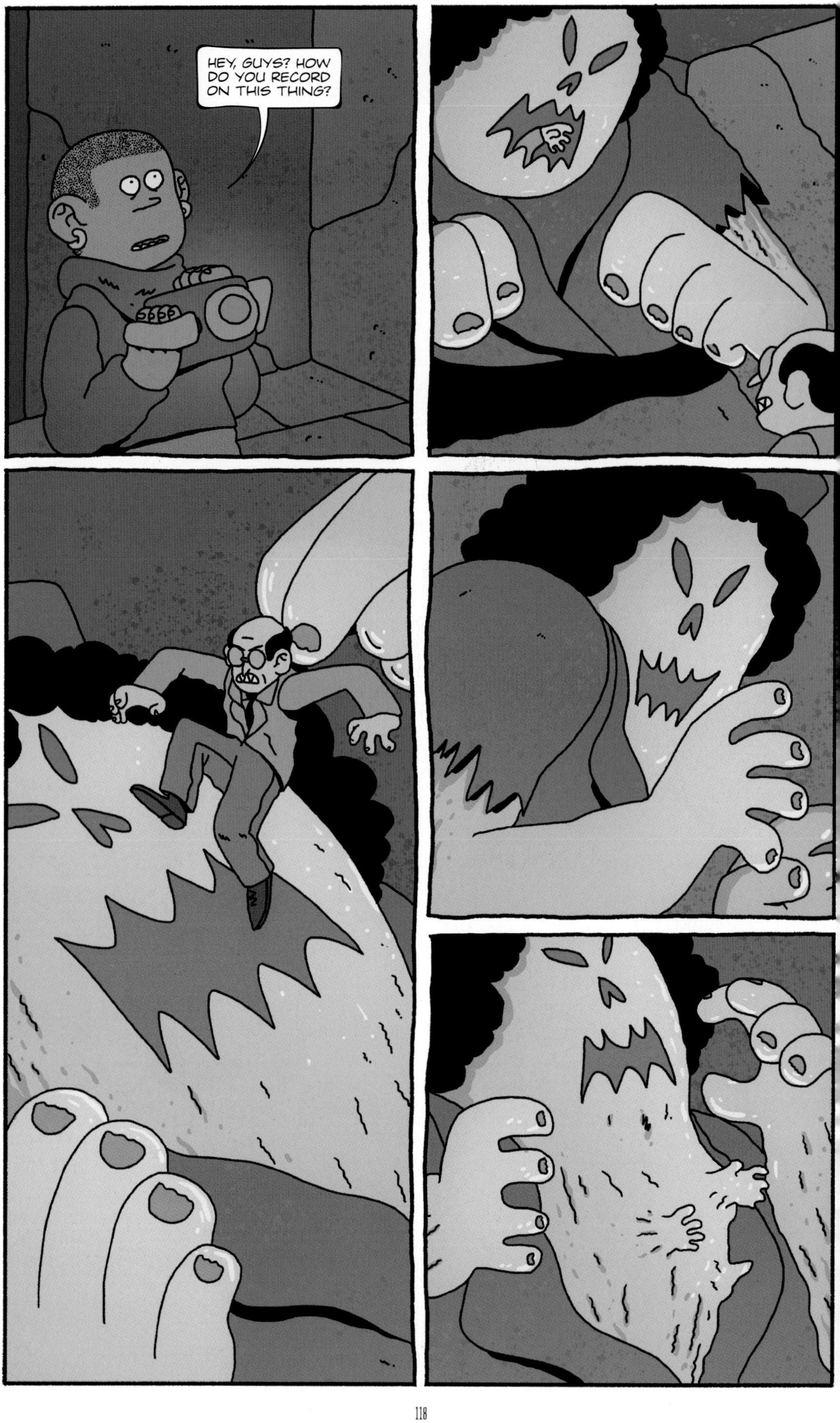
HEY, GUYS? HOW DO YOU RECORD ON THIS THING?

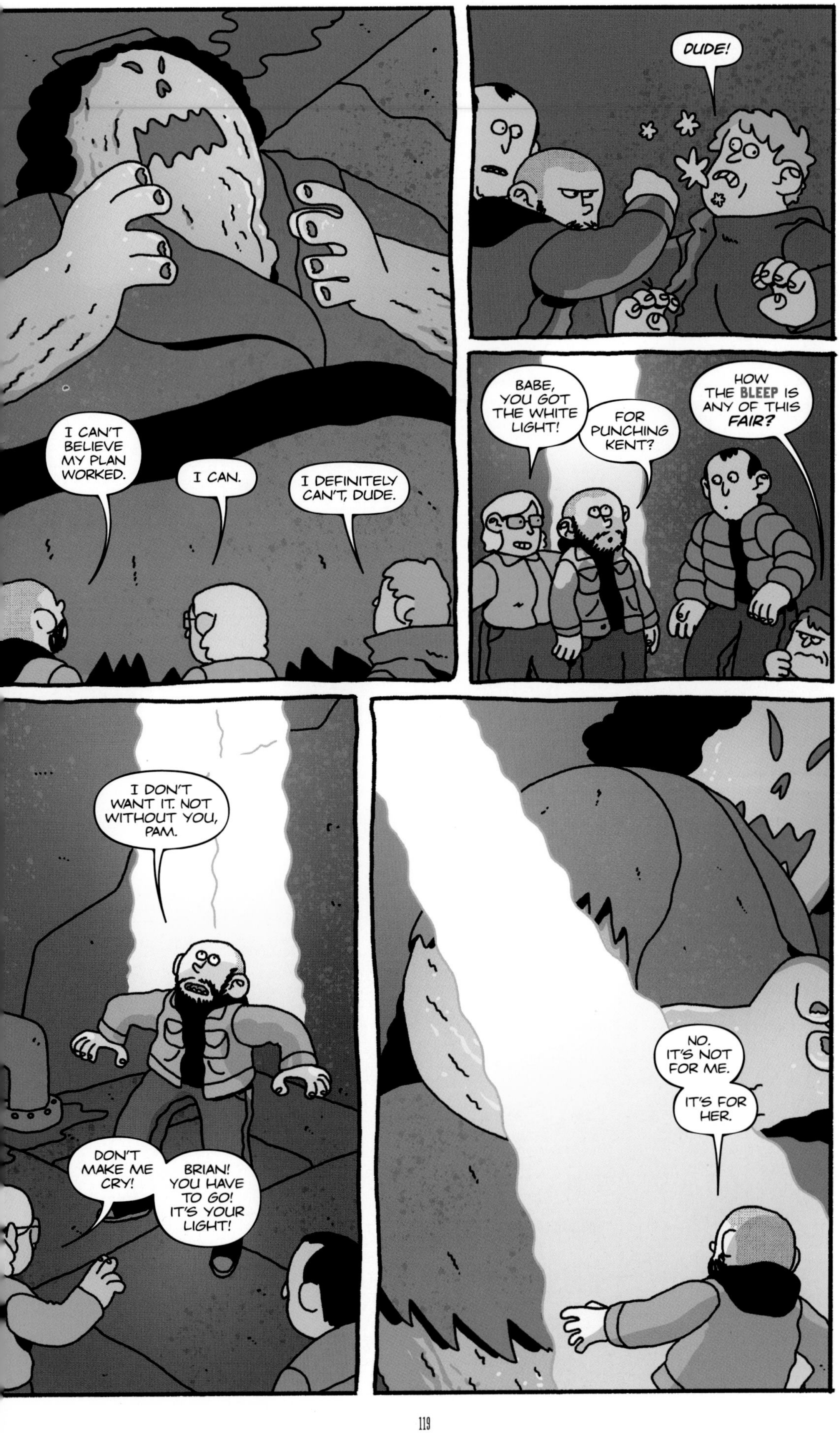
I CAN'T BELIEVE MY PLAN WORKED.
I CAN.
I DEFINITELY CAN'T, DUDE.
DUDE!
BABE, YOU GOT THE WHITE LIGHT!
FOR PUNCHING KENT?
HOW THE BLEEP IS ANY OF THIS FAIR?
I DON'T WANT IT. NOT WITHOUT YOU, PAM.
DON'T MAKE ME CRY!
BRIAN! YOU HAVE TO GO! IT'S YOUR LIGHT!
NO. IT'S NOT FOR ME.
IT'S FOR HER.

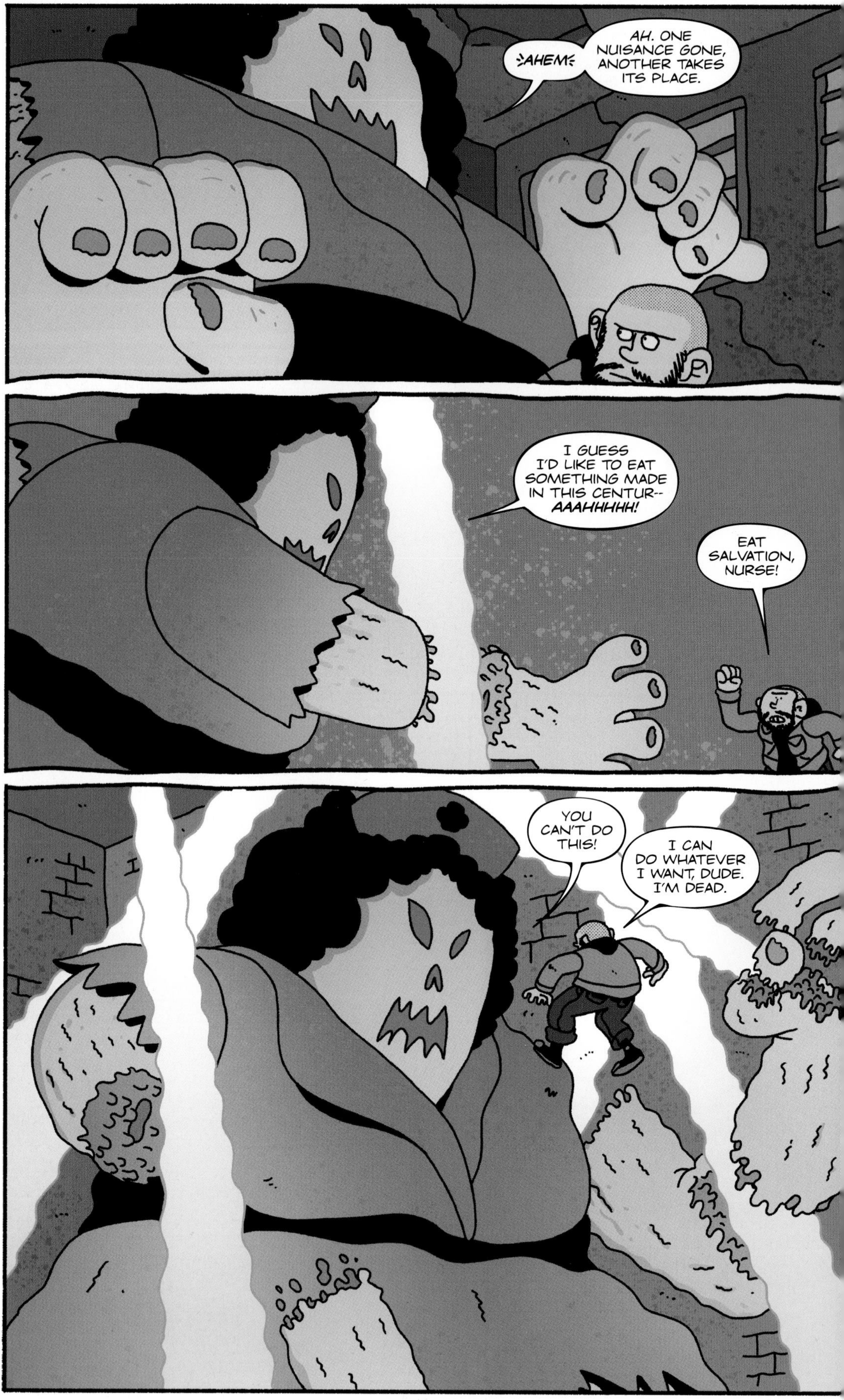

AHEM
AH. ONE NUISANCE GONE, ANOTHER TAKES ITS PLACE.
I GUESS I'D LIKE TO EAT SOMETHING MADE IN THIS CENTUR-- **AAAHHHHH!**
EAT SALVATION, NURSE!
YOU CAN'T DO THIS!
I CAN DO WHATEVER I WANT, DUDE. I'M DEAD.

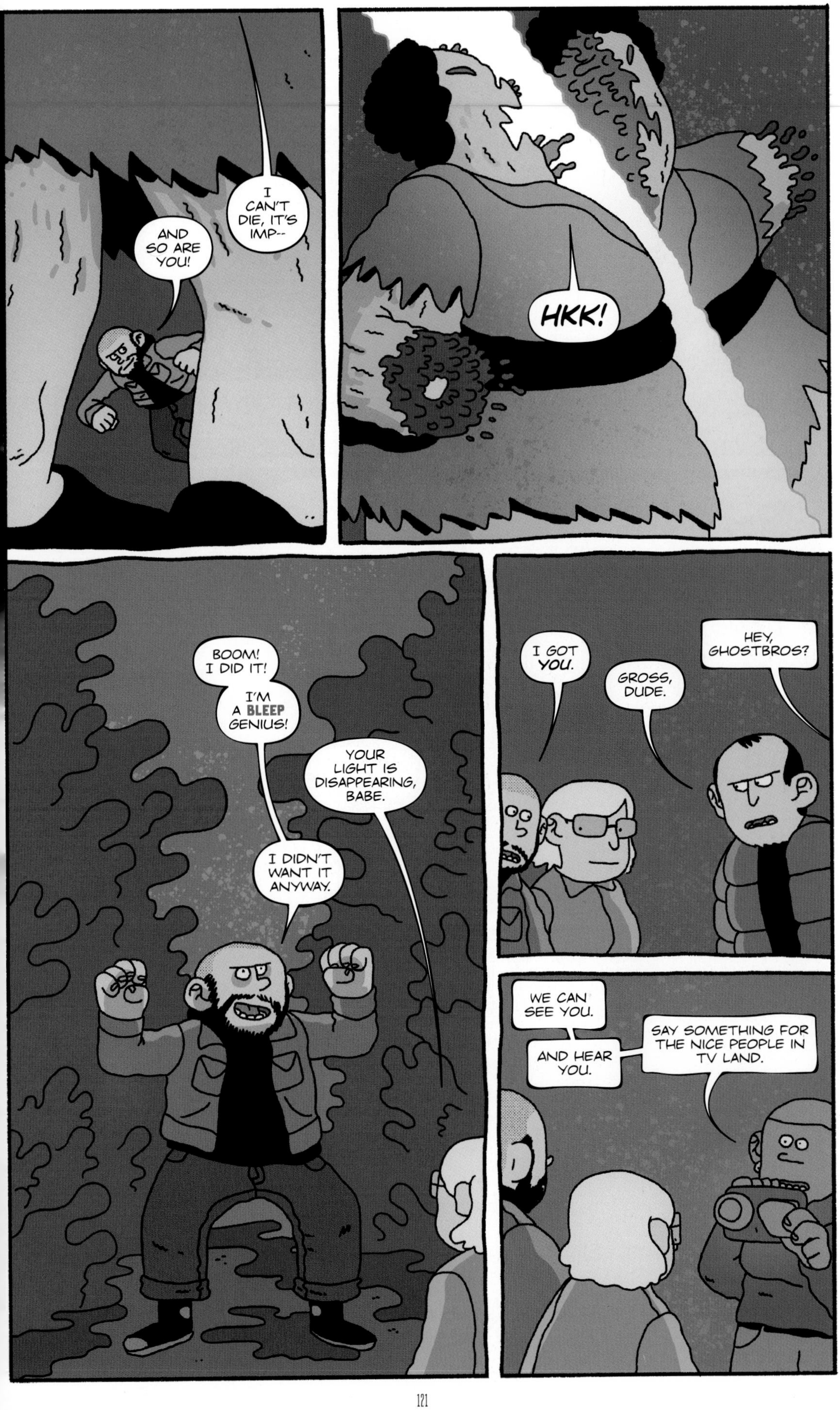
AND SO ARE YOU!
I CAN'T DIE, IT'S IMP--
HKK!
BOOM! I DID IT!
I'M A BLEEP GENIUS!
YOUR LIGHT IS DISAPPEARING, BABE.
I DIDN'T WANT IT ANYWAY.
I GOT YOU.
GROSS, DUDE.
HEY, GHOSTBROS?
WE CAN SEE YOU.
AND HEAR YOU.
SAY SOMETHING FOR THE NICE PEOPLE IN TV LAND.

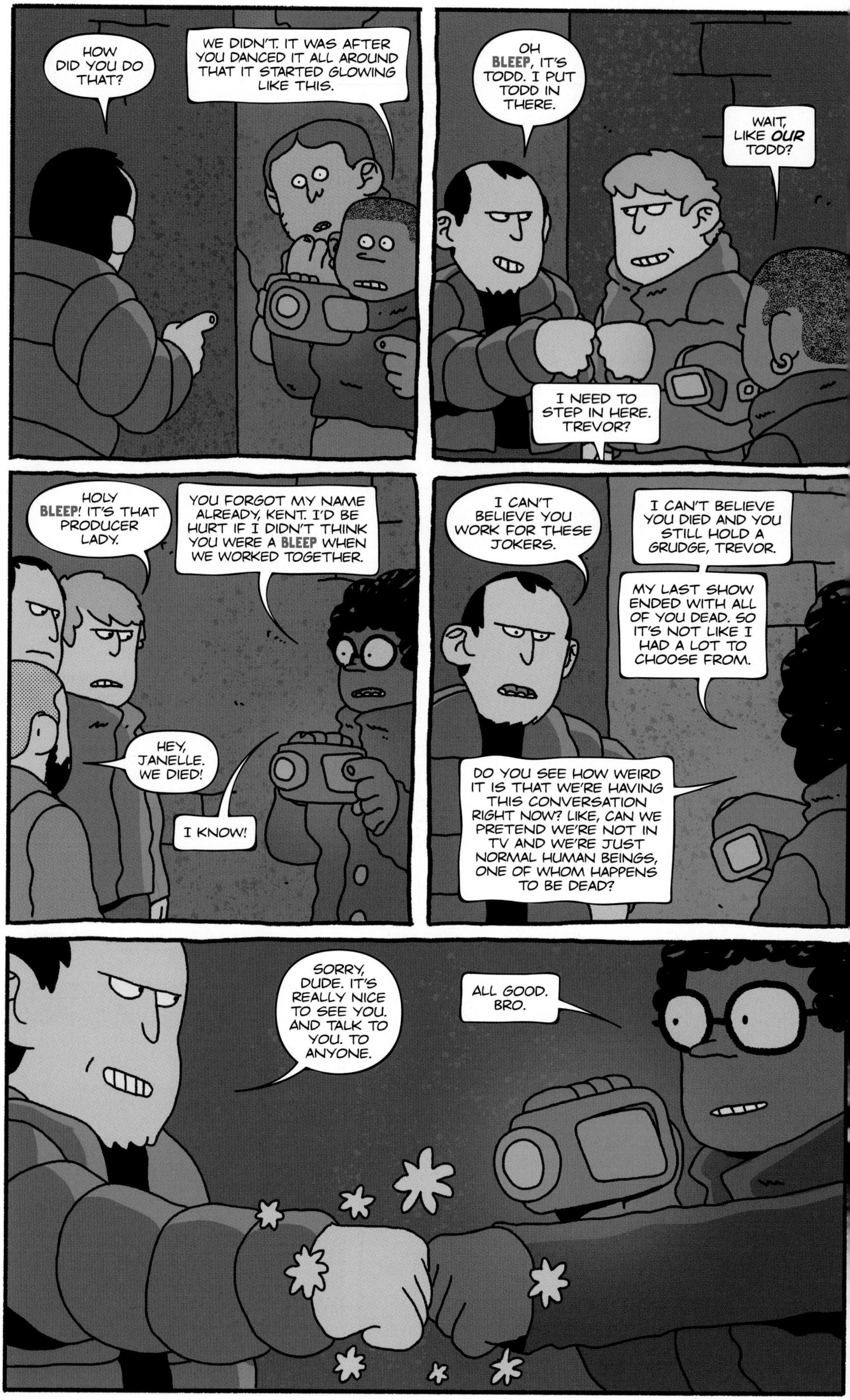

HOW DID YOU DO THAT?
WE DIDN'T. IT WAS AFTER YOU DANCED IT ALL AROUND THAT IT STARTED GLOWING LIKE THIS.
OH BLEEP, IT'S TODD. I PUT TODD IN THERE.
WAIT, LIKE *OUR* TODD?
I NEED TO STEP IN HERE. TREVOR?
HOLY BLEEP! IT'S THAT PRODUCER LADY.
YOU FORGOT MY NAME ALREADY, KENT. I'D BE HURT IF I DIDN'T THINK YOU WERE A BLEEP WHEN WE WORKED TOGETHER.
HEY, JANELLE. WE DIED!
I KNOW!
I CAN'T BELIEVE YOU WORK FOR THESE JOKERS.
I CAN'T BELIEVE YOU DIED AND YOU STILL HOLD A GRUDGE, TREVOR.
MY LAST SHOW ENDED WITH ALL OF YOU DEAD. SO IT'S NOT LIKE I HAD A LOT TO CHOOSE FROM.
DO YOU SEE HOW WEIRD IT IS THAT WE'RE HAVING THIS CONVERSATION RIGHT NOW? LIKE, CAN WE PRETEND WE'RE NOT IN TV AND WE'RE JUST NORMAL HUMAN BEINGS, ONE OF WHOM HAPPENS TO BE DEAD?
SORRY, DUDE. IT'S REALLY NICE TO SEE YOU. AND TALK TO YOU. TO ANYONE.
ALL GOOD. BRO.

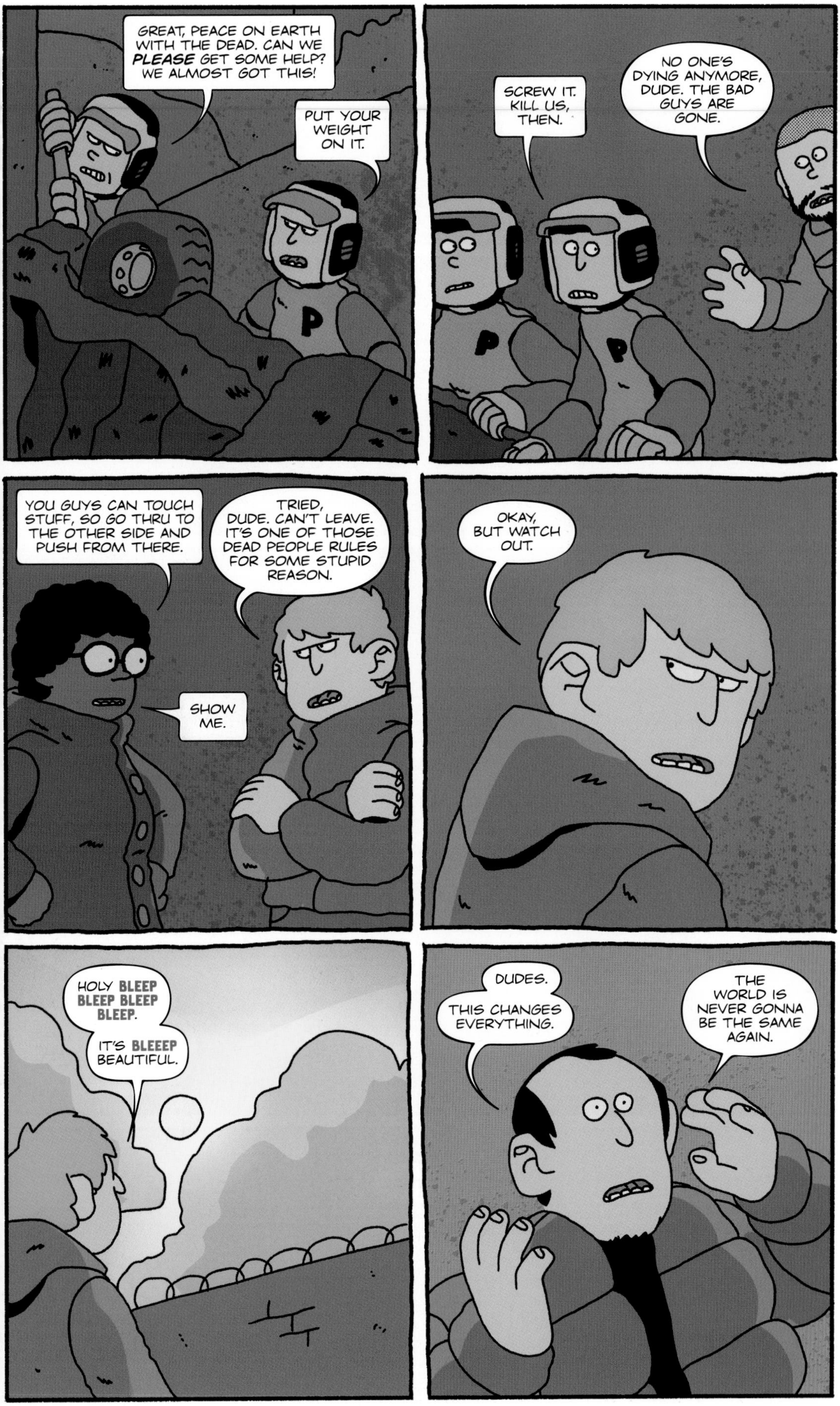
GREAT, PEACE ON EARTH WITH THE DEAD. CAN WE *PLEASE* GET SOME HELP? WE ALMOST GOT THIS!
PUT YOUR WEIGHT ON IT.
SCREW IT. KILL US, THEN.
NO ONE'S DYING ANYMORE, DUDE. THE BAD GUYS ARE GONE.
YOU GUYS CAN TOUCH STUFF, SO GO THRU TO THE OTHER SIDE AND PUSH FROM THERE.
TRIED, DUDE. CAN'T LEAVE. IT'S ONE OF THOSE DEAD PEOPLE RULES FOR SOME STUPID REASON.
SHOW ME.
OKAY, BUT WATCH OUT.
HOLY **BLEEP BLEEP BLEEP BLEEP**.
IT'S **BLEEEP** BEAUTIFUL.
DUDES.
THIS CHANGES EVERYTHING.
THE WORLD IS NEVER GONNA BE THE SAME AGAIN.

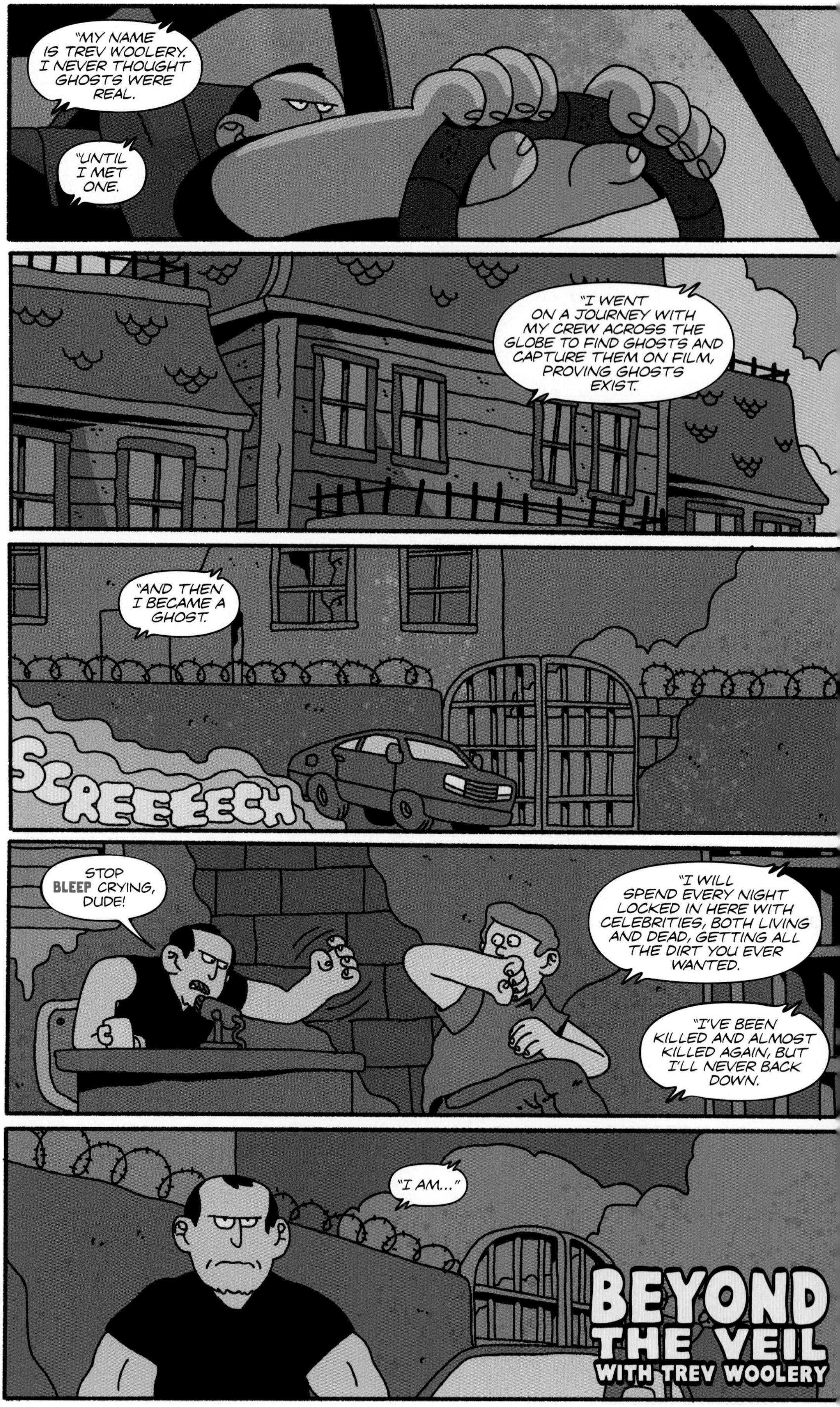
"MY NAME IS TREV WOOLERY. I NEVER THOUGHT GHOSTS WERE REAL.
"UNTIL I MET ONE.
"I WENT ON A JOURNEY WITH MY CREW ACROSS THE GLOBE TO FIND GHOSTS AND CAPTURE THEM ON FILM, PROVING GHOSTS EXIST.
"AND THEN I BECAME A GHOST.
SCREEEECH
STOP BLEEP CRYING, DUDE!
"I WILL SPEND EVERY NIGHT LOCKED IN HERE WITH CELEBRITIES, BOTH LIVING AND DEAD, GETTING ALL THE DIRT YOU EVER WANTED.
"I'VE BEEN KILLED AND ALMOST KILLED AGAIN, BUT I'LL NEVER BACK DOWN.
"I AM..."
BEYOND THE VEIL
WITH TREV WOOLERY

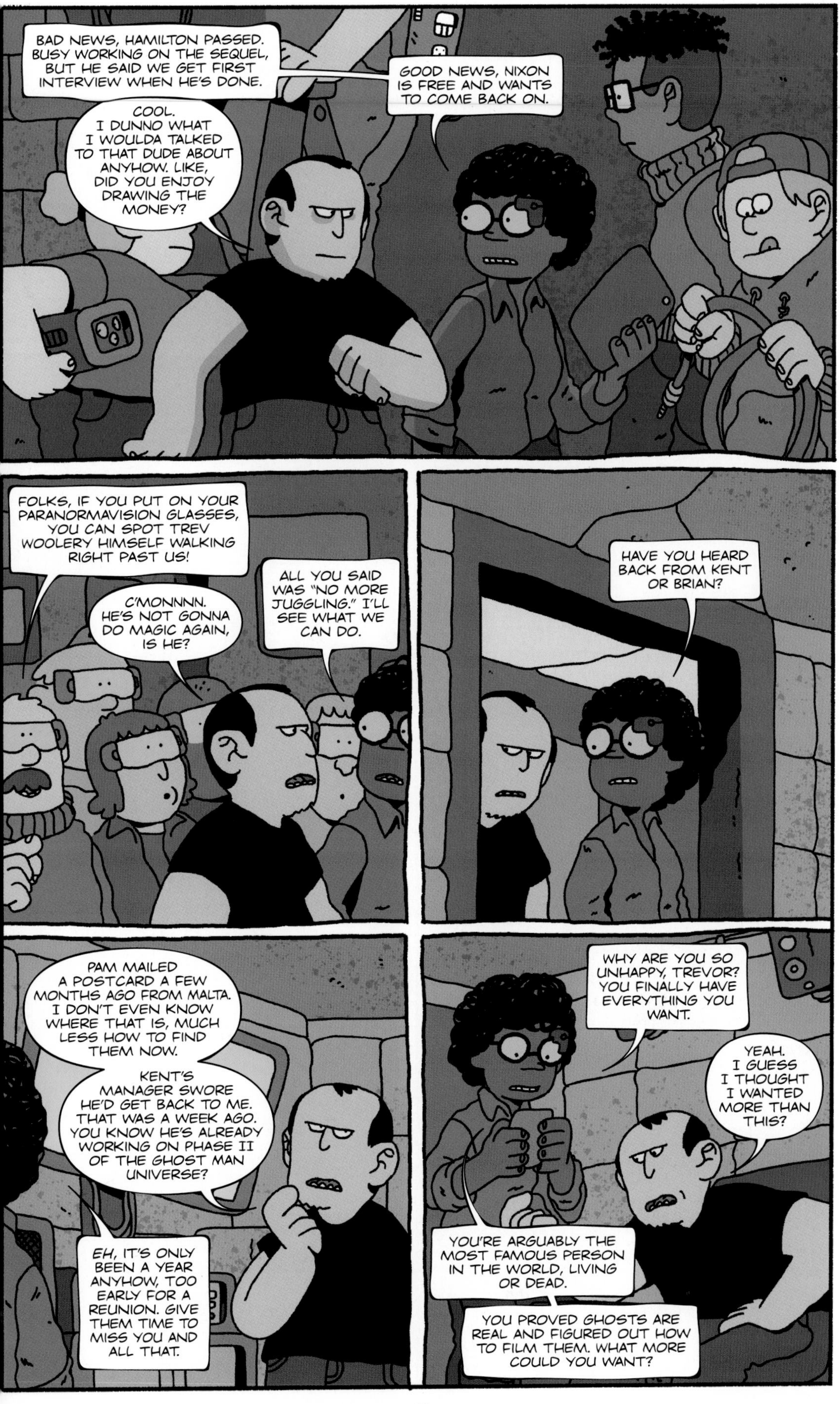
BAD NEWS, HAMILTON PASSED. BUSY WORKING ON THE SEQUEL, BUT HE SAID WE GET FIRST INTERVIEW WHEN HE'S DONE.
COOL. I DUNNO WHAT I WOULDA TALKED TO THAT DUDE ABOUT ANYHOW. LIKE, DID YOU ENJOY DRAWING THE MONEY?
GOOD NEWS, NIXON IS FREE AND WANTS TO COME BACK ON.
FOLKS, IF YOU PUT ON YOUR PARANORMAVISION GLASSES, YOU CAN SPOT TREV WOOLERY HIMSELF WALKING RIGHT PAST US!
C'MONNNN. HE'S NOT GONNA DO MAGIC AGAIN, IS HE?
ALL YOU SAID WAS "NO MORE JUGGLING." I'LL SEE WHAT WE CAN DO.
HAVE YOU HEARD BACK FROM KENT OR BRIAN?
PAM MAILED A POSTCARD A FEW MONTHS AGO FROM MALTA. I DON'T EVEN KNOW WHERE THAT IS, MUCH LESS HOW TO FIND THEM NOW.
KENT'S MANAGER SWORE HE'D GET BACK TO ME. THAT WAS A WEEK AGO. YOU KNOW HE'S ALREADY WORKING ON PHASE II OF THE GHOST MAN UNIVERSE?
EH, IT'S ONLY BEEN A YEAR ANYHOW, TOO EARLY FOR A REUNION. GIVE THEM TIME TO MISS YOU AND ALL THAT.
WHY ARE YOU SO UNHAPPY, TREVOR? YOU FINALLY HAVE EVERYTHING YOU WANT.
YEAH. I GUESS I THOUGHT I WANTED MORE THAN THIS?
YOU'RE ARGUABLY THE MOST FAMOUS PERSON IN THE WORLD, LIVING OR DEAD.
YOU PROVED GHOSTS ARE REAL AND FIGURED OUT HOW TO FILM THEM. WHAT MORE COULD YOU WANT?

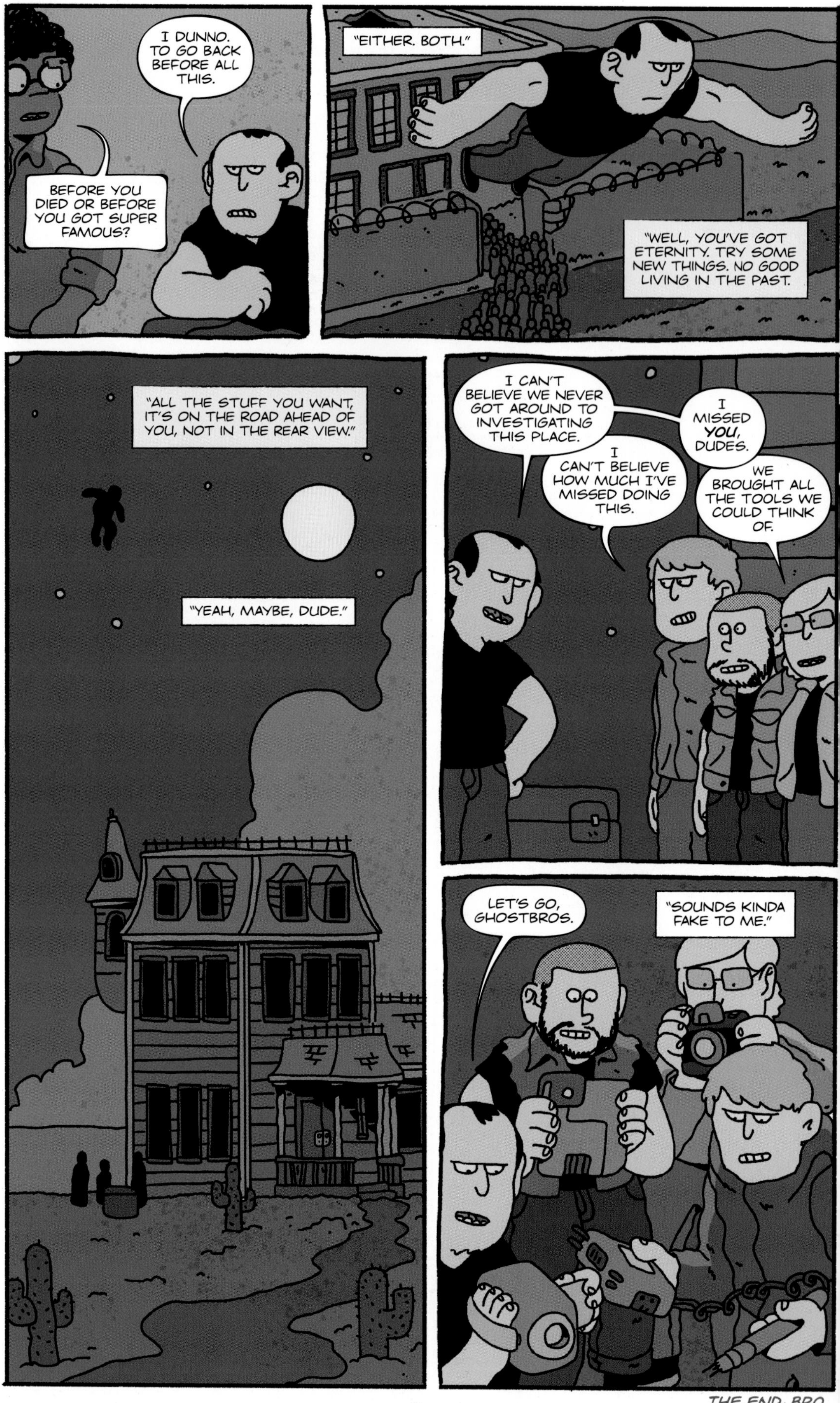
I DUNNO. TO GO BACK BEFORE ALL THIS.
BEFORE YOU DIED OR BEFORE YOU GOT SUPER FAMOUS?
"EITHER. BOTH."
"WELL, YOU'VE GOT ETERNITY. TRY SOME NEW THINGS. NO GOOD LIVING IN THE PAST.
"ALL THE STUFF YOU WANT, IT'S ON THE ROAD AHEAD OF YOU, NOT IN THE REAR VIEW."
"YEAH, MAYBE, DUDE."
I CAN'T BELIEVE WE NEVER GOT AROUND TO INVESTIGATING THIS PLACE.
I MISSED ***YOU***, DUDES.
I CAN'T BELIEVE HOW MUCH I'VE MISSED DOING THIS.
WE BROUGHT ALL THE TOOLS WE COULD THINK OF.
LET'S GO, GHOSTBROS.
"SOUNDS KINDA FAKE TO ME."

THE END, BRO.